URBAN CANADA: ITS GOVERNMENT AND POLITICS

Urban Canada
Its Government and Politics

DONALD J. H. HIGGINS

MACMILLAN OF CANADA

Canadian Cataloguing in Publication Data

Higgins, Donald J. H., 1943–
   Urban Canada

Bibliography: p.
Includes index.
ISBN 0-7705-1615-7 pa.

1. Municipal government – Canada. 2. Cities and towns – Canada. 3. Political participation – Canada. I. Title.

JS1708.H53   352′.008′0971   C77-001478-X

56, 852

Printed in Canada for
The Macmillan Company of Canada Limited
70 Bond Street
Toronto M5B 1X3

Contents

Acknowledgements

For a book such as this, an author is bound to accumulate numerous debts to others for their assistance and inspiration. This author has accumulated at least the usual share of debts, and is happy to acknowledge them. My students in urban government and politics in 1974–75 and 1975–76 deserve particular mention, for they provided stimulation and a forum in which I was able to try out and refine some of my own thoughts on the subject matter of this book. A large group of people who provided essential information were elected and appointed public officials in city halls and departments of municipal affairs across the country, and I thank them. It was gratifying to have many of them go well beyond their normal duty in compiling figures for me and supplying other material that is not ordinarily available.

Several individuals warrant special thanks: the late Kenneth Grant Crawford, who wrote in 1952 what has long remained the definitive book on municipal government in this country (*Canadian Municipal Government*) and under whom I was a student at Queen's University; Donald C. Rowat of Carleton University, under whom I also studied and who stimulated my interest in urban politics; Robert J. Jackson, also of Carleton University, who read part of an earlier draft and played a major part in having this book published; and my friend Stephen J. Ingle of the University of Hull, England. Lionel D. Feldman was enormously helpful in reading the entire first draft and in providing detailed and cogent criticisms and suggestions for improvement. Of course the responsibility for errors and deficiencies in this book remains mine. To my wife Patty are due many thanks for providing support and encouragement especially when spirits flagged. Finally, this is the first opportunity I have had to more or less publicly acknowledge the following for funding my studies and research: the Canada Council; the Central Mortgage and Housing Corporation; and the Ontario Queen Elizabeth II Scholarship Committee.

D. J. H. H.
Halifax, 1976

Introduction

It is possible to approach the area of inquiry called urban government and politics from a number of perspectives, for example with a special focus on a policy area (such as urban housing or urban planning), or on a particular level of government (federal, provincial, or municipal). In this book, the main focus is on the municipal level of government, and more specifically on "urban" municipal government. Postponing for the moment questions of definition, a "city" perspective is taken here. The term "urban government and politics" is broader than the term "municipal (or local) government and politics". The chief difference between the two is to be found in a tendency for the latter to be concerned mainly with the *internal* structures, processes, and personnel of municipalities. While the former term is indeed concerned with internal features, it extends beyond them in two ways. First, *external* structures, processes, and personnel are included, specifically the federal and provincial governments and politics. One of the aims of this book is to demonstrate the importance (past, present, and potential) of these higher levels in the urban context. Secondly, the study of urban government and politics is less confined than municipal (or local) government and politics to municipalities in the formal, legal sense. There is no necessary connection between the size and boundaries of municipalities on the one hand, and the size and boundaries of urban areas on the other. Most municipalities in this country are not urban, so they are largely outside the scope of urban government and politics. To be explicit, then, this book is concerned with government and politics relating to cities in Canada—their internal structures of government, their internal processes and political actors, and those external factors that have influence on the government and politics of cities.

From this perspective is derived the twofold purpose of the book; the first objective is to examine the frameworks of governmental structures and institutions at all levels of government (especially of cities) that are involved in making policies and decisions for urban Canada. An appreciation of those structures and institutions is required for an understanding

1

and assessment of whatever policies and decisions are actually made. How is legal power to make such decisions distributed? What is the distribution of financial resources needed to implement policies? What are the relationships among governmental institutions, both within cities, and between cities and federal/provincial institutions? In what ways have those relationships developed, and to what extent and in what directions are they evolving now? It is with such questions that the first four chapters of this book are mainly concerned.

The second purpose of the book is to go beyond *governmental* institutions and structures, and the relationships among them, to consider the *political* dimensions. Analysis of the formal governmental structures is necessary, but is insufficient because it does not necessarily describe the way things work in practice, blurs the dynamics of decision-making, and tends to distract attention away from people who do not hold formal governmental office but who have some kind of impact on the decision-making processes. For example, what about community associations and other kinds of interest groups? Where do, or where should, political parties fit in cities? What about city elections? It is with these kinds of questions, related to non-formal political roles and behaviour, that the last four chapters are mainly concerned. In fact, the eight chapters do not quite so neatly divide into government and politics. As the reader will find, there are some places in the first four chapters that include treatment of political interaction, just as there are places in the last four chapters that include formal institutional roles. A complete separation between government and politics is an artificial separation. A point that should be made explicit is that this book does not deal with areas of urban policy as such. To have done so would have required a city-by-city approach and would have required a book far longer than is practical. In any case, there is an expanding body of literature on specific issues of urban policy, and some of this literature is included in the list of Suggested Readings.

Urbanization

Since the major focus in this book is on urban municipalities—on cities— it is necessary to specify what is meant here by these and some related words:

... an urban centre is a densely settled built-up area and the urban population consists of the residents of such areas.[1]

The central attribute of modern urban systems is that they are inextricably tied to the process of economic growth and development.[2]

Urbanization is a . . . process in which the territorial units of human organization become more specialized and therefore more interdependent, and in which the social system becomes more complex.[3]

These statements are useful in pointing out that there are three main approaches to the study of urbanization: demographic, economic, and sociological respectively. Briefly, they can be summarized as follows.[4] Demography is concerned with the statistical study of population characteristics, and generally views urbanization as a process of population concentration. This involves two elements, one being an increase in the number of areas in which population is concentrated, and the other an increase in the population size of individual concentrations of people. This is generally understood to mean that the process of urbanization increases the number of cities, as well as the population size of each city. Yardsticks of measurement then become necessary—how big (in population terms) must a place be to be counted as a city? There is no commonly accepted cut-off point. For example, Statistics Canada defines as "urban" all areas that are incorporated municipalities, towns, villages, or unincorporated settlements, or built-up fringes, with a population of 1,000 or more people. The American Bureau of Census uses a cut-off figure of 2,500 people, while in other countries the cut-off figure is as high as 20,000 or more. It is often the case that *categories* of urban places are distinguished, such as Statistics Canada's agglomerations (25,000 or more people), and metropolitan areas (100,000 or more people). In any case, the demographic approach to urbanization is concerned mainly with analysis of trends in which people are concentrated in an increasing number of areas which are themselves increasing in population size (using an arbitrary population-size figure to define "urban").

The economic approach concentrates attention on urbanization as a process that expands a complex network of economic activities that *require* a concentration of production facilities (equipment, labour, buildings, and transportation facilities) and that at the same time tend to *foster* a further concentration (more purchasers must be found to buy the increased flow of goods and services). Economic growth, and therefore urbanization, is dependent on technological change as well. Industries and people tend to become more specialized and therefore more dependent on other industries and other people. These factors that increase interdependency would lead to the concentration of all urban economic activity in a single place, were it not for the fact that raw materials and finished goods must move over some distance. There is therefore a conflict between concentration (to achieve economies of scale) and dispersal (to reduce transportation costs). As Lithwick points out, the result of this conflict is that ". . . a number of production nodes will emerge, each of which provides sufficient scale economies to prevent further dispersal, but incurs high enough transport costs to preclude absorption in a larger centre."[5] In other words, economic development means that large centres will tend to grow larger, that the number of urban centres will tend to increase, and that these centres (and their respective hinterlands) will become increasingly linked to each other economically.

With regard to the sociological approach, urbanization is seen as a process that produces more complex social organization. Technological change in means of communication opens up all sorts of new possibilities for social interaction. The telephone and the car, for example, have obvious effects in greatly increasing the range of people with whom a person can interact, for people in urban areas are not limited to communication with only those other people who live close by. So the spatial patterns of social interaction grow wider and more complex, and people rely less on face-to-face contact. Increasing division of labour and specialization produce sharpened differences in social classes. For example, senior and middle-level management become more sharply distinguished from each other, and from foremen, factory floor workers, and so on. Thus the older and simpler difference between an owner/managerial class and a working class becomes a more complicated division of upper class, upper middle, middle, upper blue collar, etc. Pay differentials and differences in educational background and training needed to perform particular tasks transform what were once essentially economic class divisions into socio-economic class divisions. There is increasing social heterogeneity, and this is reinforced by immigration into urban places, for people move there not only from non-urban areas in the same country but also from other countries. Also, there is a tendency for this latter type of immigrant to become concentrated in particular kinds of occupations and in particular residential areas. Major urban centres tend to reflect their social heterogeneity and fragmentation in identifiable residential areas, partly on ethnic (and related language) grounds, and partly on social status or prestige grounds. Thus every major urban centre has more or less distinct upper-class areas, middle-class suburban areas, ethnic minority areas, low-income slum areas, and so forth. The larger the population in the urban centre, the greater the likelihood of there being more than one area of each type. While it perhaps stretches the use of the word too far beyond its normal usage, the word "ghetto" helps to indicate the increasing distinctness of such residential areas as the population increases. Some people are effectively prohibited from moving into an area because they lack the money to buy or rent a home in that area, and some people are inhibited about moving into particular residential areas because they do not speak fluently the dominant language there, or for other reasons.

Generally, these three approaches to the study of urbanization are not so distinctly and separately pursued as the above summaries might suggest. For example, there is a clear connection between urban social stratification and urban economic development, and both the economic and sociological approaches must deal with demographic urbanization. As Stone suggests, it is appropriate and useful to consider the process of urbanization as one that ". . . involves the generation and spread of characteristic features of *city life*" and that city life has (at least) three major dimensions—demographic, economic, and social/cultural.[6] How, then, can one know whether a particular place is characterized by "city life"? Are residents in all places that Statistics Canada classifies as urban (places with 1000 people or more) likely to live a "city life"? Not likely, for 1000 people is much too small a population to support an urban economic structure and complex urban social organization. And are residents of all places that are municipally incorporated as cities likely to live a "city life"? Given the fact that in British Columbia, for example, only seven of the thirty-two municipalities with city corporate status had twenty thousand residents or more in 1971, and that many had very much smaller populations than that, again the answer is "not likely". In contrast, Burlington, Ontario had a population of over 90,000 in 1973, but its municipal status was as a town. Therefore one cannot count on legal city-status as an indicator that people do or do not lead an urban way of life.

It then becomes necessary to select an arbitrary population figure to define a city as a place where people live an urban way of life. For this book, the minimum population will be 100,000. That figure has also been selected by several other authors such as Simmons and Simmons, who state that this is ". . . the point when [economically] specialized land uses and social groups clearly sort themselves out."[7] Because such a figure is arbitrary, it is not entirely satisfactory, for it leaves out those places which are approaching that figure. But some cut-off point is required. A complication arises in that much of the data needed for books like this is available only on the basis of incorporated units of government. Especially in the case of major urban centres as just defined, population settlement has overrun the political boundaries of governmental units. Such boundaries tend to be very static while patterns of population growth and settlement are dynamic. So a major urban area may have only one municipal unit of 100,000 or more people but be surrounded by a number of other municipal units, at least parts of which are densely settled, but which have fewer residents than the cut-off point. In such cases it has become necessary to rely on data only for the one municipality and ignore the others. As it happens, the municipalities in Canada that meet or exceed the 100,000 population criterion have the legal corporate status of "city" (except for the five boroughs in Metro Toronto). Therefore, the word "city" is actually used in two senses in the rest of the book: a) in a narrower sense as municipal units for the purposes of data presented; and b) in a broader sense as larger areas where the residents are likely to live an urban way of life. This may be confusing, but it should be reasonably clear in the text which sense of the word applies.

If all the data needed for analysis in this book were available for what Statistics Canada defines as a Census Metropolitan Area (CMA), this problem would be less severe. A CMA was defined for the 1971 census as the main labour market of a continuous built-up area having a population of 100,000 or more; the main labour market area corresponds to a commuting field or zone where a significant number of people are able to travel on a daily basis to workplaces in the main built-up area. The advantage of that definition is that it takes into account not only the demographic dimension of urbanization but part of the economic dimension, and would seem to be adequate for the social/cultural dimension too. However, there are advantages to looking at major urban municipalities as separate units, since almost all the CMAs include more than one municipality, and too much of the data needed are not available by CMA.

Using the arbitrary cut-off figure of 100,000 or more people, to what extent is Canada urbanized? To answer the question, one can consider either the proportion of the total Canadian population that lives in the twenty-four major urban municipalities (municipal cities and boroughs in 1971), or the proportion of the total Canadian population that lives in CMAs. This is one instance where figures for the latter are available, and they more accurately reflect urbanization. In 1973 there were twenty-two CMAs, listed in order of population in Table 1.

As this table indicates, Canada is an "urban" country demographically to the extent that there are multiple (twenty-two) areas of high concentration of people, and that some 55 per cent of the total population of Canada in 1973 resided in such areas. These figures represented an increase of five new CMAs and an increase of 10 per cent in Canada's population over the 1961 census. It was between the 1961 census and the 1966 mini-census that Canada's CMA population passed the 50 per cent mark. Between 1950 and 1970 Canada experienced one of the world's highest average annual rates of increase in the proportion of the population that resides in urban centres of 100,000 or more.[8] The extent to

---

Table 1   Population of Census Metropolitan Areas (estimates for 1973)

C.M.A.	*population*	C.M.A.	*population*
Montreal	2,775,000	Windsor	264,000
Toronto	2,692,000	Kitchener	235,000
Vancouver	1,116,000	Halifax	222,000
Ottawa–Hull	619,000	Victoria	203,000
Winnipeg	560,000	Sudbury	155,000
Edmonton	518,000	Regina	147,000
Hamilton	513,000	Chicoutimi–Jonquiere	136,000
Quebec	493,000	St. John's, Newfoundland	133,000
Calgary	431,000	Saskatoon	128,000
St. Catharines–Niagara	308,000	Thunder Bay	113,000
London	293,000	Saint John, N.B.	110.000

Total C.M.A. population: 12,164,000
Total population of Canada: 22,095,000
SOURCE: Statistics Canada, bulletin 91-207, 1973.

which Canada in 1966 was a predominantly urbanized country is dramatically illustrated in an isodemographic map prepared by the federal Department of the Environment. Usefully, this map also indicates the regional variations in degree of urbanization. In the map the geographical areas occupied by major urban census units are proportional to their total population. Thus if a major urban area has 10 per cent of Canada's total population, it is shown covering 10 per cent of Canada's total area.

A number of forecasts have been made about the proportion of Canada's total population that will reside in Census Metropolitan Areas in the future. In 1967 the Economic Council of Canada estimated that in 1980 one-third of all Canadians would reside in just the three metropolitan areas of Montreal, Toronto, and Vancouver.[9] (These three accounted for almost 30 per cent of Canadians in 1973.) Another set of projections indicates that these three CMAs together could realistically have as many as eighteen million residents, and that Montreal alone could have a population as high as 7.9 million.[10]

Governmental and Political Consequences of Urbanization

What kinds of consequences does the process of urbanization produce for governments in Canada, and how does urbanization affect political processes and personalities? Clearly, there have been benefits for Canadians both in cities and in non-urban areas, and future urbanization will add to those benefits. In social and economic terms, the results include higher levels of productivity, income, and education, a wider variety of occupations, expanded cultural and recreational possibilities, more leisure time, and so forth. But especially in political and governmental terms, the process has produced severe stresses and strains, and may be expected to accentuate them.

Lithwick has argued forcefully that these benefits are in much danger of being overrun by disadvantages or problems associated with urbanization. He has divided urban problems into two categories, those which he has termed as problems *in* the city, and those termed problems *of* the city.[11] Briefly, the distinction rests on whether the problem just happens to occur in cities, or whether it is a fundamental aspect of the actual process of urbanization. In other words, problems *of* the city are necessarily urban in their nature, whereas problems *in* the city are not. Some

Figure 1 Isodemographic Map of Canada (1966)

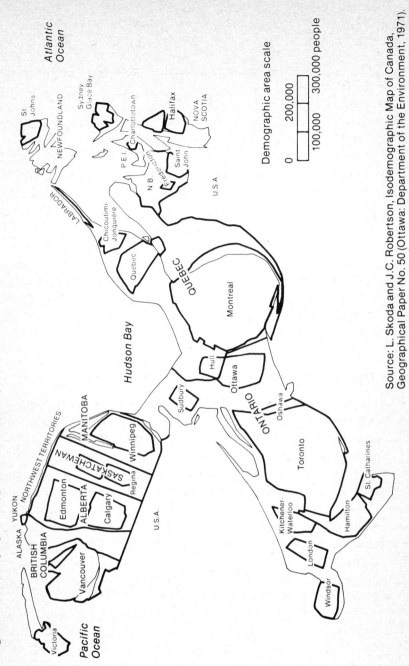

Demographic area scale

0   100,000   200,000   300,000 people

Source: L. Skoda and J.C. Robertson, Isodemographic Map of Canada, Geographical Paper No. 50 (Ottawa: Department of the Environment, 1971).

examples of the latter include environmental pollution, unemployment, inflation, poverty, high housing costs, and social unrest—these problems are indeed found in cities, but they are found elsewhere too. He has maintained that the principal problem *of* the city is the scarcity of land, which increases with growth.[12] Out of this one main difficulty flow others —transportation, availability of housing, sprawl, pollution, poverty, congestion, noise, physical decay and depopulation of the urban core, segregation of socio-economic classes—the list is almost limitless. Perhaps the most important point that Lithwick makes is that urban problems are highly interdependent. If governments attempt to deal with one situation in isolation, those attempts will tend to aggravate other problem areas.[13] Therefore what he has argued for is not better programs and policies for urban housing, for urban transportation, for urban poverty, or whatever, but a comprehensive *urban* policy, something which had never really been attempted in Canada at any level of government.[14] Lithwick's study and recommendations have had subsequent impact, and his report is considered further in Chapter 2.

The kind of problem with which Lithwick was mainly concerned, then, is one of urban *policy*, and this is certainly a consequence of urbanization that has governmental and political ramifications. If the urban policy problem is to be resolved or alleviated, only governments can do it because no one else has the capability needed. As indicated earlier, questions of urban policy are not directly pursued in this book. However, there is in addition to the matter of policy what can be termed a *process* problem of urbanization; that is to say that urbanization increases stresses and strains on governmental and political capabilities—capabilities to cope with the first kind of urban problem. The question of what governments can do in this regard is of central concern. It is with the process and capability problem that this book is mainly concerned—*how* policy decisions are made (or can be made), rather than *what* policy decisions are made (or might be made in future).

As has been noted, the scale of Canada's major cities in terms of population size and density has incessantly grown, and is likely to continue to do so in future, although perhaps at a slower rate than in recent years. The scale of urban Canada has also increased in the sense of the government of cities becoming more and more complex. Thus questions of size and complexity are useful for making connections in the diverse subject matter with which the following chapters deal.

In Chapter 1, the evolution of municipal government in Canada is examined, and it should surprise no one to find that the creation of formal institutions of municipal government is a direct function of population and patterns of settlement. Simply stated, where there are no people, or very few, in a locality, there is no need for municipal government. It more or less follows, then, that the more people there are in a locality, the more municipal government is needed, and that such government becomes bigger and more complex as population increases. Also, since municipal governments are legally subordinate to provincial governments, growing numbers of increasingly complex municipal governments raise the level of complexity of relationships between municipalities and their respective provincial masters. The larger the municipality the greater is the need for services of a wider range and higher standards. Yet Canada's municipalities are not endowed with the jurisdictional power or the financial capabilities to provide those services without the provincial governments being involved. Thus provincial–municipal relations tend to become more complicated, and the federal government adds yet another dimension to the scale of complexity in central–local relations. The nature of these connections is the concern of Chapter 2.

Again, as cities grow, their internal structures of decision making are subjected to stresses of urbanization, both in terms of having to provide new and higher levels of services to more people, and having to handle broader and more demands for services. As a result, these structures tend to become bigger (more bureaucrats, for example), and more complex (more departments, for example). It is in Chapter 3 that municipal decision-making machinery is considered. In Chapter 4 the problems of scale in urban municipal government are particularly relevant. The process of municipal reorganization in most of the country's major cities during the past twenty-five years occurred largely because the scale of city government in territorial terms had been overtaken by the scale of population and of service needs.

The first four chapters, then, are primarily (but not exclusively) concerned with urban *government*: that is, with institutions and more or less formal processes of decision making. The last four chapters are more directly concerned with urban *politics*: that is, with political behaviour in major cities. In these chapters, too, questions of scale are important.

Chapter 5 deals with some of the socio-political consequences of urbanization in so far as they establish the sort of environment of urban political life. Here, the compatibility of large-scale populations with the valued notion of "grass-roots" local government is considered, as are the effects of size or scale on such determinants of political participation as perceptions of community. As cities grow in population size and complexity of government, so does the diversity of demands for government action, and so does the need for *organization* of those demands. Only in rare instances are single individuals in major cities able to exercise effective influence on the institutional structures of decision making. Therefore, in Chapter 6 the kinds of organized-group actors that are involved in urban politics are considered, along with their varying capabilities to exercise political influence. A special kind of group actor in urban politics is the subject of Chapter 7—political parties and their involvement in urban municipal elections. It is suggested in this chapter that one possible explanation for parties' interest and activity in major cities' elections is the need for mechanisms to aggregate the diversity of interests and demands that increase as the scale of cities increases. Parties are normally thought to have interest aggregation capability. The final chapter concerns the urban politicians—the people who are charged with the primary responsibility for coping with urban problems of policy (themselves consequences of urbanization and scale) and with working the political processes wherein those problems of policy are considered.

NOTES

1. Leroy O. Stone, *Urban Development in Canada* (Ottawa: Dominion Bureau of Statistics, 1967), p. 4.
2. N. H. Lithwick, *Urban Canada: Problems and Prospects* (Ottawa: Central Mortgage and Housing Corporation, 1970), p. 46
3. George A. Nader, *Cities of Canada, Volume One: Theoretical, Historical and Planning Perspectives* (Toronto: Macmillan of Canada, 1975), p. 2.
4. For more detail see Philip M. Hauser and Leo F. Schnore, eds., *The Study of Urbanization* (New York: John Wiley and Sons, 1965), especially pp. 1–47.

5. Lithwick, *Urban Canada: Problems and Prospects*, p. 49.
6. Stone, *Urban Development in Canada*, p. 4 (emphasis mine). By "city life" he means much the same thing meant by the term "urban way of life" as used in James and Robert Simmons, *Urban Canada* (Toronto: Copp Clark, 1969), pp. 4–7.
7. James and Robert Simmons, *Urban Canada*, pp. 8–9. See also Kingsley Davis, *World Urbanization 1950–1970, Volume I: Basic Data for Cities, Countries, and Regions*, rev. ed. (Berkeley: Institute of International Studies of the University of

California at Berkeley, 1969), pp. 18–19.

8. Davis, *World Urbanization 1950–1970, Volume I*, table c, pp. 112–38. For analyses of the history of urbanization in Canada see Stone, *Urban Development in Canada*, especially Chapter 2; Nader, *Cities of Canada, Volume One*, Part Two; Lithwick, *Urban Canada: Problems and Prospects*, Chapter 2; John N. Jackson, *The Canadian City: Space, Form, Quality* (Toronto: McGraw-Hill Ryerson, 1973), Chapter 2; and Jacob Spelt, *Urban Development in South-Central Ontario* (Toronto: McClelland and Stewart, 1972), particularly chapters 3 and 6.

9. Economic Council of Canada, *Fourth Annual Review* (Ottawa, 1967), p. 190.

10. A. Goracz, I. Lithwick, and L. O. Stone, *The Urban Future* (Research Monograph 5, 1971, for Lithwick, *Urban Canada: Problems and Prospects*), Table 19, pp. 60–1.

11. Lithwick, *Urban Canada: Problems and Prospects*, pp. 13–35.

12. Ibid., pp. 15 and 102.

13. Ibid., p. 26. He demonstrates the inter-connectedness of urban problems on pp. 26–35.

14. Ibid., especially Chapter 5.

The Evolution of Municipal Government

By Canada's constitution "municipal institutions" are an exclusive responsibility of the individual provinces (in the case of the Yukon and Northwest Territories, the federal government is responsible).[1] It therefore follows that the pattern of development of municipal government in Canada has not necessarily been a uniform one. In this chapter each of the ten provinces plus the northern territories is considered separately. The focus is on the origins and later developments in municipal government up to the time that recent fundamental reorganization, if any, occurred (the latter is considered in Chapter 4).[2] While one can say that there are ten municipal systems in Canada (actually eleven or twelve, counting the northern territories), they have been characterized by several common features. These similarities, together with the more striking differences, are highlighted at the end of this chapter. The concern here is with municipalities as such; other aspects of the municipal scene such as local boards and commissions and the provincial departments of municipal affairs are examined in later chapters.

The necessity for any institutions of municipal government is a function of human settlement and patterns of settlement. Simply stated, where there are no people, or very few and evenly dispersed people, there is no need of municipal government. So municipal institutions are clearly connected to patterns of human settlement, and therefore to the process of urbanization. But the kinds of municipal institutions are a function of culture and heritage. For example, prior to the "discovery" of North America by Europeans, the aboriginal peoples of North America had well-established forms of government, but not of a sort that we normally associate with democratic local self-government. Their patterns of settlement and their cultural heritage were of a sort that neither demanded nor fostered municipal government. Therefore its evolution in Canada commenced no earlier than with the arrival in numbers of immigrants from Europe and, later, from the United States. The various traditions of government that the French, British, and Americans brought with them to Canada as part of their cultural baggage, coupled with their changing patterns of settlement (incipient urbanization), are important factors that one notes in the evolution of municipal government in this country.

The East

Since Europeans began their conquest of Canada at the eastern end of the country, it is appropriate to begin the analysis the same way.

NEWFOUNDLAND[3]

Newfoundland not only was the last province to enter Confederation but was also late in developing a system of municipal government. There were no municipalities in the province until 1938 aside from the city of St. John's. But from 1890 there did exist quasi-municipal elected district boards responsible for a limited range of local services but lacking both taxing powers of any kind and independent spending authority.

There are several reasons for the very slow development of municipal government in the province. After 1634, permanent settlement was very actively discouraged by the British, and the settlements that did eventually develop were vast in number, geographically isolated from each other, and generally tiny in population.[4] The best agricultural land, on the west coast, was not open to settlement until this century because of special fishing rights held by the French. The fishery caused the small population to disperse along the coast, resulting in the large number of small, isolated pockets of settlement, very few of which were financially able to support any form of local government. Aside from the relative poverty of Newfoundland's people, the right to own real property was not won until 1824. Bearing in mind that the traditional main source of municipal revenue in Canada has been taxation of real estate, these factors were important impediments to the introduction of municipal government. Once property ownership was granted, the property tended to be jealously guarded, especially from any form of direct taxation. Due to its geographic isolation Newfoundland also tended not to be influenced by the development of municipal government elsewhere, and the early settlers had not had prior experience with local government.

In addition to these impediments, there was only a questionable need for municipal government in much of the province. The sea provided the roadways at no cost. Education was mainly provided by churches with financial support from the government, and the range of social services was provided, if at all, by friends, family, and charities. The island's central government in St. John's provided services, such as roads, that in other provinces were provided at the local level.

The first attempt to incorporate St. John's was in 1834, and was opposed successfully on grounds of taxation. As well, there was opposition from the governor and several prominent local factions that could be called elites to placing power in elected hands. Municipal incorporation of the city occurred more than fifty years later, in 1888, when St. John's population was about 30,000, and the population of Newfoundland about 203,000. The first two decades of city status were erratic, the elected council being replaced by appointed commissions several times until a new charter was granted in 1921.

In 1933 the government passed the Local Government Act by which the Governor-in-Council could force the creation of municipalities. The Act was strongly opposed for its provision of property taxation and poll taxes, and no municipalities were created under its terms. A year later, during the Great Depression, Newfoundland's elected legislature was replaced by an appointed commission government because of the financial crisis. The commission passed the Local Administration Act of 1937–38, giving itself the power to create municipalities. None were incorporated under this act; none were forced, and none asked, again because of opposition to property tax provisions. After promises of financial assistance, several places were persuaded to incorporate beginning in 1938. By 1943 there were only four municipalities, and by 1948 still only twenty, each of which was incorporated by special charter. This process of incorporation by special charter was abandoned in 1949 when the general Local Government Act was passed, bestowing municipal status by proclamation for areas with a population of at least one thousand and providing for rural districts. This act came to apply to all municipalities other than St. John's.

Two other local government devices were developed, one of which was the local improvement district. While these districts were provided for in the Act of 1949, they were unusual in that each was created with a board of trustees appointed by the provincial government, though if several conditions were later met the district could become a municipality with an elected council. The other device was the local government community, provided for in 1952 by the Community Councils Act. This device was designed for areas with very small populations. Services to be performed were very limited, as were the sources of revenue.

The number of municipalities and quasi-municipalities in the province began to grow rapidly and steadily to the point where there were in 1975 two cities, 110 towns, eleven rural districts, 128 local government communities, thirty-nine local improvement districts, and one metropolitan area. The latter three categories are quasi-municipalities. The most populous of the municipalities is St. John's which had a 1971 population of 88,000. There remains a very large part of the province's area without any form of local government, but in 1975 about 80 per cent of the total population lived in the municipalities and quasi-municipalities. Demands for higher levels of local services and the program of closing down and consolidating coastal outports produced two recent developments. One was the commissioning of the St. John's Urban Region Study in 1968, to examine the possibilities for metropolitan government in the capital city area. The other was the appointment in 1972 of a royal commission to recommend improvements in the municipal system of the province. By 1976 there was no reorganization of that system.

NOVA SCOTIA[5]

The first municipal incorporation in Nova Scotia occurred in 1841 when Halifax, with a population of between fifteen and twenty thousand, was granted its charter. It cannot be said, though, that representative local self-government blossomed quickly, for at Confederation in 1867 Halifax remained the only incorporated municipality in the province. Though five additional municipalities received charters prior to 1879, passage that year of the County Incorporation Act marked the beginning of province-wide municipal government.

Prior to the County Act, the situation was one of local administration rather than local self-government. During the French regime, which ended in Nova Scotia except for Cape Breton Island in 1713, such local administration as there was functioned only as an extension of the central government. The British colonial authorities instituted a series of make-shift arrangements until the Courts of Quarter Sessions were established about 1750. The courts, modelled on the example of England, consisted of Justices of the Peace who were appointed by the Governor-and-Council and who performed administrative as well as judicial functions. Attached to the courts were grand juries which possessed an advisory role. The courts appointed local officials, levied taxes, issued licenses, and so on.

Considerable significance is usually attached to a wave of immigrants to Nova Scotia from New England about 1760, after the expulsion of the Acadians by the British from the province. The new settlers had been accustomed to the direct local democracy of town meetings in New England and attempted to transplant it to Nova Scotia, but with only brief success. The colonial authorities were loath to permit such a democratic practice especially after the American War of Independence. For some time, though, demands for democratic local self-government persisted, but were put down by the colonial administrators. The other main impetus for local self-government came from Halifax newspaperman Joseph Howe about 1835. He was put on trial for his condemnation of the existing state of affairs and his speech at that trial became a focus for demands for local self-government. Six years later Halifax was incorporated as a town with an elective council. However the franchise was limited to only about eight hundred people who could meet the property quali-fication, and candidates for council were also subject to a quite stringent property qualification. Hence while the 153 people of business and wealth who signed a petition in 1838, countering another petition (signed by 556 Haligonians) which had asked for incorporation, were not successful in preventing incorporation, the property qualifications ensured that the wealthy would be able to dominate the affairs of the town at least for a time.

After the coming of responsible government to Nova Scotia in 1848, the provincial assembly reversed its earlier reluctance to allow local self-government. Legislation was passed in 1855 permitting incorporation of counties and in 1856 permitting incorporation of townships. It is ironic that after the earlier demands for local self-government, Nova Scotians did not exercise the right now granted. Only one township (Yarmouth) was incorporated, but a majority vote there decided to abandon incorporation after a brief period. The earlier enthusiasm for local self-government seems to have waned in the realization by rural residents that incorporation would bring with it higher taxation.

The County Incorporation Act of 1879 was inspired by financial considerations too, this time by the provincial government which was anxious to shift some of the financial burden for local services on to local residents. The Act made municipal incorporation mandatory for rural areas, and as a consequence twelve counties were incorporated as such and the other six counties were incorporated as two districts each. The basic system of municipal government in Nova Scotia was completed in 1888 with enactment of the Towns Incorporation Act, prior to which a total of eight towns had been incorporated, each with a special charter. The Act of 1888 was enabling legislation; it permitted but did not require incorporation of towns, and it specified geographical and population size criteria which had to be met before a charter would be granted.

While there have been numerous changes over time, the structure of municipal government in Nova Scotia has remained essentially unaltered in its basic features ever since 1888. Nova Scotia in 1975 had twenty-four rural municipalities (twelve counties and twelve districts), three cities, and thirty-eight towns, and the whole population and area of the province is included in one or another of them. The twenty-five villages do not have full status as municipalities. The largest urban areas are the cities of Halifax, Dartmouth, and Sydney, with 1971 populations of 122,000, 65,000, and 33,000 respectively. In 1971 a royal commission was appointed to study the municipal system along with education and public services in Nova Scotia. By 1976 only the most tentative steps had been taken with regard to municipal reorganization in the province. The commission's proposals are described in Chapter 4.

Two interesting features of the municipal system in Nova Scotia are the fact that its direct origins were due not to any widespread acceptance of the desirability of democratic local self-government but to quite narrowly financial considerations. The other point of interest in comparing Nova Scotia to neighbouring New Brunswick is the separation of towns and cities, as urban units of local government, from the rural counties and districts. Except for possible joint expenditures for a few limited purposes, the cities and towns are completely independent of the counties politically, even though geographically enclosed by the counties.

NEW BRUNSWICK[6]

New Brunswick has the distinction of having Canada's oldest incorporated city, Saint John, which was granted a royal charter in 1785, a year after the province ceased being part of Nova Scotia. As in Nova Scotia, it cannot be said that local government blossomed quickly, for it was over sixty years before the next municipality was incorporated in the province.

The history of local government in New Brunswick quite closely parallels that of Nova Scotia in a number of respects, although most developments seem to have occurred a bit earlier in New Brunswick. Prior to 1877, most of the province was not municipally incorporated, the Courts of Quarter Sessions being the agencies of local administration. The Legislative Assembly was also greatly occupied with local matters. As in Nova Scotia the grand juries associated with the courts had a largely advisory role and provided the only semblance of citizen participation in local administration. The local citizenry seems to have been largely indifferent to the idea of democratic local self-government. This indifference is sometimes attributed (mistakenly, says Whalen) to the particular type of Loyalist immigrants from the United States. Whalen notes that only a small proportion of them came from the more southern states where the English system of Courts of Quarter Sessions had for some time been the practice.[7] Most came from the New England states with a background of town-hall meetings. Nevertheless, some of the Loyalist settlers in New Brunswick were on the whole comfortable with the courts system and did not demand democratization at the local level. There was also the French factor. The province had a substantial French population which, because of the French tradition of centralism, had not had any experience with democratic local self-government and did not push for it.

Aside from Saint John, there were by 1877 five incorporated towns and six incorporated counties. The provincial assembly passed legislation in 1851 that permitted but did not require incorporation of counties. In 1877, however, county incorporation was made mandatory, and the entire population and area of the province was thus included in one or another incorporated municipality. Such earlier demands for incorporation as had been made came mostly from the more settled areas. Each of the towns was incorporated by a separate charter until 1896 when the Towns Incorporation Act was passed. By this time there were nine towns.

The new Act provided for towns to be incorporated by simple proclamation rather than by individual special charter.

The Counties Act of 1877 and the Towns Act of 1896 established the
basic municipal system. The cities and villages round out the picture. The
cities each have separate charters of incorporation; villages were provided
for in 1920 by the Villages Act, designed to permit incorporation in cases
where the population was too small for town status. Only four villages
were incorporated under that Act, and three of those were eventually
elevated to town status. Thus there was but one incorporated village by
1961.

It is clear that the initiatives for introducing municipal government in
New Brunswick came not so much from the general populace but from
several of the chief administrators of the colony. The two main reasons
for their initiatives appear to have been the growing provincial deficit and
the legislative overload, for the legislature spent much of its time on local
matters. The implementation of municipal government in Ontario in the
1840s no doubt had a demonstration effect as well. However, people in
the rural areas remained unenthusiastic, largely on the grounds that
municipal incorporation would bring with it higher taxes. Their reluctance
was manifested in the small number of counties that were incorporated
under the permissive legislation of 1851.

One rather unusual feature of New Brunswick's municipal system was
the provision for city and town representation on county councils. The
purpose of this was to attempt to integrate urban with rural municipal
government. Representatives of cities and towns on county councils were
free to debate and vote on almost all matters but the county councils were
virtually powerless with respect to the cities and towns. This mechanism
did not produce the desired integration and the counties steadily declined
in significance. Many of them had small populations in large areas and
lacked the financial resources to provide adequate levels of services to
rural residents. In consequence the New Brunswick government launched
a program of fundamental municipal reorganization beginning in 1967
(see Chapter 4) which included abolition of the counties as municipalities. As a result of that reorganization, most of the area of the province
(about 96 per cent) in 1975 was not municipally incorporated, although
the incorporated parts accounted for about two-thirds of the total population. The municipal system in 1975 was comprised of six cities, twenty

towns, eighty-five villages, and 213 unincorporated local service districts. None of the cities has a population of 100,000, Saint John being by far the largest with 89,000 people in 1971.

PRINCE EDWARD ISLAND[8]

Prince Edward Island, like New Brunswick, was once part of the province of Nova Scotia, but was separated by the British fifteen years earlier than New Brunswick, in 1769. The small size of the island and its minuscule population (271 people in 1769) made any form of municipal government or even of decentralized administration unnecessary and impracticable. The comment that ". . . there have been no great issues of municipal reform and no significant struggles for local democracy" therefore comes as no surprise.[9] The provincial government long provided most of the usual local services for most of the province, with minor local matters being dealt with by local citizens.

The island's first experience with municipal government came in 1855 when Charlottetown was incorporated as a city. By an act of 1870, local residents could petition to be incorporated as a town or village, but because of the very small population of most settlements, such petitioning was rare. Summerside became the first incorporated town, in 1877. Six more towns were created over a period of time until the procedure of incorporation fell into disuse in 1919, finally being abolished in 1950. A new Towns Act in 1948 standardized the charters for all towns other than Summerside. The final legislative component of Prince Edward Island's local government system was the Village Services Act of 1950, but the villages so created were not real municipalities; they lacked elected councils and had instead commissioners appointed by the provincial government. The number of villages has grown steadily over time from five in 1952 to twenty-six in 1975, but the number of actual municipalities remained nine in 1975—one city and eight towns, just one more than there were in 1919. Also in 1975 there were thirty-two quasi-municipal Community Improvement Committees. Much of the island has not been municipally incorporated; about 75 per cent of the area and 45 per cent of the population in 1975 were not municipally organized. Charlottetown is the most populous municipality with a 1971 population of just over 19,000. Indeed, the entire island had only some 120,000 residents in 1971.

Due to its small area, small population, and relatively even geographical distribution of that population, Prince Edward Island's municipal system is unique in Canada. The need for municipalities has never been great nor have there been vocal demands for democratic local self-government, for the provincial legislature is quite able to itself supply most local services and respond to local input. It is therefore understandable that the province's municipalities have a narrower range of functions than usual. The island's municipal history has always been exceptionally stable and uneventful, and no substantial reorganization is foreseeable.

Quebec[10]

The history of municipal government in Quebec is generally considered to have commenced only after the French capitulation to the British forces, and even then the most significant developments occurred eighty years later, in 1840.

A number of reasons have been offered from time to time for the absence of municipal government under the French regime—the vast land area, sparse and somewhat scattered population (in 1737 the population was about 25,000, rising to about 80,000 in 1763), but undoubtedly the main reason was that municipal government was not compatible with the centralist policy and tradition of French public administration. From the founding of Quebec City in 1608 and Montreal in 1642, the French colonial administrators were no more prepared to grant local self-government than the French settlers would have been prepared to accept it. Local services were provided, if at all, either by the central government, or organized by local seigneurs and the church parishes.

It comes as a surprise therefore to find that there were several early innovations. In 1663 the Chevalier de Mezy, as Governor, provided for the election of a mayor and aldermen in Quebec City, and an election was duly held. There was also the phenomenon of "syndics d'habitations", local officers elected in the larger centres to represent local interests before the governing council. These experiments were relatively isolated though, for the French government did not approve of them. The syndics that were created by 1647 had pretty much ceased to exist by 1661. Even though they did not constitute real local self-government, these experiments represented the earliest attempts to introduce an element of local participation in decision making in colonized Canada. The intendant, as head of the civil administration, retained very strong control over local affairs through a system of local agents, particularly the road inspectors. The intendant functioned in Quebec much as the prefects did in continental France.

For three years after the capitulation, Upper and Lower Canada were under British military rule. After 1763, the British governor merely replaced the French intendant, for the form of local administration remained much as it had been, although Courts of Quarter Sessions were created. The Constitutional Act of 1791 separated Upper Canada from Lower Canada. While it granted representative government to the two provinces, the Act did not specifically provide for local self-government. However, both Montreal and Quebec City were granted charters of incorporation in 1832 after local petitioning. The charters were for only four years and were not renewed in 1836 because of the troubled political climate which culminated in the rebellion of 1837. The earliest Montreal city councils were dominated by people of Anglo-Saxon origin, reflecting the greater familiarity of such people with municipal institutions than was the case with regard to people of French origin.

The rebellion was a notable event for municipal government in the province of Quebec, for it resulted in Lord Durham's report which strongly recommended the creation of a system of municipal government. This led to the passing at the end of 1840 of an ordinance by which Lower Canada was divided into twenty-two districts, each having an elected council with special though limited powers. Montreal and Quebec City received new municipal charters that same year. It seemed as though municipal government had really arrived in Lower Canada. However, the new scheme was not greeted by all with enthusiasm. Some of the opposition was centred around a party which sprang up to sabotage the ordinance by running for election candidates who were committed, if elected, to doing nothing to put the scheme into operation. Opposition to the ordinance was based partly on the impending reunion of Lower and Upper Canada, on the fact that wardens and some other local officials were to be appointed rather than elected, and on fear of an increase in taxes. The opposition was successful and the Ordinance of 1840 was replaced five years later by the Morin Act. This established townships and parishes as municipalities and provided for the incorporation of towns and villages upon petition. In 1847 the parish and township municipalities were abolished, being replaced by larger counties. Parishes and townships were created again in 1855 by the Lower Canada Municipal and Roads Act, which also related to incorporation of towns and villages. Other acts passed in 1870, 1876, and 1903 rounded out the municipal system, but it was the legislation of 1855 which established the province's framework for municipal government. While there have been periodic adjustments to the framework, it was still largely intact in 1975 except for the process of creating regional governments and encouraging municipal amalgamation in the late 1960s and early 1970s. That process, which is described in Chapter 4, was a consequence of the enormous number of municipalities (1752 of them in 1961) in the province, many of which were very small in area and population.

In 1975 the province of Quebec had 258 cities and towns (of which about sixty-eight were cities), 248 villages, 1003 townships and parishes, seventy-two counties, and three metropolitan and regional governments. Almost all the province's population resided in municipalities but the northern fifth of the province was not municipally organized. With a population in 1971 of 1,214,000, Montreal is the most populous city. Only two others in the province had populations then in excess of 100,000: Laval and Quebec with 228,000 and 186,000 respectively.

Ontario[11]

After the French capitulation to the British in 1760, Quebec and Ontario were administered as the Province of Canada under military rule with no suggestion of local self-government. Four years later the Courts of Quarter Sessions were created as the agencies of local administration. The justices of the peace in these courts in effect ruled the administrative districts, having control over finances and over local officials, making rules and regulations, as well as dispensing justice.

Clearly one of the most important factors eventually leading to the establishment of municipal government in Ontario was the Loyalist migration during and after the American War of Independence. Those Loyalists who did not go to New Brunswick or Nova Scotia settled for the most part west of Montreal from Kingston through to the Niagara area, territory where there had been little previous settlement. Coming predominantly from the former colony of New York, the Loyalist settlers brought with them their experience of local autonomy of the New England type and thus were not likely to be content with the form of local ad- ministration then exercised by the British. After much petitioning for local self-government, the colonists succeeded first in having Upper Canada made a province separate from Lower Canada by the Constitu- tional Act of 1791. But they did not yet acquire local self-government. The British were not yet prepared to grant it, largely because the town- hall meetings of New England were considered to have been an excess of democracy and a primary cause of the American revolutionary war. Of course such democratic institutions were not yet a feature of the practice in Britain. The first bill introduced in the new legislative assembly of Upper Canada (in 1792) proposed authorizing town meetings. Although this bill was not passed, one was passed the following year which permitted ratepayers to elect certain town officials. This bill (the Parish and Town Officers Act) is sometimes viewed as the precursor of municipal govern- ment, but the town meetings had no legislative powers aside from determining the height of fences! A year later the meetings were also authorized to set the times when domestic animals could run at large. Clearly, then, the Courts of Quarter Sessions remained the main agency for local affairs, and their responsibilities were increased from time to time.

By 1812 the population of Upper Canada reached about 75,000, of which about two-thirds had immigrated from the United States. However, this fairly large population was widely dispersed. The Courts of Quarter Sessions were feeling the strain, and demands for municipal government did not diminish. Some moves were made to incorporate Kingston, but the War of 1812–14 delayed that. After the war, events began to move more swiftly. The first public school act for Upper Canada was passed in 1816 creating elective school trustee boards. In 1832 elective boards of police were permitted, the first of which was created in Brockville that year. These were misnamed, for their functions went somewhat beyond appointment of police officers. More and more towns petitioned for extended local self-government, culminating in the incorporation of York (Toronto) as a city in 1834. The financial bankruptcy of Upper Canada in 1837 provided further impetus to creating municipal governments so as to shift some of the financial burden for local works away from the provincial treasury. While the Loyalists brought with them their experience of the New England states, they also brought with them a strong antipathy to direct taxation. However, they were prepared to concede the latter in order to gain the former. By the time Lord Durham's report of 1839 stated that it was a matter of "vital importance" that a good system of municipal institutions be established, at least four municipalities had been chartered. With the failure of the Imperial Parliament to include with the legislation which reunited Upper and Lower Canada specific provision for elected local councils, it was to the new legislature that the responsibility passed. At the first session of the legislature in 1841, the District Councils Act applying to Upper Canada was passed. This Act provided for elected district councils (though the warden, clerk, and treasurer were to be appointed by the Crown) which took over all the non-judicial functions of the Courts of Quarter Sessions. The Act did not apply to incorporated cities and towns, for the larger ones already had some form of incorporation. It created only a rural form of municipal government, and of a restricted kind. The Governor-in-Council retained a considerable amount of power relative to the new districts, such as the power to dissolve a district council at any time and to disallow any by-law. This District Councils Act was the real starting point for the system of municipal government in Ontario, even though it did not entirely satisfy demands for local self-government and did not apply to cities and towns. But it signalled the end of local administration based on appointed justices of the peace and separated municipal power from judicial power.

It was the Municipal Corporations Act of 1849 (better known as the Baldwin Act) that is significant for providing for a comprehensive system of municipal government in the province. The passing of Robert Baldwin's bill abolished the districts created eight years earlier and provided for two general classes of municipalities: 1) local municipalities—cities, towns, villages, and townships; and 2) counties, made up of local municipalities. In other words the counties were second-tier municipalities, with the county council being composed of the reeves and deputy reeves of townships included in the county as well as representatives of villages and most towns. The cities and "separated" towns were excluded from the county structure. The Act provided for elected councils where none previously existed, granted the municipalities wide powers, and greatly reduced central administrative control over local affairs. Although a considerable number of adjustments were made over time, the Baldwin Act of 1849 was very durable indeed and greatly influenced the development of municipal government in other provinces.

Crawford wrote in 1952 that the municipal system in Ontario in 1849 ". . . has sustained the strains of a rapidly changing economy for over one hundred years without substantial alteration of its basic features."[12] However, it was only a year after he wrote those words that the first move was made to overhaul municipal government in the province. The reorganization is examined in Chapter Four.

In 1975 Ontario had forty-five cities (including the five boroughs in Metropolitan Toronto), 141 towns, 121 villages, twenty-seven counties, 474 townships, one metropolitan government, and eleven regional/district governments. Almost all of the northern 90 per cent of the province was not municipally organized but this area accounted for only about 1 per cent of the total population. Nine of the cities or towns had at least 100,000 residents in 1971, the City of Toronto alone having over 700,000.

The West

MANITOBA[13]

Being part of Canada's more recently settled west, Manitoba had not developed a system of municipal government prior to being admitted into Confederation in 1870. The territory was part of Rupert's Land, granted by charter in 1670 to the Hudson's Bay Company. Between 1811 and 1836 part of the land was granted to Lord Selkirk but was re-purchased by the Company until being surrendered to the government of Canada in 1870. Prior to that year local administration lay in the hands of the Hudson's Bay Company and for a time in Lord Selkirk's hands. The area's small population (numbering about 12,000 in 1870) came in large part from eastern Canada, and having had prior experience with municipal government, they were not entirely satisfied with the unrepresentative appointive basis of the Company's Council which administered the territory. This resentment showed itself in continual demands for representative government.

Once it became a province, Manitoba quite rapidly began to develop municipal structures. The first meeting of the provincial legislature passed a County Assessment Act and a Parish Assessment Act in 1871. Rather than establishing municipal governments, these two acts provided a means for compiling a provincial tax roll and for assessing residents in small localities for money required to pay for purely local improvements petitioned for by the residents. There were no elected county or parish councils.

The first attempt to create municipalities came in 1873, with Winnipeg being incorporated as a city with a population of less than 3700. A popular movement for incorporation of the city had arisen early in 1872. Public meetings were held and resolutions presented to the provincial legislature, but the legislature did not act quickly. Incorporation was apparently opposed by the Hudson's Bay Company and four property owners. These five interests owned well over half of the assessable property in the proposed city and were not pleased with the prospect of having that property taxed. After several more mass meetings, the legislature did take action but revised the draft bill presented to it by the citizens' committee in such a way as to greatly reduce the proposed city's taxing powers. After yet more mass public meetings and protests, Winnipeg was finally incorporated with a municipal structure and powers that very closely emulated the practice in Ontario.

Also in 1873 legislation was passed providing for the incorporation of other municipalities if petitioned for by residents. Only six areas became municipally incorporated under the Act. This scheme was abandoned in 1883 when the provincial government decided to impose a municipal structure for the whole province based on Ontario's county system. The province was divided into twenty-six counties which were themselves municipalities, each having from five to eight local municipalities within it. This two-tier structure did not separate local rural from urban municipalities; all were included in one county or another. The experiment was short-lived, lasting only three years. It was found to be too expensive and inefficient because of the vast area covered by some counties and because of often sparse and scattered population.

The province was then divided into rural municipalities of small areas, grouped into three judicial districts. The district boards were to provide courthouses and, later, connecting roads, ferries, and health officers. Even this was beyond the financial capacity of many local municipalities, however. The judicial boards were abandoned in 1886, and their functions were transferred to the provincial government. Thus two-tier municipal government lasted only five years. Generally speaking, the municipal system in Manitoba in 1975 was much as it was in 1886, with the municipal units being cities, towns, villages, and rural municipalities. However, just as there was much experimentation between 1873 and 1886 in Manitoba's municipal system, the period since 1960 has been one of experimentation with regard to metropolitan government in the Winnipeg area. Those experiments have been significant and have evoked widespread interest, and are examined in Chapter Four.

There were in 1975 five cities, thirty-three towns, forty villages, and 105 rural municipalities in Manitoba. Considerably less than half the province's area was municipally organized, but most of the population did live in municipalities. The most populous of them is, of course, the City of Winnipeg, with some half-million residents.

SASKATCHEWAN[14]

What is now the province of Saskatchewan was, like Manitoba, part of the lands granted to the Hudson's Bay Company in 1670, but taken over by the Canadian government in 1870. It was administered much as a colony until 1905 when it became a province. The territorial council passed the North-West Municipal Ordinance of 1883 which was patterned on the Manitoba legislation of the same year, and which in turn was based on Ontario's Baldwin Act of 1849. The Ordinance provided for the creation of municipalities, both rural and urban, if certain area and population size criteria could be met and if the citizenry in an area petitioned for municipal status. The first to be granted municipal status was Regina (as a town, in 1883) and four rural municipalities were organized the following year. The momentum was not maintained, for there were still only four rural municipalities and one additional town until 1897, when two of the rural municipalities dropped their municipal status. The problems were ones of small population (the province's population in 1881 was about 38,000) that was scattered and that lacked the financial capacity needed to support municipal government, and the considerable size (at least 144 square miles) of the rural municipalities. The experiment was not pursued. Instead, what later came to be called local improvement districts were created, beginning in 1887, primarily for the purpose of road construction. Again, these were not mandatory, and few were created until they were made mandatory in 1896.

It became the policy of the federal government to stimulate settlement of the West, and great numbers of settlers arrived from Europe and from eastern Canada. The immigrants from eastern Canada particularly had previous experience with municipal government. These factors had the effect of stimulating municipal organization in Saskatchewan so that when it became a province in 1905 there were four cities, forty-three towns, ninety-seven villages, two rural municipalities, and the non-municipal local improvement districts of which there were 359. Among the western provinces Saskatchewan was receiving the most new settlers and thus the need for municipal organization was particularly great there. The system was consolidated in 1908 and 1909 with passage of new legislation. The rural municipalities especially multiplied as a result to 200 by 1912. Nevertheless, many rural residents opposed municipal organization, usually in fear of increased taxes, and the provincial government found it necessary that year to force remaining local improvement districts (which were 144 square miles) to become rural municipalities, each being 324 square miles. Only on the prairies could such a size/shape criterion of municipal boundaries be possible with the municipalities presenting a grid pattern. While topographical features such as rivers were taken into account in laying out municipal boundaries, a map of the province showing the boundaries resembles a fishing net thrown over the province. The boundaries did not usually take into account the location of cities and towns, the size of population contained, nor the financial capacity to support municipal government.

Despite these problems, the municipal system in Saskatchewan in 1975 remained basically that of 1909, though there have been several studies proposing municipal reorganization.[15] Thus the early period of experimentation with forms of municipal government was replaced by a very long period of relative stability. The system in 1975 was comprised of eleven cities, 132 towns, 348 villages, and 292 rural municipalities. There also remained ten non-municipal local-improvement districts. About 52 per cent of the area and 6 per cent of the population was not municipally organized. There is no two-tier municipal government in the province;

however, provision is made for organizing hamlets within the rural municipalities, but only with specific regard to waterworks and sewerage systems. Regina and Saskatoon are by far the most populated municipalities, with populations of 139,000 and 126,000 respectively in 1971.

ALBERTA[16]

Since Alberta was, like Saskatchewan, part of the federally administered Northwest Territories from 1870 to 1905, Alberta's earliest experience with municipal government was the same as Saskatchewan's.

There was literally no municipal government in Alberta until 1884 when Calgary was incorporated as a town under the 1883 North-West Municipal Ordinance. The Ordinance specified minimum populations of 300 for both rural municipalities and towns, and few areas could meet that minimum. As Hanson notes, there were in Alberta in 1881 only about 18,000 people.[17] Seven years passed before Alberta's second municipality (Lethbridge) was incorporated, followed by Edmonton in 1892. The rural population was very sparse and scattered, and the fact that rural municipalities each had to have an area of at least 144 square miles prevented what few people there were from communicating with each other and developing any degree of cohesion. Therefore no petitions were presented for the creation of rural municipalities in Alberta under the Ordinance, and none were created. In most of the province the only semblance of local government was to be found in school districts and in statute labour and fire districts (later called local-improvement districts). None of these were full municipal governments for they were created for only one or two specific services and did not have elected responsible councils except for the local improvement districts after 1903.

Beginning about 1896, developments began to move quickly, due in large part to the influx of settlers in the West. While many of the new settlers were from Europe, there were substantial numbers from Nova Scotia and Ontario. These people in particular had been accustomed to local self-government and pressed for it in Alberta. By 1905 when Alberta became a province, its population had swelled to about 170,000 (about nine times as large as it was in 1881), and the municipal governments included two cities, fifteen towns, and thirty villages.

In 1912 a new and comprehensive municipal system was implemented.

The entire province was divided up in squares (1249 of them) of 324 square miles, called local improvement districts (later called municipal districts). If a district had at least 324 residents, it could be incorporated as a rural municipality. However, few incorporations were requested, largely because of fears of increased taxes. Attempts by the provincial government to stimulate incorporation had only limited success. The more settled areas of the province were more enthusiastic about municipal status, and the number of cities, towns, and villages grew rapidly prior to the First World War. Much of the province remained municipally unincorporated, though.

The municipal system remained largely unchanged until 1942 when the provincial government began to reduce the number of (rural) municipal districts by amalgamation. The depression of the 1930s financially ruined many of the municipal districts, a number of them foregoing their municipal status. Between 1942 and 1944 the number of incorporated municipal districts was reduced from 143 to sixty by amalgamation. The new units were very large in area. This fact posed some difficulties, as did the fact that the school division and hospital district boundaries did not coincide with municipal district boundaries. Tax rates within municipal districts therefore varied, and people were confused over which authority was responsible for what. These kinds of problems gave rise to rural municipal reorganization beginning in 1950. That reorganization was a novel one in Canada, for it emulated the English model whereby a single elected council in each county was responsible for all local functions including education. Two counties were established initially as a trial run, and two others shortly afterward. By 1968 the enlarged counties, which are not two-tiered, covered the majority of the province's populated rural area. The one function which remained outside county council jurisdiction was hospitals, for the county and hospital district boundaries could not be made to coincide.

Generally speaking Alberta is one of those provinces that experimented considerably with forms of municipal government, the system being reorganized several times. Like Manitoba, the early attempts to replicate Ontario's municipal system were unsuccessful in Alberta, in large part because the population was too small and too evenly scattered to be able to support that fairly elaborate system.

In 1975 Alberta had ten cities, 103 towns, 167 villages, and thirty counties. About two-thirds of the area and some 5 per cent of the total population were not municipally organized. The cities of Edmonton and Calgary are by far the most populous municipalities, having populations in 1971 of 438,000 and 403,000 respectively.

BRITISH COLUMBIA[18]

After the voyage of Captain Cook to Vancouver Island in 1778, colonization of what is now British Columbia proceeded slowly until the discovery of gold in California in 1848. That discovery resulted in a general movement of people, especially Americans, to the west coast of the continent, and British Columbia was not unaffected. Victoria in particular became an important centre of trade. Somewhat anxious to counterbalance the increasing strength of the Americans in the area, the British took over Vancouver Island from the Hudson's Bay Company in 1849 and attempted to establish a "flourishing" British colony beginning in 1850. But colonization did not flourish, for in 1853 there were still only some 450 white settlers on the island. On the mainland, the discovery of gold on the Fraser River in 1858 produced a mass influx of over 30,000 miners and others. Although most of those people stayed only temporarily, some 4000 remained in scattered areas on the mainland.

The Hudson's Bay Company's lease on the mainland expired in 1858, and the mainland became a second British colony, separate from Vancouver Island. The pre-colonial period in both colonies was marked by a total absence of municipal government. Local administration lay in the hands of Company personnel. Between the pre-colonial period and British Columbia's entry into Confederation in 1871, the first provision was made for municipalities. The City of New Westminster (capital of the mainland colony) was created as a municipality in 1860, and Victoria (capital of the Vancouver Island colony) was incorporated as a town in 1862 with a white population of about 3500. It became a city in 1867, with a permanent population of over 6000. The two colonies had been united the previous year.

Shortly after British Columbia became a province in Confederation the provincial legislature passed the Consolidated Municipal Act of 1872 by which people in an area of not more than ten square miles and having at least thirty adult male residents could petition for municipal incorporation. The rugged geography, difficult communications, and sparse population in most of the province account for the minimal population criterion. By the end of 1874 there were five municipalities in the province. Vancouver was incorporated as a city in 1886.

Several acts were passed from time to time regarding municipalities, including the Municipal Clauses Act of 1896 which adapted the 1849 Baldwin scheme of Ontario to British Columbia's circumstances. By 1900 there were some fifty-two municipalities of two classes—cities and municipal districts. While city status was presumably intended for the more densely populated settlements and district municipalities for rural areas, such a distinction became lost over time. Some cities had as few as two hundred residents, and some districts close to forty thousand people.

A very large portion of the province remained municipally unorganized. Because of the topography, settlements still tended to be scattered and isolated. The population was also not especially large (about 179,000 people in 1901) and few of the residents had much previous experience with municipal government. It was decided in 1920 to create a new category, villages. By 1948 there were still only the three categories of municipalities—thirty-five cities, thirty-seven villages, and twenty-seven municipal districts. Although the municipalities covered 78 per cent of the province's population in 1947, they covered only half of 1 per cent of the land area. The first towns were not created under the Municipal Act of 1957 until 1958.

Still, 99 per cent of the territory of the province remained municipally unorganized prior to the implementation of regional districts. Consequently, the provincial government in British Columbia itself was responsible for providing local services to almost the entire area of the province, and what municipalities existed tended to be very small. The regional districts scheme was implemented in stages beginning in 1965 (see Chapter 4 for details). Virtually the entire province was by 1975 included in one or another of the twenty-eight regional districts. In addition there were in 1975 thirty-seven municipal districts, fifty-eight villages, eleven towns, and thirty-two cities. Only about seven of the cities had 1971 populations of at least 20,000, and only one (the City of Vancouver, with 426,000) had over 100,000 residents.

The Northern Territories[19]

The Yukon and Northwest Territories were also controlled by the Hudson's Bay Company until 1870 when the land was acquired by the federal government. The territories were then governed in a more or less colonial fashion by the federally appointed lieutenant-governor, and municipal government was non-existent, obviously due to the enormous area and its extremely small and very highly dispersed population. The land area has been reduced several times—in 1870 when Manitoba became a province, in 1905 when Alberta and Saskatchewan were carved out as provinces, and in 1912 when the northern boundaries of Quebec, Ontario, and Manitoba were moved north to their present positions.

Gold was discovered in the Klondike in 1896 and the population of what is now the Yukon rapidly swelled, resulting in the creation of the Yukon as a separate territory in 1898. By 1901 the population of the Yukon was over 27,000, most of whom were recent arrivals who had earlier experience with representative government and demanded it for the Yukon. Gradually the appointive and advisory territorial council acquired a legislative function and an increasing portion of its seats became elective. The territorial administration provided what local services there were until the demands of the people in Dawson for self-government could no longer be contained, especially after 1900 when they were taxed for local improvements. Dawson was granted a charter of incorporation as a city in 1901, having then a population of over 9000. However, the charter was revoked in 1904 after a plebiscite which was conducted in a somewhat suspicious manner, and provision of local services relapsed into the hands of the territorial administration. Provision was also made in 1901 for unincorporated towns to be established upon petition. But this was not full-fledged municipal government, for residents could elect only one official (an overseer), and the range of services that could be provided was very narrow. One unincorporated town was created (Grand Forks) but it too reverted to territorial administration when its population filtered away. The beginnings of municipal government were thus short-lived.

Both the Northwest and Yukon territories now have municipal ordinances which establish frameworks for municipal government. Because of a number of unique characteristics of the North, there is considerable variety in types of municipal and quasi-municipal government, but some of the population and almost all the land area of the two territories remain without any form of municipal government. In the Northwest Territories only a miniscule proportion of the area had municipal government in 1975, but about 72 per cent of the Northwest Territories' population lived in incorporated settlements. Some 83 per cent of the Yukon's population lived in incorporated municipalities in 1975, covering only a fraction of 1 per cent of the land mass. The traditional nomadic lifestyle of the native people, the traditional practices of selecting authority figures, the often temporary nature of settlements such as the Distant Early Warning (DEW) radar installations, and so on clearly make it inappropriate and difficult to superimpose on the North a pattern of municipal government of the sort that characterizes southern Canada. The territories have had to be adaptive and innovative. Rather than creating the more usual types of responsible local self-government, emphasis has been placed on decentralization of the territorial administration and on more or less official committees of elected local residents to advise the resident administrators. Local-improvement districts are of this type. The few cities, towns, and villages that are incorporated in the two territories tend to follow the structure of local government in southern Canada. Indicative of the policy to create larger numbers of smaller municipalities was the introduction of village status in 1964 and hamlet status in 1969. There were only four municipalities or quasi-municipalities in the two territories in 1964 but by 1975 there were twenty-three in all: three cities (Dawson, Whitehorse, and Yellowknife), five towns, two villages, nine hamlets, and four local improvement districts. The most populated were the cities of Whitehorse (Yukon) with a 1971 population of 11,200, and Yellowknife (North West Territories) with 6100.

Overview

As the foregoing indicates, the pattern of evolution of municipal government in Canada has been far from uniform, but there are similarities. Although there are a few exceptions (notably New Brunswick and Prince Edward Island), in most provinces municipal government was developed only through struggles. But it was not always a case of the general citizenry struggling to be granted municipal government by reluctant colonial or provincial authorities; there were times and places when the central governments had to struggle to get municipal government implemented, sometimes in the face of opposition from the imperial government, sometimes from powerful minority interests, and sometimes from the general populace. It was particularly in those provinces which earliest developed any forms of municipal government that there was a struggle between government and the citizenry. Typically in these provinces it was the residents of more settled, more urbanized places that struggled for municipal government while rural residents struggled against it, and the provincial governments often imposed it.

In present times, when local self-government is taken for granted and often considered to be a cornerstone of democracy—"grass-roots" democracy[20]—it comes as something of a surprise to find that there were in fact some citizens who were indifferent to it and others who opposed it. But one must take into account the political values that were common until well into the nineteenth century, the heritage of the earlier settlers, and the patterns of settlement. "Democracy" has not always been a valued concept, particularly among the more affluent citizenry who feared that representative and responsible government based on a wide franchise would lead to unprincipled and spendthrift rule by the mob, to the detriment of the more materially privileged minority. There certainly is evidence to suggest that economically powerful minorities, especially in urban areas such as St. John's, Halifax, and Winnipeg, did indeed delay the introduction of municipal government in those places. Even when stalling tactics could no longer be sustained the effect of such interests could be seen in the municipal franchise limited by property qualifications, and the even more restrictive property qualifications for candidates for councils. Hence the earlier municipal governments in Canada were far from *popular* governments. Mob rule was not to be permitted and the wealthy minorities could be assured that there would not be spendthrift municipal government which would expropriate the wealth of the minority by confiscatory taxation of property.

It was not only the economically advantaged minority who opposed democratic local self-government, though. The larger group of less materially advantaged citizens, especially in rural areas, who owned little but the piece of land they had worked hard to clear and cultivate, also tended to oppose the introduction of municipal government. Once acquired, that land was jealously guarded particularly from direct taxation. Their fear was not of mob rule but simply of taxation. Since the bulk of municipal revenue has traditionally come from direct taxation of real estate, and since in some provinces the colonial/provincial governments sought to shift the financial burden for the provision of local services away from the central treasury, the fears of these people were not groundless. Those who pressed most for democratic local self-government tended to be the property-less urbanites.

The cultural heritage of the earlier immigrants also played an important part as has already been suggested. Prior to the waves of mass immigration in the last decade of the nineteenth century and early decades of the twentieth century, the three most important cultural influences were French, British, and American. Of these three only the United Empire Loyalists from the United States had had experience with more or less democratic local self-government, and even in their case it was only those Loyalists from the New England states that had such a heritage.

The early French colonists had no background in self-government. Administration in New France, as in France itself, was highly centralized in the hands of the governors and also of the church. This was reflected in an absence of demands for the introduction of municipal government and in a disinterest or outright opposition to it once provision was made for municipal institutions. Fear of taxation seems to have played a considerably less important part in their disinterest or opposition than the incongruity between their heritage and the notion of self-government. For their part, the British immigrants left Britain when the Courts of Quarter Sessions were still the mechanism for administration of local affairs in England, so these people too had no prior experience with democratic local self-government. Indeed it is the case that municipal government evolved in Britain after it had done so in much of Canada. The United Empire Loyalists who immigrated to Canada from other than the New England states had been used to local administration patterned on the English model. Hence the cultural heritages of those Loyalists and immigrants from Britain were fairly similar but not necessarily incompatible with local self-government. Considerable significance must therefore be attached to the Loyalists from New England.

Upper Canada was not among the provinces that were settled earliest, yet Ontario really was the first of the provinces to develop a more or less full-fledged system of municipal government. There is little doubt that this was due much to the Loyalists there who constituted a very large portion of the population and who had already been experienced in local self-government. Their demands for it in Ontario were particularly vocal. That, coupled with Lord Durham's endorsement in his report following the rebellion of 1837, is important in accounting for the early organization of municipal government there. The Maritime provinces too had an influx of Loyalist settlers, but in New Brunswick and Nova Scotia they did not constitute so large a segment of the population. In an indirect way, therefore, the American War of Independence had a double influence on the evolution of municipal government in Canada. First, it had a negative influence, in that the British colonial administrators were determined not to allow a repeat performance in Canada of the American independence movement, a movement which the British thought was due to an excess of democracy in the former American colonies. But the American war of independence had the later effect of quickening the pace of municipal organization in Canada when the demands of the Loyalists could no longer be contained and the New England model of local self-government had a stronger demonstration effect.

The evidence is compelling that patterns of settlement have played a major role as well in fostering municipal government. Especially in the East, in Quebec, and in Ontario the earliest municipalities were created in the most urbanized areas of the time—St. John's, Halifax, Montreal, Quebec City, Brockville, Toronto, and so on. Concentrations of people produce problems (such as waste disposal, water supply, crime, and fires) of a range and scale that require some fairly elaborate structures of decision making, and as the number of concentrations of people increased the capability of provincial legislatures and colonial authorities to oversee and control local administration was reduced. Also, the pattern of early settlement in Canada was characterized by a highly dispersed population over a massive land area. Given the problems of communication and transportation as well as often limited familiarity of central decision-makers with local conditions in remote areas, the desirability or necessity of rural municipal units became obvious to them, even if or when the rural dwellers were opposed. Hence there was a marked difference between urban and rural residents; the urban people demanded local self-government for which there was a demonstrable need, while rural residents frequently had such government forced upon them.

While these three factors of changing political values, cultural heritage, and patterns of settlement seem to have been particularly important east of Manitoba (though of some relevance westward), their importance is probably overshadowed in the West by the timing of settlement there and the demonstration effect of the Ontario system after 1849. But like most of the provinces, the western four experienced periods of experimentation with different sizes and forms of municipal government, finding their earliest attempts, which were largely copies or adaptations of the Ontario system, to be too elaborate and inappropriate for them.

Although most provinces made periodic adjustments to their systems of municipal government after the early experimentation, the relative durability of the municipal systems is quite startling. One wonders whether this durability was due as much to excellence of the municipal systems (as Crawford suggests, in writing that the Baldwin plan was "soundly conceived"[21]) as to the political difficulties involved in provincial governments overhauling their municipal systems.

Only passing mention has been made in this chapter of the relationships between the provincial governments and their respective municipalities. Since the reorganizations examined in Chapter 4 have been partly a consequence of the nature of such relationships, it is necessary to consider first the relationships between municipal governments and senior levels of government.

NOTES

1. British North America Act, 1867, section 92, subsection 8. Subsections 2, 7, and 9 are relevant too.
2. In addition to the sources listed for each province the following works have been used for this chapter: K. Grant Crawford, *Canadian Municipal Government* (Toronto: University of Toronto Press, 1954); H. L. Brittain, *Local Government in Canada* (Toronto: Ryerson Press, 1951); S. Morley Wickett, ed., *Municipal Government in Canada* (Toronto: University of Toronto Library, 1907). All departments of municipal affairs provided additional documents and figures.
3. The material for this section is drawn mostly from J. C. Crosbie, "Local Government in Newfoundland," *Canadian Journal of Economics and Political Science*, vol. XXIII, no. 3 (August, 1956), pp. 332–46; and *Report of the Royal Commission on Municipal Government in Newfoundland and Labrador* (St. John's, 1974), Chapter 1. See also S. J. R. Noel, *Politics in Newfoundland* (Toronto: University of Toronto Press, 1971).

4. Noel, in *Politics in Newfoundland* (p. 18), notes that in 1901 of more than 1300 settlements only eighteen had a population of one thousand or more; and Crosbie, in "Local Government in Newfoundland" (p. 341), notes that in 1945 there were only thirty-six settlements of this size.

5. A particularly good account of the history of municipal government in Nova Scotia is J. M. Beck, *The Evolution of Municipal Government in Nova Scotia 1749–1973*, a study prepared for the Nova Scotia Royal Commission on Education, Public Services and Provincial–Municipal Relations (Halifax, 1973). See also J. M. Beck, *The Government of Nova Scotia* (Toronto: University of Toronto Press, 1957), Chapter XIX; and C. B. Fergusson, *Local Government in Nova Scotia* (Halifax: Institute of Public Affairs of Dalhousie University, 1961).

6. A good account of municipal history in New Brunswick is the study prepared by Hugh Whalen included as Chapter II in the *Report of the Royal Commission on Finance and Municipal Taxation in New Brunswick* (Fredericton, 1963). His study also appears as H. J. Whalen, *The Development of Local Government in New Brunswick* (Fredericton, 1963).

7. Whalen, in *Finance and Municipal Taxation*, p. 45.

8. This section is derived mainly from Frank MacKinnon, *The Government of Prince Edward Island* (Toronto: University of Toronto Press, 1951), Chapter XIII.

9. Ibid., p. 274.

10. The material in this section is drawn mostly from the general references cited in footnote 2. See also Guy Bourassa, "Les Élites politiques de Montréal: de l'aristocratie à la démocratie," *Canadian Journal of Economics and Political Science*, vol. XXXI, no. 1 (February, 1965), pp. 35–51. His article also appears in Jack K. Masson and James D. Anderson, eds., *Emerging Party Politics in Urban Canada* (Toronto: McClelland and Stewart, 1972), pp. 87–109.

11. In addition to the general sources cited in footnote 2, see Romaine K. Ross, *Local Government in Ontario*, 2nd ed. (Toronto: Canada Law Book Company, 1962); Terry T. Ferris, "Local Government Reform in Upper Canada," *Canadian Public Administration*, vol. XII, no. 3 (1969), pp. 387–410; and J. H. Aitchison, "The Development of Local Government in Upper Canada, 1783–1850" (unpublished Ph.D. thesis, University of Toronto, 1953), especially parts I and V.

12. Crawford, *Canadian Municipal Government*, p. 32.

13. The material for this section comes mostly from M. S. Donnelly, *The Government of Manitoba* (Toronto: University of Toronto Press, 1963), Chapter 9. See also Alan F. J. Artibise, *Winnipeg: A Social History of Urban Growth 1874–1914* (Montreal: McGill-Queen's University Press, 1975), especially Chapter 1.

14. The following material is drawn largely from the Saskatchewan Royal Commission on Agriculture and Rural Life, *Report 4: Rural Roads and Local Government* (Regina: Queen's Printer, 1955); the Saskatchewan Local Government Continuing Committee, *Local Government in Saskatchewan* (Regina: Queen's Printer, 1961), especially Chapter 2; and George F. Dawson, *The Municipal System of Saskatchewan*, 3rd ed. (Regina: Department of Municipal Affairs, 1955).

15. See the reports of the Saskatchewan Royal Commission on Agriculture and Rural Life (Regina: Queen's Printer, 1955–1957); and Saskatchewan Local Government Continuing Committee, *Local Government in Saskatchewan*.

16. Much of the material in this section is drawn from Eric Hanson, *Local Government in Alberta* (Toronto: McClelland and Stewart, 1956).

17. Ibid., footnote 3 of Chapter I, p. 127.

18. Most of the material that follows is drawn from the general references cited in footnote 2. Some information was found in British Columbia Royal Commission, *Report on Provincial-Municipal Relations* (Victoria: King's Printer, 1947); and in Alexander Begg, *History of British Columbia* (Toronto: William Briggs, 1894).

19. In addition to the Wickett book cited in footnote 2, see Canada Advisory Commission on the Development of Government in the Northwest Territories, *Report*, 3 volumes (Ottawa, 1966), Volume I, sections B and c3.

20. See Chapter 5 on this.

21. Crawford, *Canadian Municipal Government*, p. 32.

Relationships between Canada's municipalities and their respective provincial governments are not like those between the federal government and the provincial governments. The dissimilarity stems simply from the fact that the latter relationships are founded on a federal form of government in both theory and practice, whereas the former are not, either in theory or in practice.

As Simeon has pointed out, the subject of federalism has been approached from two main perspectives.[1] One of these is the cultural/sociological approach—cultural diversity within a more or less limited context of unity, in which the federal form of government is the mechanism for protecting and expressing the diverse qualities and desires within the society that has a degree of unity of objectives. There are no convincing grounds for holding that this approach is of any utility for examining relationships between municipalities and senior government. The origins of Canada's municipalities are not to be found in cultural differences within provinces; they are to be found in a belief that local government is somehow connected to the fostering and maintenance of democracy, and in the recognition that administration of some public affairs is facilitated by the existence of local agencies of administration.

The second main approach to federalism is a legal/institutional one, which is basically concerned with questions of division of power. This approach is exemplified by K. C. Wheare, who defined federalism as a form of government in which powers are divided between two or more governments in such a way that each is co-ordinate and independent.[2] By "co-ordinate" Wheare means that people anywhere in a federal country will be directly and simultaneously affected by two (or more) levels of government. By "independent" he means simply that the two (or more) governments are not in a hierarchical or superior–subordinate relationship with each other in exercising whatever powers they have. Municipal government in Canada meets the "co-ordinate" criterion of federalism, but not the "independent" criterion, either in theory or in practice. For this reason, the kind of analysis conducted by Simeon into federal-provincial relations has little utility in analysis of provincial-municipal relations.

The fact that Canada has a federal form of government is relevant to an understanding of the role and position of municipalities, however. Municipalities are most directly affected by their respective provincial government, but they are also affected by the Government of Canada. As a consequence, the nature of the relationships between municipal governments on the one hand and the senior governments (both provincial and federal) on the other hand is complex. The term "central-local relations" is used here because it is a generic term, applicable to provincial-municipal, federal-municipal, and tri-level relations.

Local Government and Local Self-Government: Models of Central-Local Relations

It is useful to distinguish "local government" from "local self-government" because the nature of central-local relationships depends on the distinction.[3] The terms tend to be used interchangeably, but the former term can simply mean that the central government deconcentrates public administration through the operation of branch offices that are geographically dispersed. Each of the local offices of government administers policy that is formulated by the central government; there is a minimum of discretion delegated to local administrative officials; there need not be any locally elected councils, and if there are any such councils, they may have little more to do than to advise the centrally-appointed local officials and to act as a communication link between the general public in the area and the central government. Local councils (if there are any) may be delegated additional functions such as raising revenue required to pay for local services, or perhaps even deciding within more or less clearly defined limits the particular kinds and levels of services to be provided in the area. But if such added functions are delegated to them by the central governments, that delegation is not permanent and any decisions taken locally are subject to ratification, veto, or alteration by the central government. The central government supervises, directs, and controls local administration closely, and there is therefore a clearly hierarchical relationship between the organs of local government and the central government. The relationship is one in which the central government is always superior relative to the subordinate local government organs, and the nature of the relationship is apparent in the day-to-day operations of local government.

Because the structure of government in France illustrates this model reasonably well, and also because of the early influence of that structure in the province of Quebec, it is useful to describe briefly the nature of central-local relations in France.[4] The French system of local government is still based on Napoleon's framework of 1799, and is characterized by close linkages between the organs of the central government and the units of local government. From top to bottom, the hierarchy includes the central government, regions (dating largely from 1948), départements, arrondissements, cantons, and communes. The arrondissements and cantons have declined in importance, and the regions are concerned mainly with economic planning and development, so the most important levels in the hierarchy are the central government, the départements, and the communes. The départements (some hundred of them) and the communes (more than 37,000 of them) do have elected councils, but are clearly subordinate to the central government. With regard to personnel, for example, the heads of the départements (prefects) are appointed by the central government and can also be viewed as the field representatives of the Ministry of the Interior. Prefects are not subject to dismissal by département councils. Although mayors of communes are locally elected, for some purposes they function as agents of the central government and are therefore subject to prefectoral/central direction.

With regard to functions, central supervision of local affairs extends beyond the service functions that communes *must* perform (such as education, police and fire protection, and cemeteries) to include whatever things that communes do under their general grant of power. With respect to finance, all communal budgets require the prefect's approval; the prefect can add to the communal budget and increase local taxes; local taxes are collected by the central government; communal accounts are audited by the central government; and the communes are dependent on the central government for conditional grants-in-aid. Finally, communes can be abolished, altered, or created at will, and their elected councils dissolved (several hundred each year) by the central government. In sum, central-local relations in France come close to "local government" in the sense of deconcentrated public administration, exemplified by the word *tutelage*, which means that organs of local government are under the guardianship of the central government. Yet in France the nature of central-local relations is not simply and purely one of deconcentrated administration, for communal councils do have a legislative function, and therefore have a degree of discretion which has resulted in wide variations in the kinds and levels of services provided across the country.

In contrast to the administrative agency emphasis in the term "local government" is the political entity emphasis in the term "local self-government". In this model, central-local relations are not characterized by direction and control from above but by relative independence of the local organs, allowing them to establish their own priorities according to local circumstances and local desires. Whatever control is exerted emanates from within the local governmental unit rather than from outside it, and relations with central government are characterized by diplomacy. Hence local policies are formulated internally; there is a high degree of discretion in implementing policy; decisions are taken either by a local elected council or by town-hall direct democracy meetings; and the range and standard of service functions performed locally is limited mainly by local desires and the ability of the local citizenry to pay for the services. Local services and decisions are not subject to central supervision or control, nor are they dependent upon finances (with conditions attached) from central government. In other words there is a very high degree of local initiative, a very low degree of intervention or interference in local affairs by central government, and local decisions may have as much effect on the central government as central decisions have on local government. Both local and central governments are politically independent of each other (one might say that both are sovereign governments). Since neither can impose its will on the other, the relationship between central and local governments would be comparable to federal-provincial relations in Canada.

This model of central-local relations was approximated in Prussia after the reforms of 1808, for example, and also bears some resemblance to the notion of "home rule" in the United States. Again because municipal government in Canada has been affected by American experience, it is useful to employ that notion to illustrate this model of central-local relations.

As Wickwar has written, the notion of home rule holds that:

. . . the principle of self-government could best be saved by applying it more systematically to the cities. By 'municipal home rule,' these must be allowed to organize themselves. They must be freed from State legislative interference. They must be given the powers and resources needed for their policing and the assuring of public and social services. Their rights, rather than their limitations, must be enshrined into State constitutions, so that State judges might have positive ground for liberal rather than restrictive interpretation of municipal powers. If checks on power were needed the State as then constituted would be less able here [in the USA] than in Europe to supply a continuing supervision from above; in its place, local checks could be built in . . . . The freeing of the cities for self-government might even reduce the States to being little more than outgrown intermediaries.[5]

In the technical sense, "home rule" in the United States refers to the power that some municipalities have to frame, adopt, and amend a charter for their government.[6] As this definition implies, home rule has reference to the *machinery* of local government, but not to the functional powers of local government. In other words, municipalities in the United States that have home rule have discretion over *how* things are done, but little discretion over *what* is done. Therefore the American example is not completely synonymous with the term "local self-government", for local discretion is not unlimited under home rule, and the nature of central-local relations for most purposes is not such that home-rule municipalities are politically independent of their respective state government.

The fact that one must search for examples that come at all close to illustrating these two models of central-local relations is indicative that neither model is presently in operation in a pure form. Municipalities everywhere are subject to a greater or lesser degree of control by central government, and at the same time municipalities everywhere have a greater or lesser degree of initiative and discretion that distinguishes them from central government. Variations in the level of central control over municipalities and in the level of local autonomy or initiative are partly a function of variations in material circumstances of different central government jurisdictions, but they are also a function of values. As explained further in later chapters (especially Chapter 4), there are two dominant perspectives in the desired role and function of units of local (self) government. The local-government-as-administrative-agency model of central-local relations emphasizes a *service* value, which entails the provision of services that are generally deemed necessary or desirable. Associated with this service perspective is the adequacy of finance to provide services locally. The local-self-government-as-political-entity model emphasizes what can be called a *grass-roots* value, wherein local self-reliance and initiative are considered important, if not essential, to the maintenance of democracy within the overall political system.

The service-value perspective recognizes that there are general needs for services which apply regardless of the particular locality within the central government's jurisdiction, but that the provision of these services either requires or is facilitated by local administration. This perspective also recognizes that while the need is a general one, not everyone in all localities will see it as such, or that people in different localities will not necessarily agree on the priority that should be assigned to one service relative to others. Public education and social welfare are two useful examples—in localities that have strong economic bases with little unemployment, lower priority is likely to be given by the local populace to social welfare rather than education, while the reverse will likely be the case in localities with high unemployment. Furthermore, there may very well be locality inequalities in terms of ability to finance services, to the extent that even those services identified as high priorities by people in the locality may be inadequately performed. Hence the service perspective involves a recognition that at least some services which can be administered locally should not be allowed to result in gross variations and inequalities, and that such inequalities can be mitigated or removed only by central direction, control, and supervision of their administration. Thus standards are set centrally, and priorities are uniform throughout the central government's jurisdiction.

A problem with this service perspective is that it does not allow people in localities to make their own substantial decisions. They have little discretion, little initiative, and little opportunity to tailor services to fit with local circumstances. Lacking the power to make their own decisions —to govern themselves—local government as an administrative agency is not democratic in terms of popular participation, power-sharing, and especially liberty.[7] As Whalen has pointed out, the grass-roots perspective is derived from an assertion of the ultimate and absolute priority of liberty, in the sense of an absence of compusion or restraint.[8] With regard to units of local self-government, this means that liberty is served (and therefore democracy fostered) when people that are organized into a local political authority are free both from compulsion and from restraints imposed by central government. Therefore if the people in one locality do not desire the same services in the same scheme of priorities and at the same level as people in another locality desire, then the people in each locality should have the liberty to go their separate ways; that is to say that the units of local self-government should be autonomous relative to central government.

These two values cannot be completely fulfilled simultaneously in a system of local self-government. Both values have compelling features, but there is inherent conflict between the two. This conflict necessitates some sort of compromise, a compromise which either seeks to achieve a balance between the two, or which tends to favour one or the other of the two values. In the French system the service value tends to dominate, while the grass-roots value tends to dominate in the practice of home rule in some American municipalities. There are several means of trying to achieve a balance between the values, but most common is a division of powers, by which the central government retains direct responsibility for those service functions (such as regulation of trade and commerce, and defense) which it considers of especially great importance. Perhaps those service functions can only be financed by the central government; perhaps they are implicit in the central government's general goals and objectives; or perhaps severe variations in the standard of those services within its geographical jurisdiction would be detrimental to the general interest. Other service functions which are of a localized nature (especially such services to property as water supply, sewage disposal, and local streets) are delegated to municipalities, which have a considerable measure of discretion in the performance of those functions. While the central government retains the right to intervene in these service functions, such intervention is usually minimal. Finally, there is a range of service functions (such as education and social welfare) in which the municipalities are delegated some administrative responsibilities while the central government retains for itself the primary responsibility to make policy.

With regard to the first and second categories of service functions, central-local relations need not be highly complex, but the relations are likely to be complex regarding the third category of service functions, especially if local authorities lack the financial capacity to perform those service functions. This kind of an attempt to balance the two values or perspectives of service and grass-roots generally characterizes the nature of central-local relations in Britain, for example, which has had strong influence on the situation in Canada. (It is not possible here to describe in sufficient detail the British experience.)[9]

In considering the nature of central-local relations in Canada, the federal form of government makes it necessary to look not only at connections between provinces and their municipalities but also at federal-municipal relations and the recent phenomenon of tri-level relationships. It is also important to consider the actors involved and the circumstances of their relationships. Central-local relations in Canada are so complex that it would take a book in itself to describe them fully. In the context of this present study, it is possible to present only an overview of those relations.

Provincial-Municipal Relations

The precise nature of provincial-municipal relations in Canada varies from province to province, yet the similarities are strong. It is with the general features that are similar rather than with the detailed differences that the concern is here, with particular emphasis on service functions, finance, and the mechanisms whereby provincial governments and their agencies exert control over the municipalities. A further aspect of provincial-municipal relations, municipal reorganization, is dealt with in Chapter 4.

By virtue of the British North America Act of 1867, municipalities are clearly the concern and responsibility of provincial governments rather than of the federal government, except in the cases of the Yukon and Northwest Territories. Any powers that municipalities have to raise finance by direct taxation, issuance of licences, or borrowing are clearly within the realm of provincial responsibility according to the Act, as are any powers that municipalities have to make decisions regarding property, hospitals, justice, and all "local works". The subsection referring to "municipal institutions" gives to the provinces the unrestrained power to create, alter, and abolish municipalities, and to exercise whatever degree and methods of control over municipalities and over actions taken by municipalities that the provincial government cares to implement. It is therefore clear that even the mere existence of municipalities is not their legal right. Provincial dissolution of municipalities happens rarely in Canada, but does occur. Also, as Chapter 4 indicates, programs to re-organize municipalities have in most cases been initiated and sometimes unilaterally imposed on municipalities by the provincial governments. Thus the legal/constitutional position of all municipalities is one in which they could be subjected to any whim and fancy of their provincial gov-ernment. Alternatively, there are no legal/constitutional prohibitions preventing provincial governments from granting home rule status to municipalities. Of course the provinces have not granted home rule to municipalities any more than they tend to subject municipalities to whim and fancy. Canadian municipalities fit in neither the purely local-govern-ment model nor the purely autonomous local self-government model of central-local relations. Provincial-municipal links in Canada typify at-tempts to achieve some sort of balance between the service and grass-roots values, and while it is technically correct to refer to municipalities as "creatures" of the province, the implications of that word do not usually apply in the general conduct of provincial-municipal relations.

Municipalities are created by the provinces by one or another of two kinds of provincial statute. One method of incorporation in Canada has been to grant a special charter to each municipality separately. While this method of granting municipalities a legal existence as a corporate body has not completely abandoned in all those provinces that have used it, it is used rather more sparingly than it once was. It clutters up legisla-tive order papers, especially as requested changes to any municipality's charter necessitate another special act of the provincial legislature. Charters also make it difficult for the provincial government to deal with all municipalities in a common way. As a consequence, the practice of granting separate charters to municipalities has generally been abandoned in favour of the provinces passing general municipal acts which apply either to all classes of municipalities in a province or to particular classes (cities, towns, and so on). General municipal acts typically specify the service functions that can or must be performed by municipalities, the structure of municipal decision making, terms of office of elected councillors, qualifications for voters and candidates, and the extent of municipal powers to raise revenue. Among the earlier general municipal acts was Ontario's Baldwin Act of 1849, to which reference has already been made.

While special municipal charters or generally applicable municipal acts are the key documents determining the nature of provincial-municipal relations, each province has numerous other provincial statutes and regulations that affect those relations, such as police acts, education acts, health acts, planning acts, environmental pollution acts, and assessment acts. The sheer number and range of charters, general municipal acts, other provincial statutes, and regulations make the legal/constitutional context of provincial-municipal relations very complex. Many of the general municipal acts and other statutes are in themselves complex and lengthy documents. For example, Saskatchewan's Urban Municipalities Act of 1970 has 431 sections in 207 pages, plus ten appendices and at least three subsequent amendments.

SERVICE FUNCTIONS

Municipalities are required to perform some service functions, may provide others if they decide to do so, and cannot perform other functions which the provincial government reserves to itself. Thus municipalities can do nothing that is not delegated to them, and it goes without saying that no province can delegate to municipalities functions which that province does not itself have by virtue of the Canadian constitution or by virtue of federal-provincial agreements. But a province can delegate to municipalities any of its own powers and functions that it chooses to delegate.

What the provinces have granted they can take away (or add to). The history of municipal government in Canada is generally one of steady and continual reduction in the scope of functions delegated to municipalities, both rural and urban. As Beck stated, "The responsibilities of rural municipalities in Nova Scotia were at their apex in 1879"[10] and have been reduced ever since. Paradoxically, municipalities are now involved in a far wider range of functions than they were a century ago, when their main concerns were with provision of roadways, some policing, public schools, and rudimentary social services. This apparent paradox is resolved by the distinction between what service functions municipalities did perform and what service functions they were permitted to perform. It is simply the case that what they did by no means exhausted the possibilities of what they were allowed to do. The expectations, demands and objective needs of society a century ago for municipal services were very modest, conditioned by fear of increased taxes and by a general view that the best form of government (including municipal government) was minimal government. It is also fair to state that municipal councils accepted such a view, since the municipal franchise usually had a property qualification attached and since the bulk of municipal revenue was derived from direct taxation on property. Therefore it was those people who would be most directly affected by increased municipal expenditures (and taxes) that elected councillors not unlike themselves who would be sensitive to their concerns. In any case, municipal councils tended to use their spending and taxing powers modestly, more modestly than their grant of powers and functions made necessary.

Even with a broadened municipal franchise, greater expectations and demands, and the needs produced by urbanization for a greater range and higher levels of municipal services, many municipalities do not take full advantage of the possibilities. The directness, immediacy, and visibility of property taxation and high dependence on it sometimes even leads municipalities to ask that the provincial and/or federal government assume at least partial responsibility for service functions that municipalities can otherwise legally perform. Although sometimes with reluctance, provincial governments have tended to agree to such requests, resulting in an erosion of municipal functional responsibilities. The initiative in eroding these responsibilities has by no means come exclusively from the municipalities. In some situations it has been seen by provincial governments to be in the general interest to remove responsibilities for service functions from the municipalities—situations where the local authority has been financially unable or unwilling to provide a particular service at all or at standard levels; situations where there are gross variations in the kinds and levels of services provided; or situations where province-wide planning and development policies require very close control over service functions. Hence the last decade has witnessed such reductions in the functional responsibilities of municipalities as the almost total removal of municipal control over public education in New Brunswick under the Program for Equal Opportunity, resumption by the provinces of Ontario and Nova Scotia of responsibility for property assessment, the Ontario government's take-over in 1968 of responsibility for the administration of justice, or requests by some smaller municipalities which have in the past provided their own police for the provincial police or RCMP to take over local policing.

More often than not, the reduction in municipal responsibilities takes the form of greater provincial intervention rather than complete provincial control. This has led to an increasing number of *joint* responsibilities, as indicated below. The fact that municipalities may continue to have some involvement in joint responsibilities does not negate the fact that they have less functional discretion—less autonomy—than they have had historically. A second consequence of increasing provincial involvement in the form of joint responsibilities is considerable confusion in the minds of the public. Which government is responsible for what? Which government can or should be held accountable by the electorate? This confusion is compounded in the growing number of two-tier municipalities in Canada. A resident of the City of Toronto, for example, can readily be excused for not knowing whether it is the city, the Ontario government, Metropolitan Toronto, or some quasi-independent agency of government that should be called if his sewer backs up. In other words, municipal government and the nature of provincial-municipal relations have become increasingly unintelligible to the citizenry, and in a country where federal-provincial responsibilities and relations are so complex and confusing enough. What clearly emerges from the changes in municipalities' responsibilities for service functions is that the changes tend to be designed from provincial perspectives of administrative ease and efficiency, financial considerations, and standards of services, rather than from the perspective of the citizen and his or her relations with government. As legitimate as the dominant perspectives may be, they leave the citizen perplexed and baffled.

Service functions delegated in whole or in part by provinces to their municipalities are shown in Table 2:1.

Omitted from this table are municipal powers to raise revenue. Finance is considered below, but it is worth noting that in the provinces of Alberta, British Columbia, and Newfoundland municipal borrowing is channelled through provincial agencies. This table adopts the now rather common distinction between *general* and *local* services. The former refer to matters of province-wide concern in that all residents of a province are considered to be directly or indirectly affected by their quality and effectiveness, whereas the latter type are matters seen to be of more clearly local concern and impact and can be allowed to vary according to local conditions. In so far as municipalities have much functional autonomy, it is likely to be found in the powers and functions classified as local, but even in these cases municipalities must often work within narrow limits since standards are set by the province and enforced through financial transfers. The diminution of municipal functional autonomy has been occurring most obviously in the services and powers classified by provinces as of general concern.

Two points that are not readily apparent in the table are that the range of service functions that can be performed by municipalities varies somewhat according to the class of the municipality. Generally, smaller (especially rural) municipalities are most restricted in the range of services they can provide, and the range tends to increase as the municipality progresses through town then city status. For example, if the boroughs of Metropolitan Toronto were to be elevated to city status, they could require property owners to make changes in the structure of their buildings, designate highways for fast driving, and appoint their own hydro-electric commissions, things they are not allowed to do with borough status. Also, the table is not complete, which disguises the fact that some municipalities in some provinces directly perform a wider range of functions than most other municipalities. It is often the case, especially in the cities of the western provinces, that municipalities own and operate their own utilities, such as electricity generating stations in Edmonton.

The table is useful, though, in pointing out how complex are the functional responsibilities of municipalities in Canada, and the generally low level of clear and direct municipal functional autonomy. Even in situations where legal responsibility for a particular service can be easily located, the picture becomes greatly clouded by intervening financial relationships, as is discussed below. But it can be stated generally here that provincial financial assistance to specific municipal service functions frequently brings with it the imposition of provincial standards, procedures, and detailed regulations, all of which blur the legal responsibility

Table 2:1 Allocation of Functions, by Province, 1973

a)

GENERAL FUNCTIONS	Newfoundland	P.E.I.	Nova Scotia	New Brunswick	Quebec	Ontario	Manitoba	Saskatchewan	Alberta	B.C.
education	P, minor L	L supplement, P grants	L, P grants	P, L supplement	L, P grants	L, P grants	L, P grants	L, P grants	L, P grants	L, P grants
public health	P	minor M	P, minor M	P	M, P grants	M, P grants	M, P grants	P, M, P grants	P, M, P grants	P, M levy, P grants
hospitals	P	P	P, M, P grants	P	P, M, P grants	P, M	M, P grants	M, P grants	M, P grants	M, P grants
mental hospitals	P	P	P, M, P grants	P	P	P	P	P	P	P
ambulances	P, service clubs M	private, P grants	P & private, P grants	private, volunteer M	private	private, P, M, volunteer	P, private	private, M subsidies	private	private, service club, M
general welfare	P	P	P, M, P grants	P	P	M, P grants	minor M	P-cities, M contribute, P grants	M, P grants	P, M, P grants
juvenile corrections	P	P	P, M grants	P	P	P	P	P	P	P
child welfare	P	P	P, C.A., M grants	P	private, P grants	C.A. plus, P & M grants	C.A., P, P grants	P	P	C.A. plus, P & M grants
courts	P	P	P, M	P	P	P	P, Winnipeg	P, city	P	P, M
registries of deeds	P	P	P, M	P	P	P	P	P	P	P
corrections	P	P	M, P grants	P	P	P	P	P	P	P

b) LOCAL FUNCTIONS

	1	2	3	4	5	6	7	8	9	10
police	P	M	M, P grants	M	M	M	M	M, P grants	M, P grants	M
fire	M, P grants; St.John's = P	M, P grants	M, P grants	P grants	M, P supervise, P grants	M, P supervise	M, P supervise, P grants	M	M	M
street lighting	M	M	M, P grants	M	M	M	M	M	M	M
emergency measures	P	P	P, minor M	P	P, M	P, M	P, M	P, M	P, M	P, M
main highways	P	P	P	P	P	P	P	P	P	P
rural roads	M, P grants	P	P	P	P, M; P grants	M; P grants	P; M	P, M; P grants	M; P grants	P, M; P grants
urban streets	M, P grants	M	M, P grants	M	M, P grants	M, P grants	M, P grants	M	M	M
public transit	M	M	M	M	M	M, P grants	M, P grants	M	M	P Crown corp.
garbage	M	M	M, P grants	M	M	M	M	M	M	M
sewers	M	M, P grants	M, P grants	M, P grants	M	M, P aid	M	M, P grants	M	M
water	M	M	M, P grants	M	M	M, P aid	M	M, P grants	M	M
assessment	M; P grants	P	M-R; P grants	P	M	P	P, Winnipeg; M pays	M; P	M; P grants	P; M
tax collection	M	P	M	P	M	M	M	M	M	M

P = provincial M = municipal L = local R = regional C.A. = children's aid society
SOURCE: *Report of the Nova Scotia Royal Commission on Education, Public Services and Provincial-Municipal Relations*, Vol. IV, Appendix 4, tables IV-4-1, IV-4-2.

of municipalities for the performance of functions and exercise of powers and which therefore reduce municipal discretion. Many municipal councils from time to time protest to their citizens that their hands are tied— that they lack the jurisdictional competence to meet requests and demands from their citizenry for this or that. While this confused allocation of responsibilities is not infrequently used by municipal councils as an excuse for inaction, it remains the case that the functional autonomy of municipalities is much restricted, and that accusations of merely finding excuses for inaction are not always fair.

The final point that needs to be made with reference to municipal functional autonomy is that even when the municipalities have the legal power to make decisions, that power is not absolute. Municipal decisions are of course subject to courts of law, but more importantly they are in all cases, and everywhere in Canada, subject to provincial government approval. The delegation of service functions by the provinces to the municipalities is never exclusive, for the provincial government retains the legal right to veto, amend, or substitute local councils' actions, and to regulate and supervise all actions of all municipalities in the performance of those functions. Provincial action always takes precedence over municipal action. The actions of municipal councils are generally assumed to be approved by the respective provincial government in the absence of word to the contrary, and it certainly is the case that almost all municipal decisions are allowed to stand. Thus the Ontario government's celebrated announcement in 1971 of a halt to Toronto's Spadina Expressway is noteworthy as a rare exception to the general practice. While controversy certainly arose over whether the Ontario cabinet should halt the expressway, there was no controversy over the legal right of the cabinet to do what it did.

FINANCE

Financially, municipalities in Canada have never had a great degree of autonomy, and the tendency has been decidedly one of a steady worsening of their financial position in the sense of an increasing dependency on provincial contributions.

To put the financial position of Canada's municipalities as a whole into perspective, their revenues and expenditures can be compared with

Table 2:2 Expenditures by Level of Government ($ million, and % of total)

year	before intergovernment transfers[1]						after intergovernment transfers[2]					
	federal		provincial		local		federal		provincial		local	
	$	%	$	%	$	%	$	%	$	%	$	%
1950	2,370	58.1	969	23.8	741	18.1	2,119	51.9	1,059	26.0	902	22.1
1956	5,100	62.0	1,622	19.7	1,502	18.3	4,615	56.1	1,754	21.3	1,855	22.6
1962	7,486	56.7	3,372	25.6	2,277	17.3	6,352	48.1	2,632	20.0	3,356	25.4
1968	12,229	50.0	8,010	32.7	4,094	16.7	9,857	40.3	6,330	25.9	6,384	26.1
1974	28,760	52.3	18,832	34.2	6,820	12.4	22,614	41.1	15,903	28.9	12,003	21.8

1. Transfers paid to other governments are included as expenditure of the source government but excluded as expenditure of the recipient government.
2. Transfers paid to other governments are excluded as expenditure of the source government but included as expenditure of the recipient government.

Percentages for 1962–74 do not total 100 because hospital expenditure is excluded.

SOURCE: derived from *Report of the Tri-Level Task Force on Public Finance* (Toronto, February 1976), Volume II, Table 5, page 38.

the revenues and expenditures of all provincial governments and of the federal government. In the following three tables "local" includes municipalities and school boards.

Table 2:2 indicates that while in 1950 expenditures by the three levels of government were marked by some differences, the magnitude of those differences was greatly increased over time. For example, in 1950 the difference between total provincial and total local expenditures before transfers was $228 million, but by 1974 the difference had ballooned to over $12 billion. Also, the 1950 difference between federal expenditure and local expenditure of $1629 million had by 1974 swelled to almost $22 billion. The left-hand side of Table 2:2 also indicates that local government in Canada accounted for a considerably smaller proportion of total government expenditure in 1974 than was the case in 1950. It can therefore be concluded from this table that the financial impact of local government in Canada in terms of expenditures has been diminished compared to the other two levels of government. And the trend indicates a probable further erosion in the impact of local government in the future.

Expenditure is only one side of the picture. As shown in Table 2:3, local government revenue has increased at a lower rate than provincial and federal government revenues have over the same time period, and local revenue before transfers has diminished as a proportion of total governmental revenue in Canada, dropping from 14 per cent in 1950 to just over 10 per cent in 1974. Of particular importance is a comparison of the revenue and expenditure tables, for such a comparison shows not only that local government is continually in a deficit financial situation and that the size of local government deficits is increasing over time (an after-transfer deficit of $92 million in 1950, rising to $933 million in 1974), but that local government over that time period has become increasingly dependent financially on other levels of government. In other words, there is a continual imbalance between the revenue that local government raises itself (before transfers), and the expenditure that local government makes (after transfers). The actual imbalances are given in Table 2:4. By 1974, local governments in Canada were meeting less than half their total expenditures out of their own revenue sources, the remainder being made up by grant transfers from the federal and provincial governments, and by borrowing. If this situation were a short-term one, there might not be any great cause for concern. But the situation has

Table 2:3 Revenue by Level of Government ($ million, and % of total)

year	before intergovernment transfers[1]						after intergovernment transfers[2]					
	federal		provincial		local		federal		provincial		local	
	$	%	$	%	$	%	$	%	$	%	$	%
1950	3,020	65.2	965	20.8	649	14.0	2,769	59.7	1,055	22.8	810	17.5
1956	5,698	67.1	1,578	18.6	1,220	14.3	5,213	61.4	1,710	20.1	1,573	18.5
1962	6,979	55.9	3,316	26.5	2,142	17.2	5,845	46.8	2,576	20.6	3,221	25.8
1968	12,218	48.9	7,966	31.9	3,658	14.6	9,846	39.4	6,274	25.1	5,948	23.8
1974	29,353	51.5	19,242	33.8	5,887	10.3	23,207	40.7	16,313	28.6	11,070	19.4

1. Transfers paid to other governments are included as revenue of the source government but excluded from revenue of the recipient government.
2. Transfers paid to other governments are excluded from revenue of the source government but included as revenue of the recipient government.

Percentages for 1962–74 do not total 100 because hospital revenue is excluded.

SOURCE: derived from *Report of the Tri-Level Task Force on Public Finance* (Toronto, February, 1976), Volume II, Table 4, page 37.

Table 2:4   Local Revenue (own source) and Total Local Expenditure ($ million)

year	local revenue (before transfers)	local expenditure (after transfers)	shortfall
1950	649	902	253
1956	1,220	1,855	635
1962	2,142	3,356	1,214
1968	3,658	6,384	2,726
1974	5,887	12,003	6,116

not been temporary, and shows little sign of being reversed.[11] On the contrary, if present trends continue, the situation will become even worse. It is this realization which prompted the Canadian Federation of Mayors and Municipalities to write its *Puppets on a Shoestring* brief in 1976.[12]

There are three main ways in which the financial plight of local governments in Canada can be alleviated. These three approaches can be used singly or in combination. One of them is to reduce the need of municipalities for finance by having the provinces take over direct responsibility for some service functions which municipalities perform. As indicated earlier (and in Chapter 4), some moves have already been taken in this regard, and more can be expected in the future. The danger inherent in this approach is that municipalities may become so denuded of responsibilities as to become functionally insignificant as governments. A second approach would be to transfer additional funds from the federal and/or provincial governments to the municipalities. As will be explained shortly, there are several ways of transferring funds to municipalities, but the only method of transferral without further reduction of the financial autonomy of municipalities is to guarantee them set levels of provincial and/or federal tax revenues, with no strings attached. As noted below, some moves have been made in this direction too. The third approach to alleviating the financial plight of municipalities is for them to simply increase their own levels of taxation on those revenue sources which they now have available. But the problem with this approach lies in the nature of municipalities' tax base.[13]

Municipal government in Canada is the level of government that is most limited in sources of revenue available to it that are more or less independent of other governments. Since the provinces are confined by the British North America Act of 1867 (section 92, subsection 2) to only direct forms of taxation (only the federal government can levy indirect taxes), sale of licenses (subsection 9), and imposition of fines and penalties (subsection 15), so too are the municipalities restricted. And they are further restricted to only those sources explicitly granted to them by the provinces. The three primary municipal revenue-raising powers are the taxation of property, the issuance of permits and licenses, and the levying of fines and other penalties. Of these three, the first is by far the most significant as a source of revenue.

All classes of municipalities are delegated the power to levy taxes on *assessable* real property located within the boundaries of the municipality, that is, on land and buildings. In some provinces municipalities are also allowed to tax personal property such as farmers' equipment and fishermen's gear. All property owned by the federal government and its agencies is excluded from assessment, and provincial statutes exclude other types of property from taxation as well—churches, universities, schools, and property owned by provincial governments and their agencies. For some municipalities, the exclusions pose enormous restrictions on their financial autonomy, especially in smaller centres that are university towns or that have military bases, for example.

All municipalities are allowed to issue licenses and permits for a fee, and the range of licenses and permits that can be issued is wide—dog licenses, building permits, bicycle licenses, demolition permits, licenses to operate certain kinds of businesses such as amusements and massage parlours, permits to connect property to water and sewer lines, etc. The third major revenue-raising power granted to all municipalities is the power to levy fines and penalties—traffic fines, penalty for late payment of property taxes, fines for letting animals run at large or for letting noxious weeds grow, and generally fines and penalties for infractions of municipal by-laws.

In addition to these three universally granted municipal powers, some local governments (particularly in the western provinces) levy rates for the supply of public utilities beyond just water and sewerage. As noted earlier, Edmonton is one city that operates its own electricity generating stations, and is therefore allowed to charge for electrical supply.

A source of revenue that municipalities once commonly had was the poll tax (sometimes called a service fee). This was a head tax on a flat rate (that is, it did not take into account the ability of the person to pay), and was usually fairly small, ranging from $1 to $12 per person but sometimes as high as $40. The application of poll taxes varied from province to province, sometimes applying to everyone, sometimes restricted to adults, sometimes applying only to males, and sometimes excluding housewives and the elderly. The poll tax is not widely used in Canada now, exceptions being most municipalities in Newfoundland and some in Quebec and Saskatchewan, since most provinces have now prohibited its use. Nova Scotia's government, one of the last holdouts, abolished poll taxes in 1971, five years after they were last seen in New Brunswick.

The most important indicator of any municipality's financial autonomy is the proportion of its total revenue raised on its own accord from the three major sources referred to above. The higher the proportion of its total revenue a municipality raises itself, the greater its financial independence; and the higher the proportion of its total revenue that comes in the form of grants from the federal and provincial governments, the lower its financial autonomy, particularly when that income is in the form of *conditional* grants (grants-in-aid that have strings attached as to expenditure). The alternative to conditional grants are general-purpose transfers to the municipality. Such transfers can be spent in any way at the discretion of the recipient municipality, and can therefore be termed unconditional. They pose a lesser constraint on municipal autonomy than do conditional grants, but since municipalities lack long-term guarantees that unconditional grants will continue to be paid at all, and continue to be paid at set rates by the federal and provincial governments, autonomy is actually lowered by dependence on such grants. Presumably, municipalities that receive significant proportions of their total revenue in the form of unconditional transfers would be more wary of entering into long-term financial commitments than they would be if all or almost all of their revenue came from their own sources.

Several important points emerge from an examination of sources of local government revenue. First, in the five-year period up to 1974, the extent to which local governments relied on their own sources of revenue diminished appreciably, to the point where less than half their total revenue was generated internally. This decrease in financial independence

Table 2:5   Total Local Government Revenue, by Source ($ million, and % of total)

source	1969		1974	
	$	*%*	*$*	*%*
FROM OWN SOURCES				
property taxes	3,019	43.1	4,103	35.9
business taxes	263	3.8	378	3.3
other taxes	37	.5	38	.3
licenses and permits etc.	73	1.0	71	.6
revenue from utilities	331	4.7	722	6.3
investment returns etc.	237	3.4	278	2.4
total own sources	3,955	56.5	5,590	48.9
FROM OTHER SOURCES				
grants in lieu of taxes				
federal government	41	.6	56	.5
provincial government	17	.2	48	.4
federal/provincial enterprises	35	.5	59	.5
other	—	—	41	.4
unconditional grants from province	290	4.1	668	5.9
conditional grants				
federal government	37	.5	125	1.1
provincial government	2,633	37.6	4,841	42.4
total conditional grants	2,670	38.1	4,966	43.5
total revenue	7,006	100.0	11,426	100.0

SOURCE: adapted from *Report of the Tri-Level Task Force on Public Finance* (Toronto, February, 1976), Volume II, Table 10, page 48.

is a continuation of a longer trend. Using a different method of calculating sources of local government revenue, it has been found that the percentage of total revenue raised by local governments from their own sources has decreased from 62.1 per cent in 1950 to 44.6 per cent in 1974, and shows a continuing downward trend.[14] Since all other local government revenue comes in the form of transfers from other governments, it is clear that local authorities are continuing to become more dependent financially. Secondly, it can be seen that local governments

have a very narrow tax base. Revenue from utilities and returns on invest-
ment are not, strictly speaking, taxes. Therefore the heavy dependence
of local government on just one tax—property tax—becomes apparent.
Both in 1969 and 1974 local governments derived 90 per cent of their
own revenue from taxation of property, so their dependence on this one
tax has not diminished. For any level of government to rely so heavily on
a single tax is dangerous, especially when property taxes are so widely
condemned as being inflexible, inequitable, and regressive. This form of
taxation is not as well related as income tax, for example, to the ability
of people to pay. Finally, Table 2:5 demonstrates not only that local
governments are becoming increasingly dependent on other governments
for revenue but also that this increasing dependence is of the sort that
most erodes local autonomy. That is to say that *conditional* grants are
increasing as a proportion of total local government revenue. Even over
the short five-year period 1969–74, conditional grants increased from
38.1 per cent of total local government revenue to 43.5 per cent. Although the proportion increased somewhat, unconditional grants still
accounted for only a small part of total local government revenue in
1974.[15]

It is instructive to consider also the ways in which municipalities spend
the revenue they receive from one source or another. As Table 2:6 indicates, by far the largest item of local government expenditure is education. Although spending on education dropped as a proportion of the
municipal total between 1969 and 1974, it still accounted for almost 42
per cent, three times as much as its nearest rival for local government
money. If one adds to education the money spent on health and social
services, it is found that over half of all local government expenditure in
1974 was directed to what have earlier been called "general" services as
distinct from local ones. While there are now few service functions performed by local government that are not to some extent dependent on
federal or, especially, provincial transfers of money, it is these three
general services that are most dependent on such funding. In 1974 the
percentages of total local government expenditure on health, social
services, and education that came from provincial governments were
74.8 per cent, 62.3 per cent, and 66.1 per cent respectively.[16] This money
is virtually all in the form of conditional grants rather than without strings
attached. Therefore the municipalities have little or no real discretion

Table 2:6 Total Local Government Expenditure, By Function or Program ($ million, and % of total)

function or program	1969		1974	
	$	%	$	%
general government	314	4.2	526	4.3
protection (police, fire etc.)	500	6.7	948	7.8
transportation and communication				
(mainly road transport)	917	12.3	1,649	13.5
health (mainly hospitals)	394	5.3	588	4.8
social services (mainly welfare)	206	2.8	480	3.9
education	3,683	49.4	5,075	41.7
recreation and culture	262	3.5	677	5.6
environment				
water supply	221	3.0	369	3.0
sewage	229	3.1	469	3.8
other	90	1.2	156	1.3
housing	42	.6	166	1.4
financial services	492	6.6	858	7.0
other	103	1.4	226	1.9
total	7,452	100.0	12,184	100.0

SOURCE: *Report of the Tri-Level Task Force on Public Finance* (Toronto, February, 1976), Volume II, Table 15, page 59.

over how that money is spent. In company with these conditional grants come regulations and standards which must be fulfilled by local governments. Frequently, the conditions are prescribed in absurdly minute detail. For example, in Nova Scotia the type and composition of municipal police uniforms are prescribed by the provincial government, right down to the socks.

It therefore becomes apparent that local governments in Canada are locked into much of their expenditure, and that they really do have very little room to manoeuvre. This has long been the case, but severe limitations on local government expenditure have become more severe as a consequence of the federal government's implementation of the anti-inflation program in October of 1975. As the provincial governments signed agreements with Ottawa whereby the public sector in the provinces came under the federal jurisdiction, the municipalities were affected.

There have been numerous results of this, such as the Ontario government's imposition of a 5 to 6 per cent ceiling on the annual rate of increase of payments from the province to the municipalities (later increased to 8 per cent); the Alberta government's decision to limit increases in grants to municipalities to 11 per cent; imposition by the New Brunswick government of a 14 per cent ceiling on total municipal expenditure and an increase of only 5 to 6 per cent on the province's unconditional grants to the City of Saint John (the province rejected the City's budget for 1976 because it exceeded Anti-Inflation Board guidelines); and so on. What all this indicates is that municipalities either must cut back on those few service functions in which they have any room to manoeuvre, or that they will have to increase the property tax substantially.

Prospects for improvement in the financial autonomy of Canada's municipalities do not seem bright, although it is unlikely (because of provincial controls) that the kind of financial collapse experienced by New York City in 1974–76 will afflict Canadian municipalities. But it is apparent that municipal government is to an increasing extent becoming more of an administrative agency of provincial governments than has traditionally been the case. There are a few rays of hope, but they are few. For example, the Premier of Manitoba announced in his 1975 budget speech that the province's municipalities would be allocated a share of the province's income tax beginning in 1976: 2 per cent of personal income tax, and 1 per cent of corporate income tax. In his 1976 budget, Premier Schreyer announced that Manitoba's local governments would be allowed to levy their own growth taxes in the form of surtaxes on liquor, hotel accommodation, restaurant meals, and land transfers. In April of 1975 Premier Barrett of British Columbia promised the province's municipalities a one-third share of the increase in the price of natural gas. The details of the revenue-sharing scheme were worked out in consultation with the Union of British Columbia Municipalities, and the Natural Gas Revenue Sharing Act of 1975 provides for an unconditional grant of $25,000 to each municipality regardless of size or financial capacity, an unconditional grant based on municipal operating costs, and an unconditional grant calculated on the basis of $100 per housing unit start. In 1973, Ontario's provincial treasurer made a "guarantee" that provincial assistance to the province's local governments

". . . in future years will grow at a rate not less than the growth rate of Ontario's total revenues."[17] The nature of that guarantee became a matter of dispute, and by 1976 it was clear that Ontario's municipalities would be receiving increasing provincial assistance at a rate less than that of growth in the province's revenues. The apparent breaking of that guarantee is a further demonstration that local government has a low level of financial autonomy, not only in Ontario but elsewhere in Canada.

PROVINCIAL CONTROL AND SUPERVISION OF MUNICIPALITIES

Illustrating the fact that municipalities are legally and in practice subordinate to their provincial governments is the existence of agencies of all provincial governments to supervise, direct and control the municipalities. There are few departments and agencies of the provincial governments that are not somehow involved in affecting local affairs, principally through grant-in-aid programs. However, looking more specifically at the implementation and application of the provincial statutes that function as the constitutions of municipalities (general municipal acts and individual charters), the picture is less complicated. In most provinces there are two main kinds of provincial agencies that control municipalities and that therefore constitute a main means of limiting municipal autonomy.

The first type is the department of municipal affairs, headed by a cabinet minister. Each province now has one, even if its name is something other than "municipal affairs". In all the provinces other than Prince Edward Island, such departments were created by 1936, the earliest ones being in Manitoba (Department of the Municipal Commissioner, in 1886), Saskatchewan (1908), Alberta (1911), and Quebec (1918). The depression years of the 1930s witnessed the birth of such departments in most other provinces.

The creation of provincial executive departments of municipal affairs can be tied to several factors.[18] Among these was the growth in number of municipalities. The *recent* origin of such a department in Prince Edward Island is no doubt due in part to the fact that there were for a long time only eight incorporated municipalities, making it unnecessary to erect a full-fledged departmental structure to deal with them. A second factor is to be found in the ever-widening scope of governmental decision making, including that of municipal government. Thus the range and number of decisions made by municipalities became too heavy a burden for the provincial legislatures and cabinets to cope with and oversee. Thirdly and very directly connected to the blossoming of provincial departments of municipal affairs in the 1930s was the fact that the Great Depression put municipalities in constant financial difficulties, driving many to the brink of bankruptcy and some (at least thirty-nine in Ontario alone) to default on their debts. Tax revenue on property declined as property owners could not pay their taxes and forfeited their land. Municipal borrowing had to be curtailed as the bond market sagged, and municipal expenditures for relief of the poor and destitute soared. This resulted in continual appeals for financial assistance from the provinces. The provincial governments could not turn a blind eye to the financial squeeze suffered by the municipalities, and to put some semblance of order in the financial chaos, most provinces that had not already established a department of municipal affairs did so by 1936. Finally, the provincial governments needed some means of ensuring that their own programs were effectively implemented and that municipal actions would not operate at cross-purposes with provincial programs.

Departments of municipal affairs supervise local governments on a continuous day-to-day basis (rather than on an issue-by-issue basis), and usually in considerable detail. In addition to supervising and controlling municipalities (by reviewing municipal by-laws, for example), the departments are designed to give guidance and provide leadership. In many provinces the tasks of the department of municipal affairs extend to training municipal officers (often in conjunction with universities), providing the property assessment service, and aiding in the formulation of local development plans.

The other main type of provincial agency intimately involved in municipal affairs is a semi-autonomous, provincially-appointed board, examples of which are the Ontario Municipal Board, the Quebec Municipal Commission, the Local Authorities Board in Alberta, and two in Nova Scotia—the Board of Commissioners of Public Utilities and the Provincial Planning Appeal Board. Not all provinces have any such agencies, British Columbia being one. Such boards and commissions usually are separate from or only loosely connected to the province's department of municipal affairs. Generally the tasks of such boards are more narrowly defined than are those of the departments. In contrast to the departments of municipal affairs these boards deal with individual municipalities on a more sporadic and issue-by-issue basis, and typically function as a sort of court of appeal against decisions made by municipalities. It is also rather common for the provinces to delegate to such agencies a degree of power over local finances, particularly with regard to municipal debt and to borrowing for capital purposes.

Although the operation and functions of such boards and commissions vary considerably from province to province, the phenomenon can be illustrated by taking the Ontario Municipal Board as an example.[19] The OMB is the direct descendant of the Ontario Railway and Municipal Board (created in 1906), which in turn was an agency designed to centralize the functions of the Provincial Municipal Auditor (an office created in 1897 to oversee and approve municipal and school audits), the Railway Committee of the province's executive council (which reviewed municipal by-laws regarding electric railways), and several other offices. Such a centralization of provincial agencies concerned with overseeing activities of the province's municipalities was proposed as early as 1902 by the Provincial Assessment Commission and was publicly supported by the Ontario Municipal Association.

The Ontario Railway and Municipal Board was originally composed of three provincial appointees who were empowered to regulate not only local railways but were assigned, over time, power to approve municipal annexations, amalgamations, and boundary revisions; power to approve municipal by-laws regarding finance, debentures, creation of debts, public highways, streets, and bridges; the power to hear assessment appeals, and the power to approve and supervise certain municipal zoning by-laws. The Board absorbed the Bureau of Municipal Affairs in 1932, an agency which had been established in 1917 to supervise the accounts of public utilities (other than electrical utilities) controlled by municipalities. Also in 1932, the name became the Ontario Municipal Board, reflecting its greater preoccupation with municipal affairs and the demise of local railway systems. The specific powers of the OMB were discarded in favour of a general grant of power ". . . to require or forbid the doing of any act which any municipality was required to do or not to do under any Act or order of the Board or under any agreement to which the municipality was a party."[20] Specific powers were added again from time to time, such as a provision in 1935 that all municipal capital expenditures to be financed through the issue of debentures required approval from the board.

When the Department of Municipal Affairs was created in 1935, the Ontario Municipal Board was placed in the department but continued to be rather independent of it. The members of the board remained appointed by the provincial government. The supervisory powers over the municipalities that had been exercised by the OMB were largely transferred to the new department, and other powers of the board were parcelled out to several new agencies such as the Ontario Fuel Board and the Telephone Authority in 1954. The OMB was left with a more clearly quasi-judicial role (that of a tribunal) with respect to municipalities—hearing appeals to municipal zoning by-laws and hearing assessment appeals. But the board retained a supervisory role (though somewhat diminished), especially on council actions of a financial nature, and on applications for boundary revision, amalgamation, and annexation of municipalities. The OMB is given considerable discretion in its operations and decides on its own, independent of the provincial legislature,[21] what criteria to apply in reaching its decisions on such matters as revision of municipal boundaries. It also decides who it will allow to make representations to the board at its public hearings.

Despite the transfer of a number of its former duties and powers to the Department of Municipal Affairs and to other provincial agencies, the work load of the Ontario Municipal Board has continued to increase, necessitating several enlargements. It has been holding from 1500 to 2000 hearings a year. From its original three members, the board was expanded to five in 1947, to seven in 1951, to twenty-seven in 1976. (The Quebec Municipal Commission, established in 1932, consisted of fifteen members in 1976, and the chairman is a judge.) The members are appointed by the Ontario cabinet and hold office "during pleasure" rather than for fixed periods of time. Membership is supposed to be a full-time position. While the earlier provision that the chairman had to be a lawyer has been removed, the general practice of appointing as chairman someone with a legal background remains, and the board's membership is usually heavily weighted with people having backgrounds in law. The Ontario Municipal Board has come in for much criticism, most often from the municipal councils and the associations of municipalities in Ontario. The fact that this appointed board has the power (which it frequently exercises) to overturn or amend decisions made by elected municipal councils strikes many as inconsistent with the principles of representative democracy. On the other hand, there are those who support a sort of ombudsman role for the OMB, a role which was emphasized by Mr. J. A. Kennedy who retired as chairman of the board in 1972. Also, the confusion surrounding the situation wherein both the Ontario Municipal Board and the Department of Municipal Affairs have responsibility to exercise administrative supervision over municipalities seems unnecessary. One commonly proposed reform (supported by a select committee of the Ontario legislature in December, 1972) would make the OMB a purely quasi-judicial tribunal, limiting its functions mainly to the hearing of appeals on municipal decisions, while the Department would assume more complete responsibility for administrative supervision.

In Ontario, as in all provinces with agencies equivalent to the Ontario Municipal Board, the board's decisions are always subject to appeal on jurisdictional grounds to the courts of law, and to an ultimate appeal to the provincial cabinet. Such appeals are not uncommon, but it is a rare event when a provincial cabinet reverses a decision of such agencies. Again, the controversial case of the Spadina Expressway, in which the cabinet reversed a decision of the OMB (the OMB had supported Metro Toronto's decision to proceed with construction of the expressway), is notable as an exception to the rule. Having such quasi-independent agencies to oversee municipalities can at times be very convenient to provincial cabinets and legislatures, because public outcries about overturned municipal decisions can be deflected away from the governing political party.

In sum, the pattern of provincial-municipal relations in most provinces is complex, involving the legislature, the cabinet, a department of municipal affairs, most other provincial ministries, one or more quasi-independent provincial agencies, and of course the municipalities. One final factor of note in this regard is the existence in each province (even in Prince Edward Island) of associations of municipalities. These bodies function as interest groups to represent the municipal point of view to their provincial governments. In most cases such associations have become viewed by the provincial governments as so legitimate that the provinces often consult them before introducing legislation, setting forth new regulations affecting municipalities, or naming people to assorted committees. Ontario alone has at least seven—the Association of Counties and Regions of Ontario, the Association of Municipalities of Ontario, the Federation of Northern Ontario Municipalities, the Northeastern Ontario Municipal Association, the Northwestern Ontario Municipal Association, the Ontario Association of Rural Municipalities, and the Organization of Small Urban Municipalities. The remaining provinces generally have only one or two such associations which meet more or less regularly with provincial cabinets, ministers of municipal affairs, and department officials.

Federal-Municipal Relations

Even though municipalities are constitutionally created by and are subordinate to the provincial governments, one must not overlook the involvement of the federal government in matters affecting local governments. It has three main types of impact on municipalities. First is the sheer physical presence of the federal government. The Ottawa-area municipalities in both Quebec and Ontario are the most obvious examples, where the federal government is by far the largest employer, the biggest land owner, the biggest developer, and intimately involved in municipal affairs through its National Capital Commission. This presence poses special problems for the municipalities in the Ottawa area, reflected in proposals for a federal capital territory that would be outside the jurisdiction of the provinces of Quebec and Ontario.[22] While the municipalities in the Ottawa area are the ones that most obviously experience the physical presence of the federal government, similar situations exist in other municipalities such as those where penitentiaries and military bases are located. To take the Halifax area as an example, in 1975 there were 8,250 military personnel as well as 5,660 civilian employees of the armed forces there, and the federal government's naval yards occupy a significant proportion of prized water frontage. Even the smallest towns of Canada have at least a federal post office. Add to all of that the land and buildings owned by Canadian National Railways and other federal Crown corporations, and one can begin to appreciate just how significant the physical presence of the federal government in Canadian municipalities is.

A second type of federal impact concerns financial payments made directly to municipalities. Property owned by the federal government and its enterprises is exempt from municipal property taxation. However, the property is assessed and the federal government pays to municipalities grants in lieu of property taxes (which do not necessarily equal the property taxes that would otherwise be due) under the provisions of the Municipal Finance Act. As was indicated earlier in this chapter, the total amount of money involved is modest. Aside from grants in lieu of taxes, the federal government makes only conditional grants to municipalities (about $125 million in 1974), concentrated in four functions: transportation and communications, recreation and culture, environment, and housing. As a proportion of total municipal revenue, the federal government's impact is not highly significant to municipalities overall, but only to those that have a heavy federal physical presence.

The third type of federal impact is much more profound and complex, as it involves a wide range of policies and decisions made by parliament, the departments, ministries, and federal agencies. These policies and decisions have in the past been taken unilaterally and usually without prior consultation with the municipalities affected. Yet the effects are often significant in that they set parameters within which the municipalities must operate and produce consequences with which the municipalities are left to cope. The most obvious example is the federal government's anti-inflation program of wage and price controls begun in 1975, to which reference has already been made. Some less obvious examples which illustrate the general problem are the federal departments of Transport and Regional Economic Expansion. The Department of Transport (with the Canadian Transportation Commission) implements policy decisions regarding rail line abandonment and relocation, decisions which are of crucial importance to a large number of municipalities. If a rail line is abandoned, the municipality may well be killed economically, lacking the means to get goods in and out. Relocation of rail lines in urban areas can present the cities with problems of decreased housing stock or industrial land if the lines are moved to areas already utilized for these purposes. When the lands on which the rail lines were located are redeveloped for new purposes, the city is presented with planning problems, the necessity of supplying such municipal services as water supply and sewage systems, dislocation of traffic patterns, and the like. The

Department of Regional Economic Expansion is involved with municipalities in areas designated as economically disadvantaged. In attempting
to stimulate the economy of such areas it has been very keen on developing growth centres, and it is very much up to the department to determine
which municipalities should be growth centres and which should therefore
receive grant moneys to supply new and up-graded economic infra-
structure.

There are few departments and agencies of the federal government that
do not somehow affect municipalities by their programs and decisions.
But these activities have long been conducted in an overall policy
vacuum.[23] That is to say that because the federal government lacked a
more or less explicit and comprehensive urban policy, and because of the
vertical and functional nature of the federal government's bureaucracies,
programs have been implemented in isolation from each other. Sometimes
it even seems that some programs work at cross-purposes with each other.
Some of the long standing failure of the federal government to formulate
a comprehensive urban policy can be attributed to constitutional questions of jurisdiction. Secondly, urban problems are inherently complex
and interdependent,[24] lumped together in what is commonly called "the
urban crisis". Additionally, it can be maintained that there has been a
long tradition of equating urbanization with economic growth. Economic
growth has been a very dominant value not only in the minds of governments but of the public, and there has been a general reluctance to
tamper with the forces of expansion. Finally, the federal government long
lacked any agency or mechanism to formulate and implement urban
policy. In this connection, however, two federal agencies have been
created since the Second World War, and they are worth closer consideration.

CENTRAL MORTGAGE AND HOUSING CORPORATION (CMHC)[25]

The Central Mortgage and Housing Corporation came into operation as
a federal Crown corporation on January 1, 1946, by an act of parliament,
to administer the National Housing Act of 1944. The origins of CMHC
date back to the depression year of 1935 when the federal government
passed the Dominion Housing Act as a sort of anti-depression public
works device in order to alleviate unemployment and to stimulate house

construction. This act was administered by the Housing Administration within the Department of Finance but by 1945 only 32,000 housing units had been financed. Under the system, one-quarter of a mortgage loan was financed by the federal government, the other three-quarters coming from private lending institutions. In 1941 the federal government created Wartime Housing Limited as a Crown corporation to provide housing (about 20,000 units by the end of 1945) for workers in wartime munitions plants. Under the strong influence of C. D. Howe, Minister of Reconstruction and Supply, these two streams were united in the new Central Mortgage and Housing Corporation. Howe, who had been well pleased with the concept of Crown corporations (which have considerable independence from government) as a means of achieving goals quickly, realized that the depression and war had reduced the amount of housing available. This situation was made more critical with the prospect of hundreds of thousands of discharged veterans of the war returning to Canada. Originally, CMHC had two functions: to increase the flow of mortgage capital into housing through a combination of direct federal loans and inducing private lenders to make more mortgage money available for house construction; and to increase the supply of low-cost housing. The corporation was not to determine policy; this responsibility was to remain with the minister through whom CMHC reports to parliament. In so far as there was a federal housing (or urban) policy, this was it.

Gradually the functions of CMHC were broadened to include (in 1949) a form of urban renewal, whereby the corporation split the costs of acquiring and clearing slum areas with the provinces (except that the provinces usually passed their share of the expenses on to the municipalities), on the proviso that the land had to be used exclusively as a site for low-rental housing. This proviso virtually necessitated the ill-famed "bulldozer approach" to urban renewal. In 1957 CMHC began to invest directly in mortgages, in addition to the earlier practice of channelling its mortgage money through private lending institutions. This implemented the policy decided by the new Diefenbaker government in response to a rather sudden and dramatic withdrawal by the major private lenders from the house mortgage market. Other developments have been a program whereby CMHC insures mortgages without itself having direct financial involvement, loans to municipalities for construction and expansion of sewage treatment facilities, a land assembly program, a program to provide senior citizen and student accommodation, loans for rehabilitation of existing dwellings, the Neighbourhood Improvement Program, and the Assisted Home Ownership Program.

To say that CMHC has become an extremely important actor and influence in the field of housing in Canada is an understatement. Each year since 1946 between a third and half of all housing built in Canada has been financed under provisions of the National Housing Act, and the mortgage debt under the NHA stood at $15.7 billion at the end of 1974, representing 29.5 per cent of the total mortgage debt in Canada.[26] CMHC's share of this debt was over $6.1 billion.

The corporation has periodically come in for heavy criticism,[27] some of it justified and some not. The much-criticized phenomenon of suburbs full of single-family dwellings on large lots is certainly one legacy which is posing increasing problems with which municipalities must now cope— commuter traffic and mass transit for example. The notorious bulldozer approach to urban renewal, an approach virtually necessitated by the National Housing Act until 1956 (much improved in 1964), justly deserved the criticism it received for the wholesale dislocation of neigh- bourhoods, but it is arguable how much blame for this should be borne by CMHC rather than by the federal government. The corporation has had its share of scandals involving shady doings of some employees, circum- stances which darken its public image. It has also been criticized for a failure to formulate and implement a coherent, comprehensive, long- range urban policy for Canada. However, this criticism is deserved less by the corporation than by the parliament and government of Canada. The corporation must work within the legal constraints imposed by parliament, and CMHC's terms of reference clearly limited its functions to only one aspect of urban policy—housing.

In his autobiography, Humphrey Carver relates the attempts made especially by CMHC's Advisory Group (of which he was chairman from 1955–67) to try to broaden the corporation's approach.[28] These attempts were often ill-fated, either because the minister through whom the cor- poration reported to parliament bungled or was unsympathetic, because of reluctance from provincial governments, or whatever other reason. Nevertheless, CMHC's mandate continued to be of a sort that very much limited the extent to which it could go in formulating and implementing policy. Also, perhaps because it is a Crown corporation and therefore somewhat isolated from departments of the federal government, CMHC was not in a position to influence heavily those government departments such as Transport, Environment, and Regional Economic Expansion which would need to be brought in to formulate urban policy. Still, the corporation can be faulted for having taken an unnecessarily reactive role rather than using innovation and initiative. Particularly in its earlier years, it measured its success in terms of the *number* of housing units it provided, with little concern about what was behind those front doors.[29] For too long it was seen as a bed partner of the house construction industry and of private lending institutions. The task of formulating urban policy was never assigned to CMHC.

THE MINISTRY OF STATE FOR URBAN AFFAIRS[30]

The excessive caution of the Central Mortgage and Housing Corporation, its limited mandate, and an awakening both inside and outside government to the increasingly critical need for urban policy[31] resulted in the formal creation of the Ministry of State for Urban Affairs in June of 1971. This was a direct result of two reports, the first being that of the much publicized Federal Task Force on Housing and Urban Development, conceived and headed by Paul Hellyer.[32]

Mr. Hellyer was Minister of Transport in the federal cabinet, and the minister through whom the Central Mortgage and Housing Corporation reported to parliament. He was determined to put an end to CMHC's relative isolation (having recently ended the isolation of the three branches of the armed forces through unification when he was Minister of National Defence), and in July of 1968 he received approval from cabinet to establish a task force on housing. It was to report back to cabinet by February 1969. Unhappy with what he viewed as terms of reference that were too narrow, Hellyer expanded its mandate to include "urban development". The actual terms of reference drawn up by Mr. Hellyer were:

. . . to examine housing and urban development in Canada and to report on ways in which the federal government, in company with other levels of government and the private sector, can help meet the housing needs of all Canadians and contribute to the development of modern, vital cities.[33]

Hellyer embarked with his task-force colleagues (none of whom were from CMHC or from any federal, provincial, or municipal governments) on a tour of Canada, holding public hearings in twenty-seven centres and publicly soliciting briefs from any interested organizations and individuals. The task force toured various housing situations and supplemented its more formal public hearings with informal conversations and gatherings. No consultations were held with CMHC (for which Mr. Hellyer was the responsible minister), and during the task force's deliberations a freeze was imposed on all CMHC-sponsored urban-renewal projects.

In terms of political practicality, the task force was a disaster. First, its members were all "outsiders". While this ensured that the task force would have a fresh outlook, at the same time it made its recommendations suspect in the eyes of "insiders" in the federal bureaucracy, CMHC, cabinet, and some provincial governments. Second, Mr. Hellyer's personal commitment to the task force's objectives and recommendations was so intense and so public before the report was presented to cabinet that he was bound to be frustrated by opposition which the report was certain to receive. In the end, Mr. Hellyer's career as a cabinet minister ended with his resignation three months after the report was submitted, by which time it was clear that the recommendations would not be implemented as a whole. Finally, some of the report's strongly worded forty-seven recommendations flew in the face of constitutional realities; such recommendations as "Provincial governments should assume a much larger share of education costs"[34] brought forth inevitable outcries about federal intrusion in areas of provincial jurisdiction. The report also called for direct federal-municipal relations, a recommendation guaranteed to upset provincial governments.

Probably the most important aspect of the report was its recognition of a need for urban policy and its forceful recommendation that a federal Department of Housing and Urban Affairs be created. While several of its other recommendations were implemented, this particular one remained on the shelf for more than two years, being taken off the shelf only after the next report was made.

This second report was commissioned after Mr. Robert Andras became the cabinet member through whom CMHC reported to parliament. Being a minister without portfolio, Mr. Andras was in a position to devote his full attention to urban policy and CMHC. Cabinet authorized

Mr. Andras to commission a new study, but one quite different from the ill-fated Hellyer task force. This new study was to be a confidential one conducted without the hoopla that surrounded the earlier study. It was also to be broader and more thorough. Specifically, the task was to study trends in urbanization and to examine the consequences of those trends *if* the federal government continued to have no active urban policy. Dr. N. Harvey Lithwick, an economist at Carleton University and author on urban Canada,[35] was engaged to carry out the study beginning in October 1969. Lithwick commissioned six background studies of specialized subjects and presented his report in March of 1970.[36] His very well-documented report constituted a serious attack on the existing situation, particularly on the federal government's failure to integrate and co-ordinate policy decisions having urban ramifications, and on a tendency to react to symptoms of urbanization rather than dealing with their underlying causes. His report demonstrated that a continued lack of a co-ordinated urban policy would lead to the disadvantages of urbanization overtaking the advantages.

Lithwick proposed as a matter of considerable urgency the creation of a federal agency to conduct research on urbanization so as to better understand the phenomenon. He did not recommend creation of a new federal department to deal with urban policy. Instead he proposed a national urban council which ". . . would be a forum where the interests of various groups involved in the urban policy system could be presented; where objectives could be reconciled, and where feasible plans could be drawn up."[37] A technical staff of the council would then develop long-range objectives (in light of which shorter-term goals could be assessed and co-ordinated) to be presented back to the council for final examination and selection of alternatives. In proposing a national council rather than another federal department, Lithwick wanted to facilitate the greatest possible input from all possible sources, both in and outside of governments. Lithwick distinguished between *federal* urban policy and *national* urban policy. Because of divided jurisdiction, any federal policy would be inadequate; the other levels of government, as well as non-governmental groups and individuals, had to be involved in order to create a national urban policy.

While the Hellyer task force was politically inept in the way it was conducted and in the nature of some of its recommendations, its proposed federal department of housing and urban affairs was not an instance of political naivety. The Lithwick study, in contrast, showed political shrewdness in the way it was conducted (for example, in the use of acknowledged experts for preparation of the background studies), but not in its recommendation regarding a national urban council. Even in the heyday of co-operative federalism such a proposal was not practicable in the light of political/constitutional realities and obvious problems of accountability and responsibility. In consequence, the federal cabinet did not implement this proposal, but Lithwick's study was sufficiently persuasive that cabinet took another look at Hellyer's proposal for a department of urban affairs, although the new agency was not to become a department. In the Throne Speech of October 1970, the government announced its intention to create a new agency, the Ministry of State for Urban Affairs. The concept of a ministry of state in contrast to a department was a relatively new one. In general terms, the distinction between the two forms is that a ministry's function is only to formulate policy whereas departments both formulate and implement policy. Thus the new Ministry of State for Urban Affairs (MSUA) was to formulate urban policy but leave program implementation based on it to the departments and to CMHC. In addition, the ministry was to co-ordinate urban policies and to be the main medium for consultation among the three levels of government. In 1971 the MSUA absorbed an urban secretariat created in October 1970. This secretariat had two sections, one in charge of interdepartmental co-ordination, and the other (headed briefly by the discouraged Dr. Lithwick) responsible for policy formulation and research. Dr. Lithwick resigned when it became clear that his proposed National Urban Council was not going to be established.

The proclamation by which the MSUA was created defined its role as the formulation and development of policies through measures within fields of federal jurisdiction in respect of a) the most appropriate means by which the Government of Canada may have a beneficial influence on the evaluation of the process of urbanization in Canada; b) the integration of urban policy with other policies and programs of the Government of Canada; and c) the fostering of co-operative relationships in respect of urban affairs with the provinces (and, through them, their municipalities), with the public, and with private organizations. While this description of its assigned role was hardly specific, it did make it clear that the

MSUA was only to formulate (and, all being well, to co-ordinate) policy, not implement it.

If the ministry must be assessed on the basis of outcomes of its work to date, its performance could not be judged a wild success, for the results have been few and relatively modest. However, it is easy to expect too much of a young agency, and other factors need to be taken into account. Policy outcomes remain few, but in large part this can be attributed to the fact that the policy and research wing of the MSUA needed time to build up a research data base for policy formulation. Secondly, much of the work of the co-ordination wing of the ministry is not publicly visible, such as the Senior Interdepartmental Committee on Urban Affairs which was established in July 1973, and which consists of the deputy heads of fifteen federal departments and agencies.

When the Ministry of State for Urban Affairs was established, it did not absorb the Central Mortgage and Housing Corporation. The reasons why the federal government chose to have two separate agencies dealing with urban affairs (but having both of them responsible to the same minister) have never been satisfactorily explained. To separate policy formulation and co-ordination from policy implementation seems some-what artificial, and is likely to increase difficulties in ensuring that objectives are reached. Carver suggests that the image of CMHC posed a problem for incorporating it into the MSUA: "To be stuck with the model of an insurance company has, in a later period of history, made it very difficult to put CMHC into the context of a Ministry of Urban Affairs."[38] His point is that CMHC had taken a role (at least up to 1954) so dom-inated by being an insurer of mortgages from insurance companies that the corporation acquired an image similar to such companies, an image reinforced by the style of headquarters building it had constructed for itself. Aside from its image, there are other factors that help explain why CMHC did not become a part of the ministry in 1971. For one thing, the corporation's operations involved it in both urban and non-urban areas. Secondly, CMHC was only one of the federal government's many agencies and departments that were involved in implementing urban-related policies. For example, before the ministry was created, there were 112 federal programs involved in financing elements of the urban process, 131 urban-oriented research programs, and twenty-seven departments and agencies with some kind of urban involvement.[39] In other words, even if CMHC were brought into the ministry, there would still remain separate many other departments and agencies somehow involved with urban-related programs. However, the separation of CMHC and the MSUA was not to last.

Mr. William Teron, a prominent house builder and land developer in the Ottawa area, was appointed president of Central Mortgage and Housing Corporation in July of 1973. After the federal general election in July of 1974, Mr. Barnett Danson replaced Mr. Ron Basford as Minister of State for Urban Affairs and the minister through whom CMHC reports to parliament. Thus the leading personnel in both agencies had changed. Then in October 1975, the secretary (equivalent to deputy minister) of the ministry became commissioner-general for the United Nations Conference on Human Settlements (Habitat) held in Vancouver in 1976, and Mr. Teron was named acting secretary of the ministry. But he retained responsibility for CMHC as well. Hence the two agencies now had not only the same minister but also the same senior official. These moves formally heralded a reorganization and amalgamation of the agencies. The reorganization was announced as an economy measure, to eliminate overlap and duplication in research, for example. However, others have interpreted the reorganization as less of an integration than of a take-over by CMHC of the ministry.[40] It is also expected that the federal Department of Public Works in Canada's urban areas will come under the policy control of the ministry/CMHC. These developments increase the potential for the federal government to co-ordinate more effectively its involvement in urban affairs.

Tri-level Inter-governmental Relations

Probably the best known work in which the Ministry of State for Urban Affairs has been intimately involved is the series of tri-level conferences. One of the ministry's stated roles was to foster co-operative relationships among the three levels of government. While there had been a number of conferences involving the provincial and federal ministers responsible for housing, the municipalities had not been invited to participate separately from the provinces. It was only after the creation of the MSUA that tri-level conferences were formally held.

There have been three different types of conferences where representatives of the federal, provincial, and municipal governments are involved. One of these is the metropolitan tri-level conference, the earliest having been established for Winnipeg in 1972. Others followed for the Quebec City area, the Halifax–Dartmouth area, and the Vancouver area, all in 1973, and other metropolitan areas later. Composed of committees of officials from all three levels of government, these conferences are supposed to operate on a regular and on-going basis (usually meeting once a month or so) and are designed to focus on local problems and plans. The conference for the Quebec City area, for example, was to be involved with the preparation of a regional growth plan and with transportation in the older part of the city. However, this type of tri-level arrangement has faltered, and only the Halifax–Dartmouth example acquired much momentum.

Another kind of arrangement is the provincial tri-level conference, but these have been few. The Ontario arrangement was begun early in 1973, involving the MSUA, the Ontario Ministry of Treasury, Economics and Inter-governmental Affairs (all one ministry), and the Ontario Municipal Liaison Committee representing the municipal associations in the province. The conference meetings are less frequent (two in 1973) and deal with rather broad issues such as housing, transportation, and the environment. At the meeting held in Sudbury in October 1974, the federal Minister of State for Urban Affairs produced plans for a program of relocation of rail lines on a split-cost basis, a plan that the Ontario municipalities viewed as far from adequate. Other provincial or regional tri-level conferences were scheduled for Alberta in September of 1975 and for the Atlantic region in April 1976.

The most prominent tri-level conferences have been of the national variety, the first of which was held in Toronto in November 1972. While much of the impetus for this type of conference came from the federal Ministry of State for Urban Affairs, the Canadian Federation of Mayors and Municipalities (CFMM) had long sought such a forum wherein municipalities would be accorded "equal partner" status with the federal and provincial governments at the conference table and a voice independent of the provinces. The enthusiasm of the municipalities stood out in rather sharp contrast to the suspicions and guarded position of some provincial governments such as British Columbia, Quebec, and Ontario. Being protective and jealous of their constitutional jurisdictions, these provinces were reluctant to short-circuit the constitution by allowing direct consultation between the federal government and their own municipalities. Even the laying of the groundwork for that first national tri-level conference proved to be difficult. Federal, provincial, and municipal representatives committed themselves in April 1971 to such a conference, and a tri-level meeting to plan the first conference was held in April 1972. Eight months later, in November, the first conference was convened, but it has not generally been judged as an outstanding success, having produced little more than agreement to meet again. However, several factors mitigated against more substantial results, including the fact that the conference was an entirely new phenomenon with no precedents to follow. The participation of some provinces (with the notable exception of Manitoba) was less than whole-hearted, and the federal government was in a weak position, having emerged from the federal election only a month earlier with a precarious minority. In the light of these circumstances, the decision of that first conference to meet again can be viewed as something of a triumph in itself. The other significant outcome was a decision to establish the metropolitan area tri-level conferences referred to above, but a proposal to create a tri-level secretariat on a continuing basis was defeated.

The second such national conference was held in Edmonton in October of 1973, with the province of Quebec absent. Much of the discussion centred around the perennial demand of the municipalities for a larger share of governmental revenue, particularly on the CFMM's proposal that municipalities be allocated a portion of income tax revenue. Such a proposal would be significant, if implemented, in terms of elevating the general status of municipal government relative to provincial and federal government. It would also increase the level of municipal financial autonomy, for the expenditure of a municipality's share of income tax revenue would be at its own discretion. The governments of Ontario and Alberta in particular supported a compromise proposal for a study of public finance in general and of the implications of allocating municipalities a share of income tax revenue. Although the federal government and most provinces were cool to the proposal, the conference reached tentative agreement to commission such a study. Its terms of reference were to be broader than those wanted by the municipal representatives since the study would consider not only local finance but provincial and federal finance as well. However, the study was to give "special reference" to the former. Under the chairmanship of Dr. John Deutsch, the Tri-Level Task Force presented its 1312-page report in 1976.[41]

The decision to commission the study was the most dramatic development from this second national tri-level conference. But other announcements were made as well, such as the decision to hold a third conference, the proposal from the Ministry of State for Urban Affairs to create a National Urban Transportation Development Corporation as a joint enterprise of the federal and provincial governments, and a revised program to assist municipalities in the construction and expansion of sewage treatment facilities. The third conference was not to be held until after the study of public finance was completed, and was scheduled for October 1976. However, it was postponed indefinitely.

Despite the facts that two national tri-level conferences have been held (with a third one planned), that the tri-level arrangement for the Halifax–Dartmouth metropolitan area has enjoyed a measure of success and continuity, and that several provincial/regional tri-level conferences have been held, it is not yet possible to say that tri-level arrangements in general have become an integral part of inter-governmental relations in Canada. Provincial governments remain unenthusiastic about municipal participation as equal partners.

At the national conferences, municipalities are represented mainly through the Canadian Federation of Mayors and Municipalities (renamed the Federation of Canadian Municipalities in 1976). This organization was formed in 1937 as a merger between an association of mayors and an association of municipalities in reaction to the financial crisis experienced by local governments during the depression. The proportion of Canada's municipalities which are members of the federation is small (about 260 out of over 4000), but its members count for more than half of Canada's total population. The budget of the organization is relatively modest, being about one-third of a million dollars a year in 1975, and Toronto alone pays about one-tenth of the membership fees. The three areas of action emphasized by the federation are disseminating information to municipalities about programs and action of parliament and of federal departments and agencies, functioning as a lobby with regard to

the federal government, and participating in the national tri-level conferences. As an interest group, the federation is not without its weak-
nesses. Among them is the small proportion of municipalities which are
members. This poses problems in the extent to which the federation can
speak as the municipal voice. Also, the federation has long been plagued
with internal dissension, particularly between the populous urban centres
and the small municipalities. This dissension has resulted in the federation being less effective than its counterparts in other countries.

Central-local relations in Canada reflect a degree of balance between
the service and grass-roots values, and therefore fit neither the local
government nor the local self-government models perfectly. As a consequence, the nature of central-local relations in Canada is complex. It is
made more so by the federal form of government, with its division of
jurisdiction between the provincial governments and Ottawa.[42] In this
chapter it has been possible to present only a sketch of the relationships
involved as they affect and involve municipalities. The kinds of constraints, especially in terms of service functions, finance, and control from
above, that surround the governments in Canada's major cities should
now be apparent—cities are not in a position to cope adequately by
themselves with problems generated by the process of urbanization, and
if recent trends persist, their capabilities are unlikely to improve.

NOTES

1. Richard Simeon, *Federal-Provincial Diplomacy: The Making of Recent Policy in Canada* (Toronto: University of Toronto Press, 1972), pp. 6–8. See also D. V. Smiley, "The Rowell-Sirois Report, Provincial Autonomy, and Post-War Canadian Federalism," *Canadian Journal of Economics and Political Science*, vol. XXVIII, no. 1 (February, 1962), pp. 54–69.

2. K. C. Wheare, *Federal Government*, 4th ed. (London: Oxford University Press, 1963), pp. 10–11.

3. Of particular interest in this connection is W. Hardy Wickwar, *The Political Theory of Local Government* (Columbia, South Carolina:

University of South Carolina Press, 1970).

4. For details see F. Ridley and J. Blondel, *Public Administration in France*, 2nd ed. (London: Routledge and Kegan Paul, 1969), especially Chapter 4; B. Chapman, *Introduction to French Local Government* (London: George Allen and Unwin, 1953); and Fred F. Ridley, "Integrated Decentralization: Models of the Prefectoral System," *Political Studies*, vol. XXI (March, 1973).

5. Wickwar, *The Political Theory of Local Government*, pp. 56–7.

6. For a general discussion of the history and operation of home rule see Charles R. Adrian, *Governing*

Urban America, 2nd ed. (New York: McGraw-Hill, 1961), Chapter 7. For a critique of home rule see Lane M. Lancaster, *Government in Rural America* (New York: Van Nostrand, 1937).

7. There has been much controversy on the question of a connection between democracy and local self-government. A useful analysis of the several sides of the debate is Hugh Whalen, "Ideology, Democracy, and the Foundations of Local Self-Government," *Canadian Journal of Economics and Political Science*, vol. 26, no. 3 (August, 1960), re-printed in Lionel D. Feldman and Michael D. Goldrick, eds., *Politics and Government of Urban Canada: Selected Readings*, 2nd ed. (Toronto: Methuen, 1972), pp. 358–79.

8. Feldman and Goldrick, *Politics and Government of Urban Canada*, p. 366.

9. For a very detailed description of central-local relations in England and Wales prior to the reforms of 1973 see J. A. G. Griffith, *Central Departments and Local Authorities* (London: George Allen and Unwin, 1966). Regarding the new post-1973 situation see Peter G. Richards, *The Reformed Local Government System* (London: George Allen and Unwin, 1973), especially chapters III, IV, V and VIII.

10. J. Murray Beck, *The Government of Nova Scotia* (Toronto: University of Toronto Press, 1957), p. 307.

11. See J. A. Johnson, "Provincial-Municipal Intergovernmental Fiscal Relations," *Canadian Public Administration*, vol. XII, no. 2 (1969), pp. 166–80.

12. Canadian Federation of Mayors and Municipalities, *Puppets on a Shoestring: The Effects on Municipal Government of Canada's System of Public Finance* (Ottawa, April 28, 1976).

13. See Allan O'Brien, "Local Government Priorities for the Eighties," *Canadian Public Administration*, vol.

19, no. 1 (Spring, 1976), pp. 105–06.

14. *Report of the Tri-Level Task Force on Public Finance* (Toronto, February, 1976), Volume II, Table B-12, p. 96.

15. For earlier figures see Bureau of of Municipal Research, *Reorganizing Local Government—A Brief Look at Four Provinces* (Toronto, 1970); and John R. Cameron, *Provincial-Municipal Relations in the Maritime Provinces* (Fredericton: Maritime Union Study, 1970), Chapter IV.

16. *Report of the Tri-Level Task Force on Public Finance*, Volume II, Table 21, p. 73.

17. Mr. Darcy McKeough, quoted in *The Globe and Mail* (Toronto), April 21, 1976, p. 5.

18. See, for example, Lionel D. Feldman, "Legislative Control of Municipalities in Ontario," *Canadian Public Administration*, vol. IV, no. 3 (September, 1961), pp. 294–301.

19. For more information refer to Romaine K. Ross, *Local Government in Ontario* (Toronto: Canada Law Book Company, 1962); Gerald M. Adler, *Land Planning by Administrative Regulation: The Policies of the Ontario Municipal Board* (Toronto: University of Toronto Press, 1971); Horace L. Brittain, *Local Government in Canada* (Toronto: Ryerson Press, 1951); K. Grant Crawford, *Canadian Municipal Government* (Toronto: University of Toronto Press, 1954); and especially Bureau of Municipal Research, *Urban Development and the Ontario Municipal Board* (Toronto, 1971).

20. Crawford, *Canadian Municipal Government*, p. 349.

21. See Feldman, "Legislative Control of Municipalities in Ontario."

22. Regarding federal involvement in the Ottawa area refer to Rowat, *The Canadian Municipal System*, Part Five; Donald C. Rowat, ed., *The Government of Federal Capitals* (Toronto: University of Toronto

Press, 1973); and Douglas H. Fullerton, *The Capital of Canada: How Should It be Governed?*, a special study on the National Capital, 2 volumes (Ottawa: Information Canada, 1974).

23. M. D. Goldrick, "Present Issues in the Growth of Cities," *Canadian Public Administration*, vol. 14, no. 3 (Fall, 1971), pp. 452–9. Also see David G. Bettison, *The Politics of Canadian Urban Development* (Edmonton: University of Alberta Press, 1975).

24. See Lithwick, *Urban Canada: Problems and Prospects.*

25. For more detail refer to Central Mortgage and Housing Corporation, *Housing in Canada, 1946–1970: A Supplement to the 25th Annual Report* (Ottawa, 1970); L. Smith, *Housing in Canada* (Research Monograph 2, 1971, for Lithwick, *Urban Canada: Problems and Prospects*; and David M. Cameron, "Urban Policy," in G. Bruce Doern and V. Seymour Wilson, eds., *Issues in Canadian Public Policy* (Toronto: Macmillan, 1974). In a much different vein see Humphrey Carver, *Compassionate Landscape* (Toronto: University of Toronto Press, 1975), chapters 8, 9, 11, 12, and 14.

26. Central Mortgage and Housing Corporation, *Annual Report, 1974* (Ottawa, 1974), p. 30.

27. See, for example, Michael Dennis and Susan Fish, *Programs in Search of a Policy: Low Income Housing in Canada* (Toronto: Hakkert, 1972).

28. Carver, *Compassionate Landscape.*

29. Ibid., p. 108.

30. For a useful description and historical setting see David M. Cameron, "Urban Policy," in Doern and Wilson, *Issues in Canadian Public Policy.*

31. See for example Hans Blumenfeld, "The Role of the Federal Government in Urban Affairs," in Feldman and Goldrick, *Politics and Government of Urban Canada.* The article first appeared in *The Journal of*

Liberal Thought, vol. 2 (Spring, 1966).

32. Canada, *Report of the Federal Task Force on Housing and Urban Development* (Ottawa: Information Canada, January, 1969). See also Lloyd Axworthy, "The Housing Task Force: A Case Study," in G. Bruce Doern and Peter Aucoin, eds., *The Structure of Policy-Making in Canada* (Toronto: Macmillan, 1971).

33. Canada, *Report of the Federal Task Force on Housing and Urban Development*, Letter of Transmittal.

34. Ibid., p. 46.

35. N. H. Lithwick and G. Paquet, eds., *Urban Studies: A Canadian Perspective* (Toronto: Methuen, 1968).

36. An edited version of his report was published as *Urban Canada: Problems and Prospects* (Ottawa: Central Mortgage and Housing Corporation, 1970). The six research monographs have been published separately.

37. Ibid., p. 215. For further explanation see N. H. Lithwick, "Political Innovation: A Case Study," *Plan Canada*, vol. 12, no. 1 (1972), pp. 45–56.

38. Carver, *Compassionate Landscape*, p. 112.

39. Cited in Bettison, *The Politics of Canadian Urban Development*, p. 280. His book offers a critique of Lithwick's report on pp. 249–69.

40. See, for example, *City Magazine*, vol. 1, no. 8 (January–February, 1976), pp. 12–16.

41. *Report of the Tri-Level Task Force on Public Finance*, 3 volumes (Toronto: February, 1976). The Task Force refrained from making recommendations.

42. In a general way, this point is made by J. Stefan Dupré, "Intergovernmental Relations and the Metropolitan Area," in Simon R. Miles, ed., *Metropolitan Problems: International Perspectives, A Search for Comprehensive Solutions* (Toronto: Methuen, 1970), p. 346.

The Structures of Municipal Decision Making

As indicated in the Introduction, the process of urbanization has two main kinds of impact on the decision-making structures of Canada's major cities. First, it is these structures more than the provincial and federal equivalents that have for long borne the main brunt of responsibility for producing decisions and policies to resolve the kinds of urban problems referred to earlier—problems of housing, transportation, urban renewal, environmental pollution control, and all the others. Even though the provincial and federal governments are increasingly intervening in the attempt to resolve these difficulties, the responsibility for their resolution continues to be left basically to the cities themselves, a responsibility compounded in its complexity by their diminishing financial independence. This kind of impact of urbanization on internal city structures can be termed the *output* impact: the need for short-term decisions and longer-term policies to flow *out*. As the previous chapter has shown, the capability of cities to cope with the output impact is greatly conditioned by senior governments, but it is also conditioned by the internal structures of the cities themselves.

The output impact actually has two dimensions—the making of policies or decisions, and administration. The first focuses on legislative outputs from council, and the second involves the implementation or administration of council's decisions on a day-to-day basis. The extent to which these two dimensions can or should be separated from each other has been a matter of considerable debate. The British tradition of local government which characterized early municipal government in Canada and which is still strong here was based on a relative fusion of the legislative and administrative functions, whereby council not only legislates but oversees the execution of the legislation. The dominant theory supporting such a fusion is that better legislation can be made when councillors are aware of the problems involved in administration and can understand the administrative ramifications of policy alternatives, and that councils must accept responsibility for administration as well as for legislation. Although it is not the case that *all* American municipalities are characterized by an attempt to separate the two functions, many do attempt to do so on the grounds that while councillors who are not technically expert can legislate, administration is best left in the hands of those who are hired for their expertise. As will be seen below, this separation between legislation and administration is most evident in the council/city manager structure of decision making which originated in the United States and has been adopted and adapted in a number of Canadian municipalities.

The other kind of impact of urbanization on a city's decision-making structures can be termed the *input* impact. As cities increase in population and as residents become increasingly aware and concerned about urban problems and the processes through which attempts are made to resolve those problems, the local authorities are faced with barrages of complaints, requests, and demands for action. Citizen participation in Canadian cities has tended to increase in scale (refer to Chapter 6) and in the kinds of tactics used to try to influence the decision-making structures. Citizen input in city government and politics is far less confined now than it was to relatively passive and relatively supportive voter turnout at municipal election time. The shift in citizen participation has tended toward more visible and vocal group activism not only at election time but on an on-going basis. The input impact therefore bears on the extent to which councils and councillors can perform a representative function —being aware of and giving proper consideration to the ideas and views of individuals and organized interests that are not formally a part of the governing process.

Both these kinds of impact raise serious questions about the capacity of existing municipal decision-making structures to cope with producing the large number of "right" legislative and administrative outputs to alleviate or resolve urban problems, and with the ever more numerous, more popular, and better organized kinds of inputs from the populace. Indeed, an inability of existing city decision-making structures to deal adequately with the two impacts can be considered an important explanation for the process of reform of municipal structures and perhaps also for the renewed interest of political parties in becoming active in urban politics. If present structures are unable to represent, aggregate, and accommodate input demands and complaints and to produce the desired outputs, why not then reorganize the structures or possibly superimpose on them an interest-aggregate function performed by political parties? These questions are pursued in chapters 4 and 7 respectively.

The municipal structures of decision making differ considerably from province to province as well as within each province, varying somewhat according to the size of the municipality. They are to some extent prescribed by provincial governments' municipal acts or by the special charters of municipal incorporation. About the only accurate generalization that can be made of them throughout the country is that each municipality has a mayor or the equivalent (such as a reeve or warden), a council of elected aldermen, committees of council, appointed personnel to administer the municipality on a day-to-day basis, and special-purpose bodies. Knowledge of the particular nature of these five components and the particular way they are combined in a municipality allows an appreciation of the extent to which municipalities can cope with input and output stresses.

The Position of Mayor

The most publicly visible component of the decision-making structure is the mayor. The office is an important one but one that is generally defined only in vague terms in provincial acts or special charters. For example, the mayors of Regina and Saskatoon are designated as the "chief executive officer" of the cities and are required by Saskatchewan's Urban Municipality Act of 1970 (section 51) to

a) be vigilant and active in causing the laws governing the municipality to be duly executed;
b) inspect the conduct of all civic officers;
c) cause all negligence, carelessness and violation of duty to be duly prosecuted and punished so far as it is in his power to do so; and
d) communicate to the council all such information, and recommend such measures, as may tend to the betterment of the finances, health, security, cleanliness, comfort, ornamentation and prosperity of the municipality.

The Act also empowers the mayors to call special meetings of council, to preside at all meetings of council, to suspend any city official (other than a city commissioner or manager) subject to later approval of council, and to appoint special constables (subject to later ratification by council). The mayor is also *ex officio* one of Saskatoon's commissioners. While the terminology and specifications vary, these duties and powers are typical of those allocated to the mayors in Canadian cities. In some cities (notably in British Columbia, Quebec, and Manitoba) mayors have expanded powers such as a veto over actions of council.

Specifications of the powers and duties of Canadian mayors certainly make them more than just one more member of council but the powers usually do not in themselves make Canadian mayors "strong" chief executives in the American tradition. For example, mayors in this country do not tend to have the legal power to unilaterally appoint civic officials. But because of the vagueness of their specified powers and duties, their relationships with other members of council can vary greatly even within a particular city when the occupant of the mayor's chair changes. The extent to which a mayor is pre-eminent in council depends much on the personality of the particular incumbent. If the mayor has a forceful personality and has developed a network of close working relationships with other members of council, then the incumbent mayor may acquire informally a position of strong leadership in council and be able to exercise the powers of a strong chief executive. Montreal's Jean Drapeau is an example of a mayor who clearly has been able to add such powers to his office informally.

It is also not unusual for certain traditions to develop around the office of mayor, traditions that in effect endow it with extra power. For example, the decision on which members of council or which non-elected citizens should sit on which committees, boards, commissions, and authorities is sometimes delegated to the mayor. Similarly, it is common for mayors to initiate much of the action in council, and to represent the city in negotiations with other governments and other outside interests, as well as to represent the city on ceremonial occasions.

Another factor that almost always puts incumbent mayors in a position where they are able to assume a role of leadership, of a fairly strong chief executive, is the fact that in larger cities, the position of mayor is considered to be a full-time job, and is paid accordingly. Aldermen are infrequently full-time and in many cases are not paid enough to make their position a full-time one. What this means is that the mayor clearly has the opportunity to become very familiar with background material and has the benefit of day-to-day contact with the civic bureaucracy. Also the mayor is usually an *ex officio* member of all committees of council and of special-purpose bodies. He or she therefore can become more expert than part-time aldermen on the broad range of matters to be brought before council. This tends to put mayors in a position from which they can often determine the particular course of action taken by council even though the mayor normally does not have a vote in council except to break a tie.

Additionally, mayors have a different and pre-eminent constituency compared to that of aldermen. Almost all of Canada's large cities (except for Vancouver, Thunder Bay, and Windsor) have the aldermen elected on a ward basis so that any one alderman represents primarily the people of his or her ward, which is only a fraction of the city's population. On the other hand, the mayors of all the larger cities are elected at large; their constituency is the whole city, and this tends to buttress the status and prestige of the mayor considerably. In those Ontario cities that have the board-of-control form of government the mayor's constituency is not a unique one, for controllers are elected at large too. Nevertheless, the mayoralty is a singular elected position, and attention, complaints, and demands tend to be focused more on the mayor than on any other member of council. If the mayor becomes a strong chief executive, the ability of the decision-making structure to cope with input stress is seriously jeopardized. No one person can satisfactorily cope with the range and number of inputs from individual citizens and organized interests in a major city. The channel of communication is likely to become constricted and restricted to inputs from selected individuals and interests. Output stress is also likely to become severe unless the mayor delegates power to appointed civic officials or to members of the mayor's personal staff.

The Council

Another aspect of the ability or inability of the cities' decision-making structures to cope with the input and output stresses posed by urbanization is the city's council. The Canadian tradition has been one of small councils, and in this regard Canada resembles the American municipal tradition more than the British tradition. Councils large enough to resemble provincial legislatures have been very rare in Canada, although Montreal at one time had a hundred members of council. Very few city councils have more than twenty members, with the norm being eleven or thirteen, including the mayor.

There is no necessary connection between population size of a city and the size of its council, as Table 3:1 indicates. It is the last two columns in the table that are of most interest here, for they give some indication of the extent to which a mass of inputs can be handled by councillors.

The question of the optimum size of a city council is one on which

Table 3:1   City Councils (1975)

city	number of councillors	population	people per councillor	electoral basis for aldermen
Montreal	56	1,250,000	22,300	19 wards
Toronto	23	700,000	30,400	11 wards
Winnipeg	51	560,000	11,000	50 wards
North York	19	528,000	27,800	14 wards
Edmonton	13	452,000	34,800	4 wards
Vancouver	11	440,000	40,000	at large
Calgary	13	440,000	33,800	6 wards
Scarborough	17	363,000	21,400	12 wards
Hamilton	21	305,000	14,500	8 wards
Ottawa	16	296,000	18,500	11 wards
Etobicoke	15	289,000	19,300	5 wards
Laval	22	242,000	11,900	8 wards
London	19	240,000	12,600	7 wards
Mississauga	10	240,000	24,000	9 wards
Windsor	9	200,000	22,200	at large
Quebec	17	188,000	11,100	7 wards
York	11	146,000	13,300	8 wards
Regina	11	145,000	13,200	10 wards
Saskatoon	11	136,000	12,400	10 wards
Kitchener	11	130,000	11,800	at large*
Halifax	11	125,000	11,400	10 wards
St. Catharines	13	117,000	9,000	6 wards
Thunder Bay	13	107,000	8,300	at large
East York	9	106,000	11,800	4 wards

*in a plebiscite in 1974 voters approved introduction of a ward system.

there is no general agreement, and debate usually centres on contrasting views of what is the most important function to be performed by a council. There are two main schools of thought. On the one hand there is the view that emphasizes the function of council as a representative body, the focus being put on what is referred to above as the input impact of urbanization. The logic of this position is that municipal government is a cornerstone of democracy, an essential feature of which is representation of population, and the more representation the better. To ensure that municipal government is "grass roots" democracy, the contact between individuals and their elected representatives should be as close as possible. The possibilities for close contact are increased when the people an elected councillor must represent are few and when the residents of a small sector (i.e. small ward) of the city can point to a particular councillor as "their" representative. Therefore, a city should be composed of a large number of elected representatives, each of whom represents a small ward.

The contrasting view emphasizes the function of council as a provider of services, and therefore focuses on the output side of the process. The argument here is that since large numbers of policies and decisions are required of council (and sometimes quickly) the decision-making process needs to be made as streamlined and speedy as possible. Since the more people there are in any group, the greater the likelihood is of opposing viewpoints requiring more time and debate to resolve, the best way of getting decisions made quickly is to keep council small, and to have council run more as a consensus-seeking and non-political corporate board of directors than as a politically oriented legislature. By extension, the resolution of any conflicts within council is made more expeditious when "parochial" concerns associated with a large number of small wards are absent from the minds of the councillors. The point is: have either no wards, or only a few very large wards.

These two positions do not appear to be compatible. It does not seem to be possible to arrive at the same optimum size and basis of election of council by emphasizing first one then the other view of the more important function of a city council. When the size of council is increased to facilitate representation, critics say it faces a crisis in decision making, and when council is reduced in size to facilitate decision making, critics say it faces a crisis in representation. The way in which the role of the mayor is performed, the presence of some kind of political parties on council, and the way in which council uses committees can lead to some common ground however.

Committees of Council

Whether a city council has committees or not, and how many, is generally a matter decided by council itself. Virtually all Canadian city councils do have committees, of which there are two main kinds besides the entirely different "committee of the whole". When council meets in a committee of the whole, the formal parliamentary rules are suspended, the mayor may leave the chair, and debate takes place among all members of council in a less formal way than is otherwise the case.

The two main kinds of committees are standing committees and special or *ad hoc* committees. Committees of both kinds are normally composed of only part of council although there are instances where all councillors sit on a particular committee. It is usual for the mayor to be an *ex officio* member of all committees. Standing committees are on-going, and the members of each standing committee are usually selected by council as a whole (sometimes by nomination of the mayor) shortly after a city election or each year. These meet regularly and their tasks or mandates are delegated to them by council. Special or *ad hoc* committees are created for a specific and usually short-term task, and occasionally have non-council members as well. Once the tasks assigned to it by council are completed, the committee is dissolved.

Standing and special committees are differentiated also by the kind of function they perform. Special committees generally have an advisory capacity only and thus have no legislative or executive authority delegated to them by council. These committees are usually created to investigate a particular problem area or policy issue and then report back to council with recommendations. An example is Toronto's 1975 Task Force on the Status of Women. The recommendations made can of course be rejected or modified by council as a whole. Standing committees do have an advisory function too but in addition they may also have some degree of executive power, especially in the first decision-making model discussed later in this chapter. The amount of executive power they have varies greatly among these models. The executive function involves the committee in overseeing the operations of one or more line departments of the city administration, or a particular policy area that straddles departments. Each of Canada's major city councils typically has from three to five standing committees. In 1975 Thunder Bay's council, for example, had five: 1) Public Works, Protection to Persons and Property; 2) Health and Social Services; 3) Parks and Recreation; 4) Planning and Zoning; and 5) Finance. In this respect Thunder Bay's council is more typical than Montreal's council, which is unusual in having only one standing committee. That committee is called the Committee on Toponymy, and its function is to decide on the names of streets.

If standing and special committees are wisely used, they can go some way toward overcoming some of the disadvantages of large city councils in terms of expeditiously producing outputs by parcelling out to specialized small committees responsibility for investigating, debating, and recommending courses of action for council to take. But the use of committees by councils of any size, and especially large ones, as a mechanism to maximize both the input and output functions of council has several dangers. Excessive use of, and delegation of power to, committees can reduce council to little more than a rubber stamp which automatically adopts committee recommendations. While this does not necessarily mean that the output function of council is poorly performed, it does detract from the performance of the input function. The problem here is that committees may be used to remove from the limelight potentially controversial issues on which there needs to be a maximum of public input. Even when they are open to the public, and even if the public is allowed to speak at them, committee meetings tend to escape public attention and coverage by the mass media. In effect, committee meetings are comparatively private. Inadequate use of committees by council can also pose dangers, especially with regard to council's output function. If council insists on repeating in full and at great length the debate which has already taken place in the smaller committees, the making of policy decisions will be unnecessarily prolonged. In other words, councils can best organize their workloads and perform their functions when they use specialized committees for the purposes of intensive investigation, soliciting and considering representations from the civic administration and the public, and recommending action for council to take, the recommendations being respected but adequately scrutinized by the full council.

The City's Bureaucracy

Appointed personnel also have an important effect on the ability of cities to cope with input and output stresses. Just as it is a myth at the provincial and federal levels of government that appointed personnel are involved only with regard to the execution and administration of actions taken by legislatures, so too is it a myth in city government. Of course such employees are fundamentally involved in policy execution and administration, but the more senior personnel are involved with regard to inputs as well, and should be. It is the technical and professional expertise that some of them possess, as well as their experience on the job, that makes them valuable aids to council in the formulation of policy. The more senior members of the city bureaucracy are particularly well-placed to advise council or committees of council on the range of policy options available and on the administrative ramifications of those options. It is with the city bureaucracy that residents of the city tend to have their most frequent contact, if only to pay water bills or to pick up social assistance cheques. Therefore the bureaucracy can function as an additional channel of communication of public inputs to council.

All this is contingent on the lines of communication between members of council and the more senior city bureaucrats being reasonably numerous and open. If contact with senior city administrators is limited to or monopolized by the mayor (and by other elected members of the city's executive committee if there is one, or by elected controllers if the city has a board of control), then the full advantage of city bureaucrats' involvement in the decision-making process will not be realized. Reference has already been made to the fact that there is sometimes an attempt made to isolate policy making from administration, especially in the council/city manager structure discussed below.

Taken as a whole, municipal bureaucracies are very large in Canada. In September of 1975 the total number of municipal employees in Canada was estimated at about 252,000 excluding teachers and employees of municipally-owned enterprises such as hospitals and transit systems. At the same time the number of employees of the federal government was 328,000, excluding personnel in the armed forces and of Crown corporations; and provincial and territorial government employees numbered about 349,000, excluding employees of provincial Crown corporations.

Table 3:2 Size of City Bureaucracies (1975)

city	1975 population	municipal employees excluding teachers	public school teachers (primary and secondary)
Edmonton	452,000	11,249	3,861
Vancouver	440,000	5,256	3,010
Calgary	440,000	7,000	4,220
Ottawa	296,000	3,400	4,000
Etobicoke	289,000	1,540	2,942
London	240,000	1,900	2,224

This last figure also excludes British Columbia, for which figures were not available.[1] Table 3:2 gives some idea of the scale of city bureaucracies, although the figures given are not fully comparable. Some cities specified that temporary employees were included but other cities did not. Also, some cities did not indicate whether employees of special-purpose bodies such as transit commissions were included or not. Finally, some did not specify if teachers in separate (i.e. Catholic) schools were included.

A municipality's bureaucracy is organized into two kinds of departments as well as into special-purpose bodies such as school boards, library boards, and public utility commissions. Line departments are those which provide a particular public service such as a fire department does, or a police department, social welfare department, parks and recreation department, and so on. Staff departments provide support services necessary to the operation of line departments and of council, and examples include personnel, purchasing, and accounting departments. The number of line and support departments that major cities in Canada have varies from about nine (in Ottawa in 1975) to twenty-five (in Calgary in 1975).

Aside from relative size, city bureaucracies differ from bureaucracies at the federal and provincial levels in several respects, but most importantly in the kinds of services performed and the nature of decisions taken. As explained in Chapter 6, local government has traditionally been associated mainly with non-controversial "housekeeping" services, especially to property—provision of water supply, sewerage collection and disposal, fire and police protection, and so on, while services to people (services which tend to be more controversial) have been most associated with the senior levels of government. However, cities are increasingly becoming more involved with controversial areas of policy such as environmental pollution control, social and physical planning, and urban transportation priorities. This shift in emphasis strains city bureaucracies and requires that new kinds of professional and technically competent personnel be hired by cities, and that the work orientation of existing personnel be altered through specialized training. The need for improved co-ordination among city departments is also apparent so as to accommodate the increasing number and range of services they must provide and to ensure that the performance of those services does not become too fragmented. The four decision-making models discussed below differ considerably in their co-ordination capabilities.

Special-purpose Bodies: The Phenomenon of Ad Hockery

> The councillors up at Pitlochry
> Believed in the creed of Ad Hockery;
> They farmed all decisions
> To boards and commissions,
> And so made their council a mockery.[2]

A characteristic of virtually all of Canada's major cities is a proliferation of assorted boards, commissions, authorities, and committees. While these are often an important part of the city's decision-making process, they usually possess a degree of independence that places them somewhat outside the formal structures discussed next. Such bodies are typically created for a single purpose, such as boards of police commissioners, of education, of health, of libraries, of parks, of transportation, of public utilities, of electrical supply, of conservation, of museums . . . the list is endless. Some special-purpose bodies are required by provincial statutes, such as the boards of police commissioners, of health, and of education in Ontario. The others are created by the city councils themselves. It is also sometimes the case that such bodies are created jointly by two or more municipalities for the purpose of fostering inter-municipal co-operation and co-ordination. The fact is that since many metropolitan areas are politically fragmented in the sense of having no one municipality to cover the entire metropolitan population, some mechanisms for co-operation and co-ordination become necessary. Such is especially the case for those kinds of urban problems that refuse to respect municipal boundaries—air and water pollution, for example. Some special-purpose bodies can only advise city councils and/or provincial governments. Most are operating agencies, having been delegated power by the city governments and/or the provincial governments. It is the latter type that is of most immediate importance in a consideration of decision-making structures and processes.

No one can specify with certainty just how many special-purpose bodies there are in the major cities or in Canada as a whole, for the count would depend on whether one includes or excludes those whose dealings are mainly with the provincial governments. But they certainly are numerous. According to the Bureau of Municipal Research, there were in Ontario alone over 3200 in 1967. Even though the list in Table 3:3 excludes a wide range of special-purpose bodies, especially advisory ones, the total is more than three times the 964 municipalities there were in the province a year later. Another study, conducted in 1975, identified 122

Table 3:3   Special-Purpose Bodies in Ontario (1967)

Utility Commissions	360	
Planning Boards	225	
Community Centre Boards	250	
Parks Commissions	150	
Public Library Boards	220	
Health Boards	270	
Police Boards	93	
Police Villages	158	
	——	
		1,726
Public School Boards	777	
Separate School Boards	482	
Secondary School Boards	235	
	——	
		1,494
		——
total		3,220

SOURCE: Bureau of Municipal Research, *Regional Government—the Key to Genuine Local Autonomy* (Toronto, May, 1968), page 10.

such bodies in Metro Toronto alone, of which nineteen were at the Metropolitan level and 103 at the city (borough) level.[3]

To take the City of Calgary as an example, its 1974 Municipal Manual lists the following special-purpose bodies: Gas and Power Committee, Industrial Expansion Committee, Calgary Taxi Commission, Council-School Boards Liaison Committee, Building Appeal Board, Development Appeal Board, Gas Approval Board, Calgary Parking Authority, Calgary Regional Planning Commission, Transportation and Development Authority, Boxing and Wrestling Commission, Calgary Area Emergency Measures Organization, Calgary Regional Arts Foundation, Board of Health, Parks and Recreation Board, Landlord and Tenant Advisory Board, Weeds Appeal Board, 1975 Centennial Committee, Calgary Exhibition and Stampede Board, Tourist and Convention Association, Calgary Zoological Society, Heritage Park Society, Library Board, McMahon Stadium Board, Hospitals Board, Auxiliary and Nursing Home District Board, Metro Calgary and Rural General Hospital District Board, Metropolitan Calgary Foundation, Planning Commission, Police Commission, Scholarship Committee, Campaigns for Public Contributions Approving Authority, Ad Hoc Planning Advisory Committee, Housing Committee, Intergovernmental Housing Committee, Mayor's Pollution Committee, and the Trade Market and Convention Centre Authority, plus the Calgary Board of Education and the Calgary Roman Catholic Separate School Board.[4]

Boards of education constitute the most numerous category of special-purpose bodies, most municipalities in Canada having at least one, though in New Brunswick education has become largely a provincial concern and in Alberta the counties do not have boards of education because the county councils themselves are responsible for education. Public education has therefore been singled out in most provinces for special attention, there being provincial statutes requiring boards of education entirely or partly separate from municipal councils, and with low or no council control over the operation or financing of the schools. In most cases the city's education budget is drawn up entirely by the board of education and presented to council which cannot alter that budget. In other words, all that most councils do in respect of the city schools is to collect tax revenue for the school board. The independence of the school boards from municipal councils in this country has on the whole been unquestioned, following the Ryerson tradition established more than a century ago.

The reason for separating boards of education in particular from city councils is to be found in the notion that there are certain local functions into which politics should not enter, especially not into education. This notion holds that education, among other functions, is too important to be subjected to the vagaries of politicians or would-be politicians. Perhaps the single most popular promise of candidates at civic election time is to reduce taxes. Since education constitutes by far the largest single item of expenditure in cities' budgets, it would be the most obvious target for penny-wise local politicians. Hence the conclusion follows that control of local education should be de-politicized. Also, special-purpose bodies like boards of education can function as a means whereby provincial governments can ensure a degree of policy control. In Nova Scotia, for example, the provincial government appoints some of the members of school boards. Over time, these arguments have come to be applied to a wide range of other local functions, police protection being a particular case in point. The logic has a certain compelling force to it, for accounts of cities which at one time had police protection directly under the control of the city council show that enforcement (or lack of it) of municipal by-laws was sometimes rather selective.[5]

The present-day situation with regard to special-purpose bodies is one of very considerable complexity and fragmentation of the decision-making process in most of the major cities. While granting that there may be some measure of validity to the notion that some local functions need to be especially protected from improper influence, some serious questions arise. Is separate status really essential for all the local functions to which it is extended (bearing in mind the list for Calgary)? How seriously do they detract from local autonomy? Can city councils exercise adequate control, over the finances for example, of all these agencies? Without control, can councils adequately establish priorities? Can special-purpose bodies be adequately co-ordinated with line and staff departments? And is there any adequate and effective means whereby the public can hold such bodies accountable, especially where there is a distinction between responsibility for spending money and for raising the money? As has been pointed out elsewhere,[6] the proliferation of special-purpose bodies presents serious problems in terms of efficiency (duplication, voids, too many players, and lack of co-ordination among them), public control (isolating the citizenry from the decision-making process, loss of public input through lack of information about such bodies, and having so many positions on such bodies being appointive rather than elective), and a general weakening of municipal government.

The Decision-making Models[7]

Having considered separately each of the five structural components of the decision-making process in cities, it is necessary to examine the ways in which they are put together. To describe here in detail the internal structure in each of Canada's major cities is an impossible task. While each is unique in some respects, almost all of Canada's major cities can be typed as utilizing one or another of four basic structural models. Some cities combine features from one model with features from another. Winnipeg, for example, has a board of (appointed) commissioners as well as an executive committee of elected councillors, and London has an (elected) board of control as well as an appointed chief administrative officer that functions like a city manager. One city has been selected to illustrate each of the four basic models and the characteristics of the models that bear on their capabilities to cope with input and output stresses.

THE COUNCIL/COMMITTEE STRUCTURE

Although only one of the twenty-four urban municipalities that had a population of at least 100,000 in 1971 retains this model, it remains the most common in Canadian municipalities overall. Thus it is smaller municipalities that utilize this structure, the exception being the Borough of East York in Metropolitan Toronto. It is derived from the British experience, and as the diagram illustrates it is characterized by the elected council meeting both as a whole and in a number of smaller committees. In East York there are eight standing committees that are relatively permanent and that deal with a particular area of administration and policy. There can be any number of temporary special committees as well. One or more departments of the civic bureaucracy reports to and is supervised by each standing committee. As the diagram suggests, there is no necessary connection between the number and titles of committees of council and the number and titles of departments. Some departments

Figure 3:1 East York's Council/Committee Structure (1975)

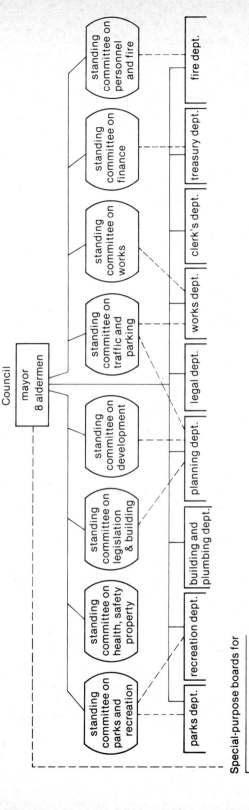

Council

mayor
8 aldermen

standing committee on parks and recreation

standing committee on health, safety property

standing committee on legislation & building

standing committee on development

standing committee on traffic and parking

standing committee on works

standing committee on finance

standing committee on personnel and fire

parks dept.

recreation dept.

building and plumbing dept.

planning dept.

legal dept.

works dept.

clerk's dept.

treasury dept.

fire dept.

Special-purpose boards for

- education
- health
- libraries
- planning
- parks
- rinks
- hydro electric
- community gardens
- historical and arts
- safety
- recreation centre

may be responsible to council through one committee for some purposes, and through another committee for other purposes.

Committees of council in this kind of decision-making structure have both input and output functions. After consultation with the appropriate appointed department heads and sometimes after receiving representations from interested groups and individuals, the standing committees propose action for council to take. It is not always the case, though, that committee meetings are open to public attendance or to public participation. In a sense the committees aggregate interests; that is, they weigh competing viewpoints and alternative courses of action, attempt to reconcile them, and then present their recommendations to council as a whole. The committees are also involved on the output side of the process in that they are supposed to oversee the operations of the departments which execute the decisions taken by council. However, committees are not normally delegated much authority, so that except for minor matters their actions require the sanction of council. Therefore standing committees can function as a strong liaison mechanism between council as the legislative body and the civic bureaucracy as the administrative agency.

The council/committee model has a number of advantages and disadvantages with regard to capacity to cope with input and output stresses. Looking first at the advantages, the diagram indicates that there are multiple channels for communication between council itself and the administrative departments through the standing committees. Some of the other decision-making models are much more deficient in this regard. In the council/committee model these multiple channels can facilitate both the input and output functions. The role of the committees in proposing action to council is enhanced by the communication channels. Having a number of committees may (if the meetings are open to public attendance and participation) also increase the possibility of private individuals and organized interests being able to exert influence on council because of the number of points of access and because of their relative specialization. If a group seeks to have council alter a zoning by-law for example, the group perhaps need choose only one of several points of access— the particular standing committee that deals with planning and zoning—and can focus their efforts only on the members of that one committee rather than having to attempt to persuade all members of council. If the members of the committee can be persuaded of the group's position, council is likely to do the same, for councils usually accept committee recommendations. Another advantage of this decision-making structure that affects both the input and output functions is the fact that members of council have the opportunity to specialize in particular areas of policy and administration, and to apply such expertise as they already have.

Among the disadvantages of the council/committee model is the tendency for the number of committees to increase over time, particularly as the council becomes involved in additional areas of decision making. This can put an increased burden on the members of council who have to spread their time and talents more thinly. Hence they are likely to be less able to consider in depth both inputs and outputs. Also, the decision-making process itself tends to get slowed down, in that what gets debated in committee is often debated all over again in council, even though council usually ends up accepting committee recommendations. Thus the time lag between initiation and implementation of action in council may be increased somewhat in this model. The lengthening lag between input and output is also attributable to willingness by some councils to shunt particularly controversial matters on to a committee for "further study", a tactic that is at times entirely justified for complex matters but is rather too convenient a means of postponing or evading unpopular decisions. Another aspect of this matter is that even when committee meetings are not actually closed to the public, they are generally held outside the glare of publicity and media coverage, thereby diminishing the possibility of the public being adequately informed.

Usually considered to be the most serious shortcoming of the council/ committee structure is the lack of any strong co-ordinating mechanism. The danger is that ramifications and inter-connections of matters considered by committees are less likely to be examined than in other decision-making models, for each committee is quite specialized and only some members of council sit on any one committee. For example, a standing committee on housing may initiate action in council to stimulate residential construction in a particular part of the city but may not fully appreciate the consequences of their recommendations with regard to the need for additional public transportation facilities, parks, water supply, etc., for these matters would be the concern of other committees. The mayor is almost always the only member of council who sits on all committees, and it is impractical to entrust to this one individual the responsibility for ensuring that matters are properly dealt with in a wider context. If the municipality performs only a few service functions and has only a few administrative departments, this disadvantage may not be severe. But in a major city the problems are important. It is not surprising therefore that the council/committee model is used primarily in municipalities with fairly small populations.

THE COUNCIL/COMMISSION STRUCTURE

Although this model of decision-making is not the most common in Canada's municipalities taken as a whole, it is used in a number of Canada's major cities, particularly in the three most western provinces. Four of the twenty-four urban municipalities with 1971 populations of over 100,000 use this structure or a variation on it.[8] Edmonton is used to illustrate.

As Figure 3:2 indicates, the basic features of the council/commission model are an elected council and an appointed board of commissioners. The commissioners are appointed by council and each is responsible for a number of particular departments and/or utilities. There are at least two commissioners in this structure, and the mayor is a commissioner *ex officio*. It is not an essential feature to have either a chief commissioner or standing committees of council, but all four cities do have both these features. In the case of Edmonton the appropriate commissioner sits on "his" standing committee, and the committees meet regularly to consider matters referred to them by council and to make recommendations back to council. The standing committees have only a modest mandate to oversee civic administration for they do not have the power to act on their own on major matters. Nevertheless, the fact that the appropriate commissioner attends and participates in the committee proceedings facilitates the working out of an informal mechanism whereby the committees can oversee in some detail the operations of the civic administration. Therefore the committees are not entirely limited to performing only an input advisory role.

The board of commissioners is responsible to council as a whole, normally through the mayor, and sometimes through the chief commissioner as well if one is so designated. The department heads are responsible to council through the appropriate commissioner and through the

Figure 3:2 Edmonton's Council/Commission Structure (1975)

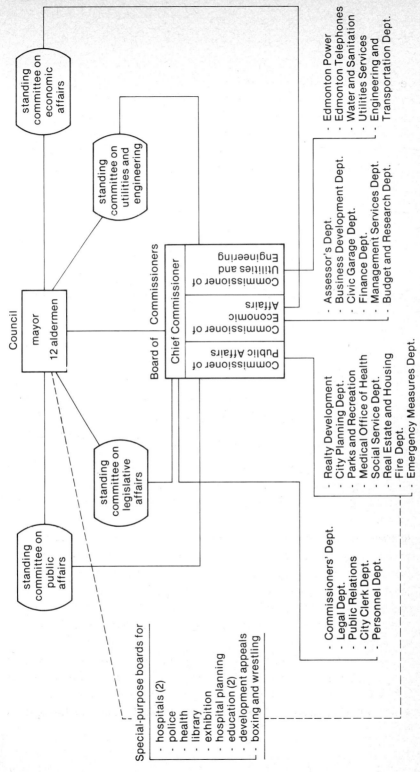

Council

mayor
12 aldermen

standing committee on economic affairs

standing committee on utilities and engineering

standing committee on public affairs

standing committee on legislative affairs

Board of Commissioners

Chief Commissioner

Commissioner of Public Affairs

Commissioner of Economic Affairs

Commissioner of Utilities and Engineering

- Commissioners' Dept.
- Legal Dept.
- Public Relations
- City Clerk Dept.
- Personnel Dept.

- Realty Development
- City Planning Dept.
- Parks and Recreation
- Medical Office of Health
- Social Service Dept.
- Real Estate and Housing
- Fire Dept.
- Emergency Measures Dept.

- Assessor's Dept.
- Business Development Dept.
- Civic Garage Dept.
- Finance Dept.
- Management Services Dept.
- Budget and Research Dept.

- Edmonton Power
- Edmonton Telephones
- Water and Sanitation
- Utilities Services
- Engineering and Transportation Dept.

Special-purpose boards for

- hospitals (2)
- police
- health
- library
- exhibition
- hospital planning
- education (2)
- development appeals
- boxing and wrestling

board of commissioners as a whole. The commissioners, who are hired and dismissed by council, function as a small executive group interposed between the legislating council and the administrative departments.

The council/commission structure has advantages and disadvantages in its capacity to cope with input and output stress. Principal among the advantages is the fact that a board of commissioners is in a position to co-ordinate programs and policies because of its small size and its collective responsibility to council. As non-elected personnel, the commissioners are not likely to be competing with each other. The board is not so large as to be unwieldly and cumbersome, yet having more than one senior administrative officer helps to ensure that diverse areas of expertise are brought to bear on particular matters, thereby aiding an appreciation of the ramifications of decisions and proposals. An advantage can also be found in the mayor's being an *ex officio* member of the board of commissioners, for this provides a degree of fusion between the council as a political legislative body and the administration. Thus a means is available for council to direct and control the administration more effectively. While the number of channels of communication between council and the administration is smaller in this model than in the council/committee model discussed above, there is at least more than one such channel.

Among the disadvantages of the council/commissioner arrangement is the fact that power and influence tends to be concentrated in the small group of commissioners. Even though they lack the formal power to actually make city policy, the influence they can exert on policy formulation and implementation is indeed considerable. Also, the board of commissioners is an additional level in the decision-making structure, and there is therefore some risk that council may be somewhat isolated from the departments, especially if the two bodies communicate only through the commissioners. Further difficulties might arise if the mayor as an *ex officio* commissioner takes on an active role as one commissioner rather than limiting himself to being primarily the board's spokesman in council.

The number of departments in the four cities that use this model is relatively large, ranging from Saskatoon's seventeen to Calgary's twenty-five. It is chiefly the fact that the model has inherent in it a co-ordinating mechanism that has made it a fairly common and appropriate structure in cities that provide a wide range of services through a rather large number of civic departments.

THE COUNCIL/BOARD OF CONTROL STRUCTURE

This model of decision-making is found only in Ontario but is rather closely paralleled by what is called the council/executive committee structure in the province of Quebec.[9] It is this organizational structure, particularly the executive committee variant, that comes closest of any of the models to resembling the cabinet form of government. Ontario's controllers (six of the seven cities have four controllers, while the Borough of York has only two) are not chosen either by the mayor or by council, but are directly elected. The executive committee variant has its members (usually four or six plus the mayor) chosen by council from among the elected aldermen. When a city council is dominated by a particularly strong mayor such as Jean Drapeau in Montreal, the mayor, in effect, chooses the other members of the executive committee much like a prime minister or premier chooses a cabinet. The means of selection is the main factor that distinguishes boards of control from executive committees. Ottawa's council/board of control structure is used to illustrate how the model works. (See Figure 3:3.)

The model's essential feature is the fusion of administration with council as a legislative body, and it is this fusion that differentiates it from the council/commissioner model. There need not be any standing committees of council but there is always one or a few. Although they run for election separately from aldermen, members of the board of control (which includes the mayor) are full members of council. But members of the board of control or executive committee generally have responsibilities that no other members of council have—to formulate recommendations to council and to co-ordinate and supervise all departments and their operations. Among other things, controllers are responsible for preparing budget estimates for council's consideration, preparing specifications for tenders, and nominating appointed personnel. All matters to be referred to council are referred to the board of control first. Recommendations from the board to council can be rejected only by a two-thirds vote of council as a whole (including votes cast by the mayor and controllers). Therefore such recommendations are not often rejected.

Figure 3:3 Ottawa's Council/Board of control Structure (1975)

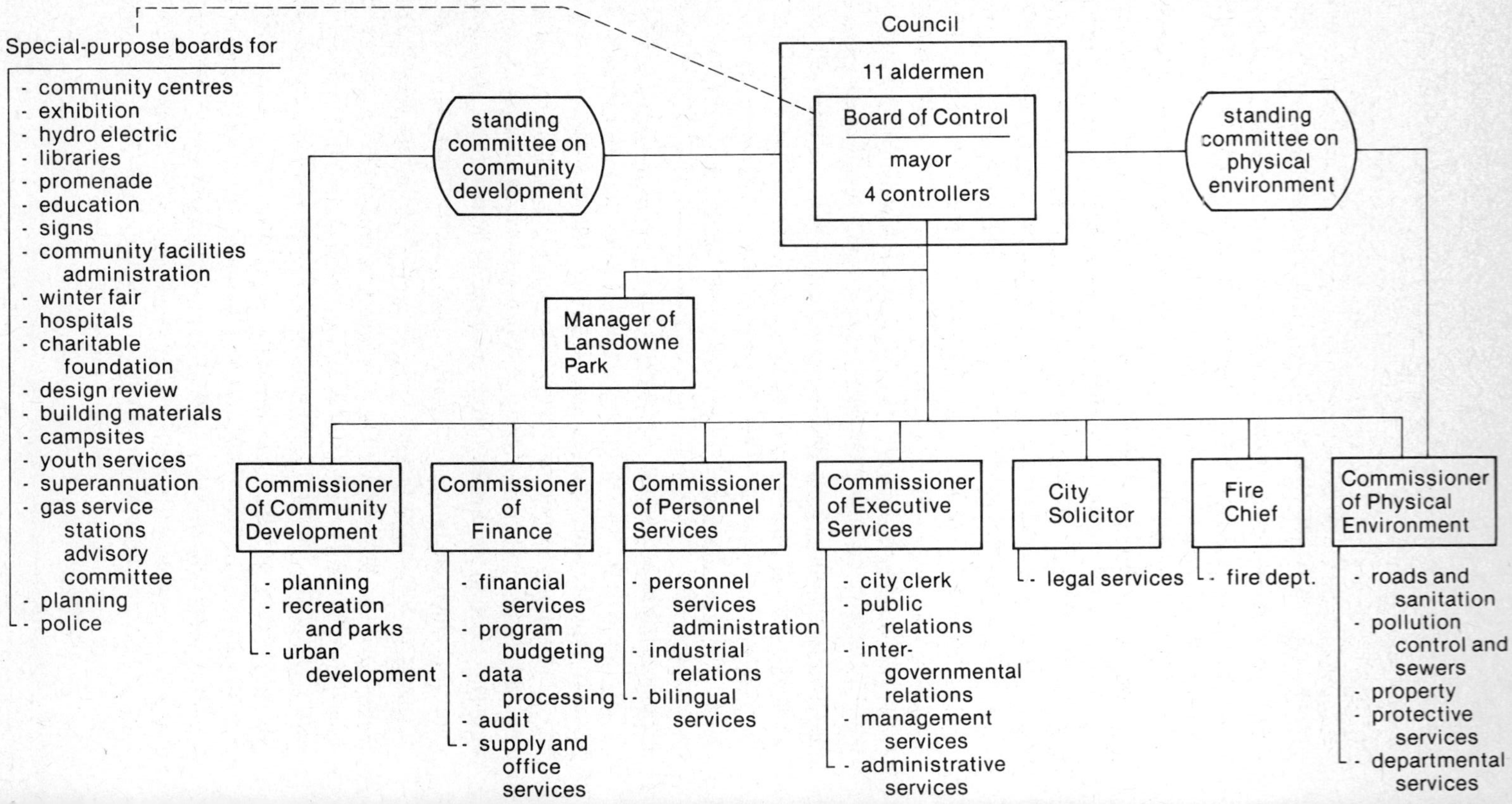

It has also become customary in some cities, at least informally, to allocate among the controllers specific responsibility for several departments. Thus controllers can specialize in particular areas of policy and administration, although the board of control normally reports and recommends collectively to council.

In Ottawa, two of the department heads meet regularly with the two standing committees which are composed of the mayor *ex officio* and five or six aldermen. Controllers are not members of these committees. Department heads attend the weekly board of control meetings on request, as well as the meetings of full council as requested.

In terms of this model's capacity to cope with input and output stresses, the most readily apparent advantage is the degree of co-ordination made possible. The relatively small size of the board of control or executive committee, the fact that it generally meets more frequently than council, and the possibilities available for the board or committee members to acquire and apply detailed information and experience in particular areas of policy and administration, make the potential for co-ordinating council's outputs superior to that of other decision-making structures. However, this particular advantage has several disadvantages associated with it, as noted below. A second advantage of this model is the fact that since members of the board of control or executive committee are, in effect, the most senior civic administrators and are at the same time a part of council, the latter is not so forced to deal with administrators at arm's length as in the council/manager model particularly. The senior civic administrators can therefore be held directly accountable to council as a whole, particularly in those cases where members of the board of control or executive committee have what amounts to a portfolio—particular responsibility for one or more areas of policy and administration. In such cases several department heads report to individual members of the board, and because controllers are members of council too, the channels of communication are increased compared to the council/manager model. This facilitates input from the civic bureaucracy to council.

There are, however, disadvantages, namely that the possibilities of co-ordination are to some extent counter-balanced by the fact that the board of control or executive committee is elevated relative to the rest of council. While members of the select group may not monopolize the information flowing upward from the civic bureaucracy, the rest of council is not likely to be as well informed as the controllers or executive members can be. It may be at least partly this possibility that accounts for the creation of standing committees of council which can enable the rest of council to acquaint themselves with the bases for administrative decisions and policy recommendations. But the select group still has the advantage.

Further, the possibilities for effective co-ordination are contingent on the board of control or executive committee being able to function as a team. In this regard, the executive committee variation is preferable to the board of control because while the former is chosen from among those people already elected as ordinary aldermen, board members have a special mandate that no alderman has. Controllers run for office as controllers and are elected on an at-large basis. This gives them a mandate that can be considered superior to that of aldermen and matched only by that of the mayor. Frequently, controllers have once been ordinary aldermen, and also have aspirations to be mayor. Thus, in those cities with the council/board of control structure, there is a sort of step-ladder to the mayor's chair—ambitious aldermen run for election to board of control, and ambitious controllers later tend to run for election as mayor. As a consequence, the board may be subject to an internal competition that is neither conducive to the kind of solidarity that an executive committee can attain, or to effective co-ordination. The difference in mandate between aldermen and controllers can also lead to strained relations between the board and the rest of council. While aldermen are unlikely to view the controllers' mandate as superior, members of boards of control do have an electoral status and prestige that exceeds that of aldermen. That factor and the difference in detailed information available to the two groups tends to diminish the role and status of aldermen.

Finally, regarding the translation of inputs into outputs, the council/board of control model presents the same kind of extra hurdle that the council/commission structure has. Since all matters to be referred to council are first referred to board of control, inputs from the general public via aldermen have to go through an extra step before possibly becoming outputs from council in the form of policy. This can increase the time lag between initiation and implementation. The two-thirds vote requirement also increases the possibility of a discordance between inputs and outputs. But the extra step may go some way to ensure that the potential consequences of proposed decisions are considered.

THE COUNCIL/MANAGER STRUCTURE[10]

This decision-making model has become rather popular in Canada's smaller cities, but a number of the larger cities have adopted it too.[11] The City of Vancouver is an example. (Figure 3:4.)

The council/city manager structure originated in the United States (Staunton, Virginia) in 1908, and was intended to transplant to local government a type of decision-making most associated with business corporations. Council was to resemble a corporate board of directors, being concerned only with matters of policy and leaving administration in the hands of the employees headed by the city manager. The manager was to resemble a corporation's general manager, overseeing and directing day-to-day operations. The intention was, quite simply, to divorce policy from administration. Thus, the basic features involved an appointed city manager and an elected council, with or without committees. Council's only administrative function was to hire and fire the city manager, who would be at the apex of the administrative structure and would appoint (and dismiss) department heads and prepare the budget.[12]

The Canadian experience with the council/manager model began in 1913 in Westmount, Quebec. The model was not quick to garner widespread adoption in Canada because the circumstances which led to its use in the United States (political patronage, corruption, and favouritism) were less prevalent here. Nonetheless, it did become popular in the 1940s and 1950s, especially in Quebec. While in its general features the Canadian version closely resembles its American counterpart, certain adaptations have been made in this country; on the whole they tend to put the position of city manager in Canada in a less powerful position relative to council. Among the modifications is less isolation of council from the civic bureaucracy, in that heads of departments frequently deal directly with committees of council rather than only indirectly through the city manager. Also, the power of the city manager to appoint and dismiss department heads is somewhat weaker in Canada; usually, he or she only recommends that council take such action, rather than making the decision unilaterally. It also tends to be the case that the role of city manager

Figure 3:4   Vancouver's Council/Manager Structure (1975)

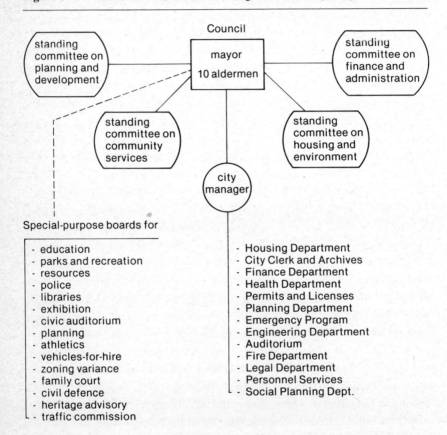

Council

standing committee on planning and development

mayor
10 aldermen

standing committee on finance and administration

standing committee on community services

standing committee on housing and environment

city manager

Special-purpose boards for

- education
- parks and recreation
- resources
- police
- libraries
- exhibition
- civic auditorium
- planning
- athletics
- vehicles-for-hire
- zoning variance
- family court
- civil defence
- heritage advisory
- traffic commission

- Housing Department
- City Clerk and Archives
- Finance Department
- Health Department
- Permits and Licenses
- Planning Department
- Emergency Program
- Engineering Department
- Auditorium
- Fire Department
- Legal Department
- Personnel Services
- Social Planning Dept.

is less limited to administration than it is in the United States. By virtue of his or her unique position at the apex of the civic administration, a city manager can have an influential role to play as a policy formulator for council. In general, the attempt to divorce the making of policy from administration in Canadian cities with a council–manager structure has been pursued less vigorously than in the United States.

Considered to be chief among the advantages of this model of decision making is the degree of co-ordination (especially of outputs) afforded by there being just one person at the head of the administration. As the diagram suggests, all lines of communication involving council and city bureaucrats are supposed to flow through the office of city manager. But Vancouver, like most Canadian cities that have a city manager, does have some direct communication between departments and committees of council, so there is not complete reliance on just one channel. Another advantage of this model is that it can diminish the administrative burden on councillors. By being released from responsibility for day-to-day administration, councillors can concentrate on broader issues of policy and in particular on contact with individuals and organized interests that are not formal parts of the decision-making structure. Also, since the city manager as chief administrative officer is appointed by council "at pleasure" (meaning that there is no set term of office and that the turn-over of city managers is quite low) and is not elected, he or she has a permanency of office that may facilitate the making of longer-range policy. This is in contrast with newly elected councillors, who have to spend a period of time familiarizing themselves with their new role and must constantly keep an eye on the date of the next city election. The city manager is free of such concern.

The fact that the city manager may have such a monopoly of access to expertise and information can lead to situations where this one appointed (and therefore not directly accountable to the electorate) individual can, in effect, predetermine action to be taken by council. Because of the volume of information available, he or she sometimes must be selective in deciding what information to pass along to council. Hence there is a danger of council being led by, rather than directing, the city manager. It requires either a vigilant council or some structural modifications (such as having standing committees of council meet frequently and regularly with heads of departments) to ensure that lines of communication are not too restricted and to minimize the danger of an excessive accumulation of influence in the hands of the city manager. Finally, it was noted earlier that major cities have quite large bureaucracies organized into as many as twenty-five departments. It is unrealistic to expect a single individual as city manager to be able to co-ordinate, administer, function as a liaison with special-purpose bodies, advise council on all matters, and hire and fire personnel, in such a context. Even the best trained and most able city manager can be strained in performing all these tasks, and that may be one reason why only one of the thirteen largest cities in Canada utilizes this decision-making model without at the same time having an executive committee of council.

The concern of this chapter has been the formal structures of decision making within cities. Certainly the five components in each model and the relationships among those components do not in themselves constitute an adequate account of the processes whereby decisions are made in cities. One must also take into account the inter-governmental context described in the previous chapter, and the political context, on which the last three chapters are focused. But before that consideration of the politics of decision-making in cities, there is one more aspect of government that needs examination—developments in municipal reorganization in Canada.

NOTES

1. Statistics Canada, bulletins 72-004, 72-007 and 72-009 for July–September, 1975.

2. Quoted from the *Report* of the Ontario government's Niagara Region Local Government Review —The Mayo Report (Toronto: Department of Municipal Affairs, 1966), p. 67.

3. Royal Commission on Metropolitan Toronto, *The Organization of Local Government in Metropolitan Toronto: Background Report* (Toronto, April, 1975), appendices VIII–X,

4. City of Calgary, *Municipal Manual* (Calgary, 1974), pp. 10–19.

5. See, for example, James H. Gray, *Red Lights on the Prairies* (Scarborough: New American Library of Canada, 1973). In his chapter "To

hell with Pearl Harbour—remember Pearl Miller!", Gray cites the difficulties encountered by Calgary's police chiefs from city council during the early part of the twentieth century over enforcement of the laws dealing with prostitution and alcohol.

6. Dominic DelGuidice and Stephen M. Zacks, *The 101 Governments of Metro Toronto* (Toronto: Bureau of Municipal Research, October, 1968). This has been reprinted in part in Lionel D. Feldman and Michael D. Goldrick, eds., *Politics and Government of Urban Canada: Selected Readings*, 2nd ed., pp. 237–47.

7. For more detail on these models refer to Thomas J. Plunkett, *Urban Canada and Its Government: A Study of Municipal Organization*

(Toronto: Macmillan, 1968),
chapters 3–5; K. Grant Crawford,
Canadian Municipal Government
(Toronto: University of Toronto
Press, 1954), chapters v and viii;
and Donald C. Rowat, *The Canadian
Municipal System: Essays on the
Improvement of Local Government*
(Toronto: McClelland and Stewart,
1969), Part One. Useful descriptions
of how the models operate in some
of Canada's larger cities are found
in the series of *Profile* publications
from the Ministry of State for Urban
Affairs. A list of the *Profiles* is
included at the end of this book. See
also the Royal Commission on
Metropolitan Toronto, *The Organization of Local Government in
Metropolitan Toronto: Background
Report* (Toronto, April, 1975).

8. They are Edmonton, Calgary,
Saskatoon, and Winnipeg. As noted
earlier, Winnipeg has the added
feature of an executive committee
of council.

9. The major cities with boards of
control are Hamilton, Ottawa,
London, and the boroughs of North
York, Scarborough, York, and
Etobicoke. The executive-committee
variation is found in Montreal,
Toronto, Laval, and Quebec City
(the latter two have the added
feature of a city manager). Some of
Ontario's metropolitan and regional
governments and Quebec's regional
and urban communities also utilize
the council/executive-committee
structure, often with a chief administrative officer (manager).

10. A somewhat one-sided but useful
account of this decision-making
structure is Orin F. Nolting, *Progress
and Impact of the Council-Manager
Plan* (Chicago: Public Administration Service, 1969).

11. Of Canada's twenty-four urban
municipalities with 1971 populations
of 100,000 or more, seven presently
employ a form of the council/
manager structure. They are Regina,
Vancouver, Windsor, Mississauga,
Halifax, St. Catharines, and Thunder
Bay. As noted earlier, other cities
and second-tier governments combine a city manager (or the equivalent) with executive committees of
council. The terms city manager,
city administrator, city co-ordinator,
and chief administrative officer all
mean the same thing.

12. Nolting, *Progress and Impact of the
Council-Manager Plan*, p. 32.

Municipal Reorganization 4

As indicated earlier, the evolution of municipal government in most provinces was characterized by a sometimes quite frantic and short period of experimentation, generally followed by a long period of maintenance of the municipal structures once the basic framework was established. Also, this evolution cannot be said to have attracted much interest outside Canada because innovation was not a feature of the Canadian example. Instead, the provinces borrowed upon the British and American experiences in local government, making modest adaptations to suit local conditions of the time. But those local conditions have been radically modified, and earlier municipal structures have been rendered archaic.

The modern period of municipal government in Canada can be said to have begun just over two decades ago as far as the larger cities are concerned. This period was heralded by the introduction of metropolitan government in the Toronto area in 1954, and the years since then have witnessed considerable activity directed toward overhauling the organization of municipal government in many provinces, particularly affecting the major cities. Further, the restructuring of Toronto did occasion some international interest, as in the United States, where Toronto became a model emulated in several cities such as Miami and Nashville. Very considerable interest and discussion has also followed the reorganization of Winnipeg, a development that can be viewed at least as innovative in 1972 as Metro Toronto was almost two decades earlier.

It is no accident that the winds of change in municipal organization have blown with the greatest velocity over the larger cities. While it is true that the rural areas and smaller cities have not been left untouched by change, they have been less significantly affected, for they have been less subjected to the kinds of pressure which are generally considered to have led to reorganization of the major cities.

Fyfe attributes the recent activity in municipal reorganization in a general way to three factors: population growth, urbanization, and technological changes and improvements.[1] Simple increase in numbers, from a Canadian population of about 5.4 million in 1901 to more than twenty-

two million in 1975, has increased the magnitude of problems encountered by all levels of government, not least municipal government. And
it has forced all governments to undertake new functions which a small
and scattered population did not require. But the population growth has
been unevenly distributed, most of it concentrated in the larger cities,
accompanied by a stable or declining population in many rural areas. Not
only does this aspect of urbanization in itself cause urban problems
(housing, for example), it also puts strains on existing municipal decision-making structures and processes in terms of their ability to cope
with the expanding number and range of inputs and outputs. It has also
complicated the relationships of city governments with other governments, both horizontally (municipality with municipality) and vertically
(for example, province with municipality). Technological change such as
improvements in communication and transportation strongly influences
the structural functioning of local governments, particularly in the more
highly urbanized areas. Technological innovation increases opportunities
for improved communication among governments of all levels and between governments and their citizenry. At the same time, though, it also
gives rise to or accentuates problems of the relationships between growing numbers of better educated, more informed, and increasingly concerned citizens on the one hand and comparatively static (often archaic)
institutions and processes of government on the other. There is always a
lag between the detection of changes in the values, beliefs, and objective
circumstances of a citizenry and the time that formal institutions and
processes of government are modified to reflect those changes. The long
persistence of the basic frameworks of municipal government in Canada
suggests that it is particularly prone to the problem of time lag.

In addition, technological change and innovation intensifies, and may
create, problems of inter-governmental relations, for some functions that
once were more or less "local" tend to become of regional or even of
provincial concern. Urban transit, urban planning and development, and
urban pollution control are all good examples. One could add to this list
such other services as social welfare, public schooling, crime prevention
and control and so on. In a major urban area that is politically fragmented, in the sense of having within the one urban complex multiple
units of municipal government that border each other, each municipality
may be a sort of political island unto itself. But this is an artificiality.

Urban dwellers and urban problems are not sealed within the confines of any single governmental unit, for urban municipalities are not walled cities. People often live in one urban municipality but work in another; polluted rivers and air carry into other municipal units effluent introduced elsewhere; crime and criminals do not respect urban municipal boundaries; and what one urban municipality does (or does not do) with regard to planning and development will have spill-over effects on its neighbours within the larger complex.

As a consequence, the political boundaries of municipalities in the major urban areas of Canada tended over time to become at best blurred, and at worst irrelevant. These boundaries ceased to reflect patterns of daily life and often began to present such problems for the provision of municipal services that either semi-autonomous inter-municipal boards and commissions had to be created, or the provincial governments had to assume responsibility for some functions previously considered to be in the municipal domain. In either case, traditional local government becomes of decreasing significance. Property assessment is a case in point. With their historic reliance on property tax revenue, the municipalities had long been responsible for assessing the value of real property for taxation purposes. But in the politically fragmented major urban areas, this began to lead to inequities in assessment and levels of taxation. Thus a house on one side of a street, being in municipality A, might be assessed at approximately market value and levied a tax rate to support an extensive range of municipal services, whereas a comparable house across the street, in municipality B, might be assessed on a different criterion and levied a tax rate to support fewer services or lower standards of them. Political fragmentation also leads to competition among municipalities within the same metropolitan area for commercial and industrial development, with the adjacent municipalities striving to out-do each other in granting reductions or exemptions from property taxes. In the end, no municipality is likely to experience much actual advantage over its neighbours.

There is also the point that the presence of large numbers of relatively small municipalities tends to increase the total costs involved in providing some municipal services, for no matter how large or small the area or population of a municipality, the mandatory services require some minimum of overhead expense for plant, equipment, and personnel.

The conclusion that one would naturally draw from these points is that there is a demonstrable need for a rationalization of municipal government in urban areas. This is often interpreted as a need to amalgamate, to centralize, or to enlarge the geographical scope of urban municipal jurisdiction so that services can be provided and functions performed in such a way as to make government more efficient and economical, to reduce inequities in the kinds and levels of services provided throughout the area, and to reflect that pattern of economic interdependency of people in the urban complex. As will become evident below, this interpretation has been and still is a very influential one, and has underpinned many of the instances of urban municipal reorganization across Canada as well as of proposals for further reorganization. But it will be pointed out in the Overview to this chapter that such an interpretation is no longer quite so dominant as it was.

The following brief description of municipal reorganization in Canada is focused on the phenomenon of metropolitan and regional municipal government, a phenomenon to which little reference has been made in the earlier chapters. Of particular concern are changes to the area and boundaries of urban municipalities, to their internal organization, and to their powers and functions. Almost all provinces have manifested some reorganization of highly urbanized municipalities, and, with the two exceptions of Prince Edward Island and Saskatchewan, the remaining provinces have at least proposed some reorganization which may yet be implemented. In the review, therefore, both actual instances of reorganization as well as proposals that may yet become fact are examined.

Newfoundland

The province of Newfoundland has not yet embarked upon any general scheme of municipal reorganization but may be expected to do so within the next few years. Professor Hugh Whalen headed a royal commission established in August of 1972 by the provincial government to study all matters pertaining to municipal government throughout the province. The report was presented to cabinet in 1974, was released to the public in September of 1975 without comment from the provincial government, and is still under consideration.[2] The Whalen Commission excluded St. John's from many of its recommendations, but it did propose in general terms the introduction of ". . . a system of regional government in the St. John's Urban Region . . .".[3] Determination of the area, boundaries, and so on of the proposed regional government for the St. John's urban area was not specified, since the area was the subject of a separate study.

That commission of inquiry, headed by Mr. A. Henley, is expected to complete its work in 1976. For much of the rest of the province, the Whalen Report recommended the gradual creation of an unspecified number (perhaps as many as twenty) of regional governments which would be created over a period of some thirty years. They would be two-tiered, with councillors at both levels being directly elected. The regions would be organized in a way somewhat similar to British Columbia's regional districts (see below) but Newfoundland's upper-tier units would have considerably more power and functions than is the case in British Columbia. The general intent of the Whalen Commission's recommendations was to greatly increase municipal self-reliance, especially with regard to finances, relative to the provincial government.

The other development of note in Newfoundland is the St. John's Urban Region Study which was completed in 1973 and which suggested three alternative schemes respecting the metropolitan St. John's area.[4] Scheme A would create an enlarged City of St. John's and separate the urban from the rural area. The latter area would be organized as a two-tiered county. Scheme B would create a two-tiered governmental structure for the metropolitan region, while Scheme C would create a single large municipality but with a number of "communities" which would function almost entirely as a basis for representation on the city council. All three schemes would cover exactly the same area, an area many times that of the present City of St. John's. The Henley Commission referred to above is considering these proposals. There is already some kind of precedent in Newfoundland for metropolitan municipal government, in the form of the St. John's Metropolitan Area Board which was created in 1963 and which covers about half the territory proposed in the three schemes for reorganization. But the Board is not a true municipality because it is an appointed body and has minimal service functions, basically planning responsibilities and administering land use and development control in areas adjacent to the City of St. John's. It also has no jurisdiction within the city.

Nova Scotia

The major urban areas in Nova Scotia had not been municipally reorganized by 1976, although the boundaries of the cities of Dartmouth and Halifax were greatly expanded through annexation in 1961 and 1969 respectively. Further growth of this kind is proposed from time to time, especially for Dartmouth. In the case of the City of Halifax, the annexation expanded it to about three and a half times its area prior to 1969. Also in 1969 a proposal was made to reorganize municipal government on Cape Breton Island substantially, but this is not pursued here because it will not be implemented.

Other than the instances of annexation, the structures of urban municipal government remain as they have been for years. However, in 1975, the Nova Scotia government began to grapple with the monumental (some seven thousand pages long) Graham Report.[5] The Royal Commission on Education, Public Services and Provincial-Municipal Relations which was established in 1971 with very broad terms of reference, proposed municipal reorganization that would affect the entire province.

Three "metropolitan counties" would be created (and eight nonmetropolitan ones), one for the Halifax–Dartmouth area combining three present municipalities, one for the industrial Cape Breton area to replace eight existing municipalities, and one for the Pictou area which would replace six municipalities. The Pictou example would scarcely be "metropolitan" as its total population would be only about 45,000 in 1971. The Halifax–Dartmouth metropolitan county would have a 1971 population of about 250,000 compared to 122,000 in the City of Halifax, and the Cape Breton metropolitan county would have a 1971 population of about 130,000.

The area and boundaries of the proposed metropolitan counties were determined primarily on considerations of the services and functions which would be performed by municipalities. Thus the Graham Commission's starting point for the recommended reorganization was a reallocation of services and functions to be administered by the province and by the new municipalities. Only after that were matters of geographic area, population size, and organization ". . . that would be best suited to those functions" examined.[6] More minor considerations that guided its recommendations with regard to area and boundaries were minimum population size of sixty thousand, and suitability for planning. The end result would be that the three metropolitan counties would each have an area of between 900 and 1000 square miles compared to the City of Halifax's area in 1975 of about 24.5 square miles.

The three metropolitan counties (and the other eight) would be unitary rather than two-tiered. A two-tiered structure was considered, but was rejected on the grounds that the province's population was too small to afford it, that it would result in a multiplicity of municipal authorities with overlapping responsibilities, and that it would not be conducive to effective and economical provision of municipal services to both urban and rural residents.[7] The commission envisaged each county having twelve wards, each of which would have one representative on council, and up to four "community associations" in each ward. These associations would be optional, being created only upon petition of people in an area, but would be designed to acquaint the county council with the views, concerns, and needs of citizens in the area, especially on matters of planning. The associations would have no functions other than this communication/advisory one.

With regard to the proposed reallocation of powers and functions between the provincial government and the municipalities, the commission's recommendations would result in a considerable reduction in the role of municipalities. The reorganized municipalities would be restricted to a list of "local" services while the province would assume responsibility for all "general" services plus such housekeeping matters as property assessment, tax billing, and tax collection. What would be lost by the municipalities are their present responsibilities for education, libraries, health and welfare services, housing, administration of justice, and some aspects of transportation services. The municipalities would acquire no responsibilities that they did not have in 1975. It was intended by the commission that the kinds and levels of services provided within the metropolitan counties would not be uniform. The range and standards of services provided in designated "city service" areas would be higher than in the designated "rural service" areas, and levels of property taxes would vary accordingly.

By early 1975 it became apparent that the Graham Commission's recommendations would not be implemented as a package. Although the provincial government introduced legislation beginning in June of 1975 that would involve the provincial government resuming responsibility for property assessment, would remove municipal power to tax non-residential property, and would have the province assume greater responsibility for costs of education, the Minister of Municipal Affairs made it clear that the Graham Report would not be implemented in total.[8] It seems unlikely that municipal government in the urban Halifax area will be fundamentally reorganized in the next few years.

New Brunswick

The most controversial aspect of municipal reorganization in New Brunswick was the Program for Equal Opportunity which commenced in 1967. The program implemented almost all of the recommendations of the Royal Commission on Finance and Municipal Taxation (the Byrne Report).[9] That reorganization applied to the entire province and the most dramatic aspects of it were the abolition of counties, the creation of a large number of villages, and a massive resumption by the provincial government of powers and functions that had been exercised by municipalities. While the City of Saint John was affected by the Program for Equal Opportunity, it was also affected by another royal commission report, conducted by Mr. Carl Goldenberg, which focused specifically on the city.[10] Goldenberg's terms of reference were limited to the question of amalgamation and boundaries, not powers and functions. Both the Byrne and Goldenberg reports were completed in 1963, the latter first. On the whole, the Byrne Report supported the Goldenberg recommendations, and the reorganization of Saint John (simple enlargement of the city) took effect at the same time as municipal reorganization was instituted in the rest of the province.

As Mr. Goldenberg recommended, municipalities in the Saint John area were amalgamated into one enlarged municipality which included the former city of Saint John, the city of Lancaster, and the parish of Symonds. The area involved was about 104 square miles and the population was some 89,000. The former city of Saint John had a 1966 population of about 52,000. The considerations that led Mr. Goldenberg to his recommendations included his view that the area constituted a single urban community, that all the people in the area shared the same heritage and had been closely interrelated for 180 years, that the area would be appropriate for provision of municipal services, and that allowance had to be made for future growth. Therefore the new boundaries were not tightly drawn around a highly urbanized core. Since what was recommended and implemented was simply amalgamation of existing municipalities, the municipal structure remained a unitary one. The only internal divisions were wards for the purposes of elections.

It is to the Byrne Report that one must turn to consider changes in the powers and functions of Saint John. Those changes applied to the entire province. The commission was greatly concerned with what it determined were gross variations in the level of municipal services among the province's municipalities. After examining per-capita expenditure by function and by type of municipality, it concluded that rural residents were especially disadvantaged. The commission seriously considered only two courses of action, possible enlargement of the existing counties being summarily dismissed as a third course of action. The first possibility was to leave the division of responsibilities as it had been but add a system of equalizing conditional grants from the province to the municipalities. The second possibility was to reallocate responsibility for services by having the provincial government assume responsibility for the expensive "general" services (education, health and hospitals, social welfare, and administration of justice) plus support services (property assessment and tax collection), leaving the municipalities responsible for "local" services such as police and fire protection, water supply, recreation, streets, sewerage, and garbage collection. It was the second course of action that was recommended in 1963 and implemented in 1967. What the commission clearly wanted was as sharply defined a division of responsibilities as possible which would simplify provincial–municipal relations and increase municipal autonomy over those services for which they were to be responsible. The first possible course of action, involving a more complex pattern of provincial–municipal relations and a more complex set of conditional grants, would not meet these ends. The result of the reorganization of 1967 was a considerable diminution of the responsibilities of the enlarged city of Saint John as well as of all other municipalities in the province. As one commentator noted, "More surprising than the revolutionary proposals of the Byrne Commission was the fact that the New Brunswick Government implemented most of the recommendations...."[11]

Quebec

At the end of 1971, only eighty-four of the 1591 municipalities in the province of Quebec had populations of over ten thousand, and only three of those had populations in excess of 100,000. Hence the municipal structure was characterized by a very large number of municipalities that were generally very small in population. The need for reorganization of the province's municipal system was becoming particularly pressing from the point of view of the provincial government.

MONTREAL

The beginning of metropolitan government in Montreal can be traced back to the creation in 1921 of the Montreal Metropolitan Commission. However, the Commission was so limited in the functions it performed that it did not constitute metropolitan municipal government. It was essentially an agency to exercise financial control over the fifteen municipalities on the Island of Montreal in response to financial difficulties experienced by several of them. The Commission, which was composed of representatives of the municipalities concerned and one representative of the province's Department of Municipal Affairs, had power to supervise the finances of the area's municipalities, especially with regard to borrowing. Its functions were gradually expanded over time to include some aspects of traffic and (briefly) planning.

The next stage was the creation in 1960 of the Montreal Metropolitan Corporation as a result of the Paquette Report.[12] The Paquette Commission was set up by the City of Montreal in 1952 with the authorization of the provincial government to study the administrative problems resulting from there being so many municipalities on the Island of Montreal. In 1955 there were thirty-six of them, fewer than half of which were members of the weak Montreal Metropolitan Commission. The Montreal Metropolitan Corporation which grew out of the Paquette report almost immediately became moribund because of dissatisfaction by the City of Montreal with its low representation on the Corporation's council compared to that of the other member municipalities which were largely suburban.

Next in the series of studies respecting the Island of Montreal was that of the Blier Commission,[13] which eventually led to the establishment by the provincial government of the Montreal Urban Community. With its terms of reference limiting the inquiry to the twenty-nine municipalities at that time on the Island of Montreal, this commission began in February of 1964 to examine problems of inter-municipal relations and was to consider the possibility of regrouping the municipalities and reorganizing the political structures on the Island. It cited evidence that residents on the Island constituted a single socio-economic whole (although it noted that such a conclusion applied less to people in the western portion of the Island), and that the then-existing municipal boundaries were "only accidental". The basic principles on which the Blier Commission made its recommendations were that the provision of services must be efficient, be assured to all citizens of the Island, and that the costs of those services be shared equitably. "Local" services were distinguished from "regional" ones, and this distinction formed the basis for dividing responsibilities between the metropolitan and lower-tier units of municipal government. In its report, the commission seemed to be leading up to a recommendation to amalgamate the twenty-nine municipalities into one huge new one, yet rejected such a proposal because of unspecified "practical difficulties". In the end, the Blier Commission recommended a regional two-tiered arrangement with an upper-tier General Council on which the twenty-nine municipalities would be represented. For the purposes of representation the member municipalities were to be grouped into four sectors. No amalgamations or boundary changes were proposed.

Legislation was passed in the Quebec National Assembly in December of 1969 to create the Montreal Urban Community to come into effect on January 1, 1970. As the Blier Commission recommended, the MUC was to be a two-tiered federation of the twenty-nine municipalities on the Island of Montreal. Rather than being grouped into four sectors, the twenty-nine were grouped into five sectors for the purposes of representation on the MUC council, with the City of Montreal being a sector by itself. The council is composed of all fifty-one members of Montreal City Council plus one delegate from each of the other municipalities, but each vote is weighted by population. The City of Montreal has a majority on council as well as more than half of the seats of the Executive Committee of the MUC council. No changes were made in the number or boundaries of the twenty-nine member municipalities but the MUC was required to propose at a future date a rearrangement and consolidation of the lower-tier units. The area involved was about 180 square miles, and had a population in 1970 of about two million.

With regard to functions, the Montreal Urban Community was to take over in phases from the municipalities responsibility for property assessment, development planning, traffic control and public transportation, area water and trunk sewers, air pollution control, garbage, public health, and co-ordination (and possibly integration) of fire and police protection. If it so decided the MUC council could also take over responsibility for parks and recreation, libraries, and subsidized housing. These were the kinds of "regional" services that the Blier Commission had in mind. The Montreal Urban Community has not enjoyed smooth sailing since it was created. There was a long and bitter battle preceding the integration of the police departments, and great concern persists among the small member municipalities about the MUC's finances, reflecting a city-suburban clash of interests.

Before turning attention to the two other main developments in reorganization of municipalities in the province, it should be noted that several instances of municipal amalgamation occurred prior to 1970. The most notable of these was the creation in 1965 of the City of Laval. It was formed by amalgamating the fourteen municipalities making up Ile Jesus beside Montreal Island as a consequence of the Sylvestre Report.[14] The area involved was ninety-eight square miles, and the population just before amalgamation was a total of 170,000.

REGIONAL GOVERNMENT

In 1970, the same year that the Montreal Urban Community came into being, regional government was instituted in the Quebec City and Hull areas. It became apparent that the two reorganizations were to be the forerunners of a more general system of regional government throughout the province. Thirty-two municipalities in the Hull area, covering 908 square miles, were federated to form the Outaouais Regional Community. The municipalities retained their separate identities but were grouped into five sectors for purposes of representation on the Executive Committee of the ORC's council. Representation on that council, as in Montreal and

Quebec, is indirect. The mayor or other council member of each of the thirty-two municipalities sits on the Outaouais Regional Community council, but votes are weighted according to population. The boundaries of the ORC, like those of the Quebec Urban Community, were determined by the provincial government after technical studies were completed. The Quebec Urban Community included what had been twenty-eight municipalities, consolidated to twenty-three in 1971, with a population of about 400,000. None of the municipalities on the Levis (south) side of the St. Lawrence River have been included. The municipalities of the QUC were grouped into five sectors for purposes of representation on the QUC's executive committee. Both the new Outaouais and Quebec structures are responsible for development planning, traffic control, public transit, assessment, and the promotion of industry and tourism. In addition, the two new structures can take over from their member municipalities responsibilities such as water supply, garbage disposal, public health, police and fire protection, low rental housing, libraries, and regional recreation and parks. However, both the QUC and the ORC have moved slowly in taking over these optional services. The QUC has assumed responsibility for garbage disposal and may be expected to take responsibility for water supply, public health, low rental housing, and police in the near future.

The provincial government was anxious to consolidate municipalities within the Outaouais Regional Community by encouraging voluntary amalgamation, with the objective of forming five large new lower-tier municipalities. The matter of voluntary amalgamation occasioned great and bitter conflict especially during 1972 and 1973, and a dozen or so of the municipalities announced that they were going to try to secede from the ORC. The provincial government set (and let slide by) several deadlines for the municipalities concerned to reach some agreement, but regroupment finally took place in January of 1975. Some reduction in the number of lower-tier units also occurred in the Quebec Urban Community, principally through the City of Quebec annexing neighbouring municipalities so that by 1973 the City's area was over four times as large as it was in 1969. In terms of the range of things that they *can* do, both the Outaouais Regional Community and the Quebec Urban Community are quite similar to the Montreal Urban Community.

REGROUPMENT

In December of 1971 the Quebec National Assembly passed Bill 276, which was an act to promote the regroupment of municipalities throughout the province. Passage of the act followed release of the government's White Paper on the reform of municipal structures, released in March that year.[15] The new program was intended to result in a dramatic reorganization of the province's municipal system by reducing the 1600 municipalities to nearly half that number within a decade, and combining them into 131 two-tier regional communities. The scheme was to be a staged one, and it was planned to encourage voluntary amalgamation with financial inducements. However, the regroupment act, which replaced the Voluntary Amalgamation of Municipalities Act of 1965, made it clear that if municipalities could not themselves reach voluntary agreement to amalgamate, the provincial government would order municipal amalgamation. Whether achieved voluntarily or by imposition, amalgamation of municipal units and federation of them into regional communities was considered necessary in order to buttress municipal autonomy relative to the provincial government and to enable municipalities to provide a better standard of services.

The provincial government made vigorous efforts in 1971 and 1972 to regroup municipalities, but their efforts produced such outcries of protest, especially from people in rural areas, that Premier Bourassa declared a moratorium on regroupment in November of 1972. He also replaced his Minister of Municipal Affairs three months later, when Dr. Victor Goldbloom succeeded Mr. Maurice Tessier. The new minister adopted a more conciliatory approach to the question. Regroupment has progressed slowly since then, and has occurred mainly in urban rather than rural areas. Between late 1974 and early 1976 some eighty municipal units had been reduced to about twenty. Few further instances of regroupment can be expected. Instead, the provincial government has begun to shift its attention more toward developing some seventy or eighty "regional centres", which would be much looser and less powerful arrangements than the regional governments. The regional centres are to focus on regional development and land-use planning. While this may entail some amalgamation of existing municipalities, amalgamation is not a central feature. The Metropolitan Council of the Upper Saguenay (in the Chicoutimi area), which came into existence in January of 1975, may be a prototype of the regional centres.

Ontario

Ontario has been in the forefront of urban municipal reorganization in Canada, a fact which is not surprising when one considers the heavily urban character of much of the province's population. The two principal developments to examine are Metro Toronto and regional government.

METRO TORONTO

The creation of a two-tiered federation of municipalities in the Toronto area beginning on January 1, 1954, is generally considered to be a milestone in Canadian municipal history, and marked the beginning of the modern era. Indeed, Metro Toronto was North America's first major metropolitan government. In 1953 the Ontario Municipal Board announced its decision concerning an application made to it by the City of Toronto to amalgamate the city with twelve other municipalities in the area.[16] The Cumming Report, as it has come to be known, turned down the application, and instead recommended the creation of a municipal federation of the thirteen municipalities concerned, a federation which would be a sort of urban equivalent of the non-urban counties. In so recommending, the OMB clearly was attempting to reach a pragmatic compromise between the position of the central city, which demanded complete amalgamation, and the position of the suburban municipalities, which demanded a retention of their autonomy and separate identities.

The alacrity with which the provincial government acted upon that report and the extent to which the recommendations in the report were accepted are remarkable. Only one month passed before legislation was introduced in the Ontario legislature to give effect to the recommendations. The Cumming Report's recommendations regarding area and external boundaries were accepted in full. The OMB appears to have given rather scant consideration to the possibility of including either a wider or a smaller area and population than that of the thirteen municipalities involved in the City of Toronto's application. The board satisfied itself that those municipalities and their residents constituted an interdependent whole, economically and socially. Other factors which confirmed the appropriateness of the outer boundaries in the board's view were the absence of open spaces and physical barriers separating the thirteen municipalities, and the large number of inter-municipal agreements of various sorts among those municipalities. In other words, there were already political connections upon which a more elaborate structure could be built. Hence both the OMB and the provincial government accepted the City of Toronto's position with regard to external boundaries, and consequently the new metropolitan structure was to include the thirteen municipalities covering some 240 square miles, with a population in 1953 of about 1,174,000.

Although the OMB and the Ontario government accepted the City of Toronto's position with respect to the outer boundaries, the city's view that all internal boundaries be discarded by amalgamation was rejected. It is clear that the objections to amalgamation raised by the other municipalities had their effect both on the board and on the provincial cabinet. The Municipal Board felt that existing municipalities should retain their separate identities because total amalgamation would involve prolonged administrative confusion, would result in a substantial increase in taxation, and that a single council for the whole area would be too remote to deal with local matters. What was therefore recommended was the two-tier federation with the thirteen existing municipalities constituting the lower tier, and a nine-member council (four from the City of Toronto, four from the other twelve municipalities, and a chairman to be appointed by the provincial government) as the second tier.

The system of representation on the Metro council was one of the most contentious issues which the Ontario Municipal Board faced. The thirteen municipalities differed vastly not only in their actual populations, but in their patterns of population growth and potential. As Smallwood has pointed out,[17] the metropolitan Toronto area in 1953 contained three concentric arches of municipalities. At the centre was the City of Toronto, with a population then of about 666,000. It was by far the most populous of the thirteen municipalities, but it had comparatively little scope for population growth. In fact, the city's population had declined about 2 per cent over the previous eight years. Next was an arch of nine suburban municipalities ranging from Swansea with a population in 1953 of only

about 8,300 to York with a population of 100,000. These nine municipalities had all been experiencing some population growth (ranging from
about 17 per cent to 81 per cent) over the previous eight years, but their
potential for further growth was somewhat limited. Beyond this arch
stretched three largely undeveloped municipalities covering 182 of the
240 square miles of metropolitan Toronto. While the populations in 1953
of these three ranged only from about seventy thousand to 110,000, they
had each experienced phenomenal population growth since 1945 (at least
225 per cent), and being of large area and comparatively undeveloped,
their potential for future population increase was very great.

What the Ontario Municipal Board had to do was arrive at equitable
representation of both the city and the suburbs on the metro council.
Recognizing that there was a serious cleavage of interests between the
two, the board recommended giving equal representation to the two
divisions, with the province appointing what would probably end up being
a referee with the deciding vote as chairman. The provincial government
decided on a somewhat larger metropolitan council. It was to have
twenty-five members of which twelve would be from the City of Toronto,
one from each of the twelve other municipalities, and Mr. Frederick G.
Gardiner as Chairman appointed by the province. Thus each of the twelve
suburban municipalities had equal representation (and unweighted votes)
despite the vast differences in their population sizes. Differences in their
population growth in future ensured that the distortion of the principle of
representation by population would become magnified as time passed.

The other particularly contentious issue faced by the Municipial Board
was the division of powers and functions between the two tiers. The
recommendations made and accepted later by the provincial government
were another clear compromise. Metro council was to be responsible for
only a few services such as capital borrowing, major roads, and property
assessment. The lower-tier units were to retain responsibility for a
similarly limited number of services, like police and fire protection,
licensing, and libraries. This left the bulk of municipal powers and
functions to be shared between the two levels on a joint basis. For
example, Metro council would be responsible for area planning while the
lower-tier municipalities were to be responsible for local planning. Also,
Metro would be responsible for wholesale water distribution and wholesale sewage disposal, while the lower-tier units were to actually supply

the water to consumers and collect sewage. Hence the division of powers and functions was not a simple, uncomplicated one. In 1957 the thirteen police forces were amalgamated, so police protection became a Metro responsibility as did pollution control the same year.

Like most experiments, over time it became evident that adjustments to the original Metro Toronto framework were desirable. In any case, the provincial government had made clear its intention that a review of the new framework would be made within five years of Metro's inception. The City of Toronto had never been happy with the new arrangement and still wanted amalgamation. This was supported by the major newspapers which viewed the federated framework as a denial of the economic and social unity which the Cumming report had discovered. A major point of dissension was representation on the Metropolitan council. The twelve smaller municipalities had never been even approximately equal in population to each other and the variations were indeed accentuated by the very high population growth rates in several of them. Yet each of them had equal representation on council (equal to each other of the twelve, that is), and the City of Toronto had twelve times the representation of any other municipality. The principles of representation by population or even representation by member unit were therefore involved in this point of contention, for neither principle was adhered to in the existing arrangement. Not surprisingly, there was not only city-suburban conflict, but conflict among the suburban ones as well. Even the forceful personality and personal influence of Mr. Gardiner as Chairman of Metro Toronto could not forge unity and overcome the cleavages between the city and the suburbs. In addition, levels of municipal services and expenditures varied considerably among the member units. Also at issue was the question of whether the chairman of the Metro council should continue to be appointed by the provincial government, or whether the office should be an elective one.

In 1957 the provincial government appointed a Commission of Inquiry headed by the same Mr. Cumming who had been the "father" of Metro Toronto. This commission reported its findings in March of 1958, and stated that the experiment was basically an overwhelming success, and that no fundamental changes should be made. With regard to representation and voting on council, the number of member municipalities, the selection of chairman, and almost everything else, the commission recommended "no change".[18] It would have come as something of a surprise perhaps had this commission recommended abandonment or substantial change to the framework of 1953, given Mr. Cumming's considerable involvement in both instances. All major points of contention remained unresolved, and in early 1963 the City of Toronto applied again to the Ontario Municipal Board for amalgamation of the thirteen municipalities.

In an unusual move, the provincial government diverted the City of Toronto's application away from the OMB by establishing a royal commission. Mr. Carl Goldenberg was appointed as the commissioner in 1963 to review Metropolitan Toronto with wide terms of reference, and presented his report in 1965.[19] As expected, he recommended reorganization but not complete amalgamation. The outer boundary of Metro Toronto would remain unchanged, but internal boundaries would be altered. Mr. Goldenberg recommended that the thirteen municipalities be consolidated into four new cities, although he, like Mr. Cumming in 1953, concluded that the whole area was an economic and social whole. In devising the recommended boundaries of the new cities, he adhered strictly to existing municipal boundaries as well as taking into account links of geography and common interests, common problems of renewal and redevelopment, levels of "maturity", administrative efficiency, geographical size, population, resources, and scale of operations. On no measures would the proposed four cities be equal, but the variations among them would be much less marked than was the case at that time. The members of Metro council would include the four mayors as well as councillors to be directly elected to sit not only on Metro council but on the city councils as well. A chairman would still be appointed by the provincial government. Mr. Goldenberg also recommended adding slightly to the powers and functions of Metro particularly with regard to planning and education finance, but the powers of the lower-tier units would remain largely intact.

It was some months later that Premier Robarts announced the government's reactions to the Goldenberg report.[20] Legislation was passed by the provincial legislature in 1966 to reorganize Metro Toronto in 1967. Mr. Goldenberg's recommendations were not accepted in their entirety, the main difference being in the degree of consolidation. Instead of consolidating the thirteen municipalities into four cities, they were consolidated into six municipalities—a slightly enlarged City of Toronto plus five "boroughs", a term new to Canada but borrowed from British practice. Because the number of lower-tier units would be different from that proposed in the Goldenberg report, the distribution of seats on Metro council was different, but based on the same principle of representation by population. The functions and powers of Metro council were increased only by the addition of responsibility for welfare, but the Metro School Board was given the power to equalize education facilities and costs.

The statement of Premier Robarts also indicated that a further review would be instituted sometime between 1972 and 1975. On September 11, 1974, this promise was fulfilled when the Premier of Ontario appointed a new Royal Commission on Metropolitan Toronto. By this time, though, Mr. Davis has succeeded Mr. Robarts as Premier, and it was Mr. Robarts himself that was named the royal commissioner for the study that he had promised nine years earlier. His report is due in 1977.

REGIONAL GOVERNMENT

The evident and generally recognized success of metropolitan government in the Toronto area, despite its problems, had a considerable demonstration effect and was obviously a factor of great importance in accounting for the development of regional government in other more or less densely settled areas of the province. Because of the number of regional governments that have been established in Ontario and because they were generally created one at a time (with considerable variations among them), it is not possible to describe here developments in each such region.[21] Separate studies have preceded each new regional government, and these governments were each created by separate statutes of the provincial legislature.

Creation of regional governments in the province was a more or less direct outgrowth of several earlier developments, besides Metro Toronto of course. In April of 1966, Premier Robarts released the first Design for Development statement which was a strategy for economic development of the province. The three categories of regions identified each had specific problems: the sustained-growth regions faced problems of urban expansion; the slow-growth regions needed buttressing; and regions with inconsistent or fluctuating growth needed assistance to even out the fluctuations. It became apparent that the regional development strategy required co-ordination with planning efforts of municipal governments. But the identified regions were municipally fragmented. Thus the concept of regional government was a mechanism for the implementation of the regional development scheme. As Mr. Robarts stated, regional government and regional development were closely associated. Second, two government reports presented in 1965 and 1967 both recommended the creation of comprehensive regional government for Ontario. The first of these was the Beckett Report (from the provincial legislature's select committee on the municipal act and related acts) which recommended two-tier regional governments based on the existing counties in order to ". . . restore responsibility to the elected representatives and increase the possibility of economical and efficient administration of municipal services. . . ."[22] The legislature's Committee on Taxation (the Smith Report) emphasized that the restructuring of municipal finance in Ontario that was needed to attain reasonable equity in local finance was contingent on a comprehensive reorganization of municipal government. That committee recommended the creation of twenty-nine regional governments to cover virtually all of the southern and some of the northern parts of the province.[23] Finally, the provincial government passed legislation that took effect in January of 1969 that consolidated into larger units the more than 1500 school boards.

The first regional government was the Ottawa–Carleton Regional Municipality which came into being in January of 1969. By the end of 1975 there were eleven such regional governments. Together, they account for only a small proportion of the province's total land area but for 35.1 per cent of Ontario's 1972 population. Including Metro Toronto (which, because of its area, cannot properly be counted as a "regional" government), close to two-thirds of the province's population at that time lived in a reorganized, two-tiered urban municipality.

Five criteria spelled out in the report of the Committee on Taxation in 1967 were supposed to be taken into consideration in determining the area and boundaries of regional governments. The criteria were: 1) a sense of community based on sociological characteristics, economics, history, and geography; 2) a *balance* of interests; 3) adequate financial base; 4) sufficient size to produce economies of scale; and 5) ability to

Table 4:1 Regional Governments in Ontario

name	date of operation	area (sq. miles)	population (1972)	units before reform	units after reform
Ottawa-Carleton	January, 1969	1,100	467,700	16	16 (11 by 1974)
Niagara (St. Catharines)	January, 1970	720	345,200	26	12
York	January, 1971	645	173,700	14	9
Muskoka	January, 1971	1,688	31,100	25	6
Waterloo (Kitchener)	January, 1973	519	258,900	15	7
Sudbury	January, 1973	1,088	167,800	15	7
Peel (Mississauga)	January, 1974	484	302,700	10	3
Halton (Burlington)	January, 1974	405	202,300	7	4
Durham (Oshawa)	January, 1974	875	220,200	21	8
Hamilton-Wentworth	January, 1974	432	398,200	11	6
Haldimand-Norfolk	April, 1974	1,117	83,900	28	6

facilitate inter-regional co-operation.[24] To these five were added three other criteria—community participation and acceptability, utility of boundaries for other institutions such as provincial departments and agencies, and the proviso that the criteria applied to one tier should also apply to the other tier.[25] However, analysis of boundary determinants used in the various studies leading to regional governments indicates that these eight criteria were not uniformly used, and that a number of other factors were sometimes more dominant.[26]

The distribution of powers and functions between the two tiers is not uniform among the regional governments, but generally the regional councils are responsible for area-wide planning while member municipalities are responsible for local planning. Water supply is usually regional with distribution being a local responsibility, and sewage services are similarly organized. Arterial or main roads are usually a regional responsibility, other roads being a responsibility of the lower-tier units. Welfare is generally a regional responsibility along with most municipal aspects of health, police protection, and emergency measures. There are, though, exceptions to almost all these generalizations.

It was originally intended that there would be regional governments across the province by 1975. However, the program never enjoyed smooth sailing or an enthusiastic response. Critics have been concerned that regional government was being imposed, was proceeding too quickly, and that it would duplicate services, place heavier burdens on the cities in order to upgrade services in rural areas, create more red tape, result in higher levels of taxation, and so on. The opposition has come from many quarters, including associations of municipalities, and especially the provincial Liberal Party. By 1973 it was apparent that the pace of regionalization would be slowed and that the provincial government was scaling down its plans for additional regional governments. In February of 1975 Premier Davis told a meeting of the Ontario Society of Regional Municipalities, "I say it here and I say it unequivocally—there will be no more new regional government in the province of Ontario, period, at this time."[27] As an alternative, the provincial government turned its attention to the possibilities of restructuring and strengthening the existing counties, and has commissioned a series of studies (twelve by late 1975) similar to the local government reviews that preceded the formation of each regional government. In addition, in 1974 and 1975 the Ontario government commissioned reviews of the two regional governments created earliest—Ottawa–Carleton (reviewed by Dr. Henry Mayo, who did the study that preceded creation of the Niagara Region), and Niagara (reviewed by former Toronto councillor Mr. William Archer). These reviews can be expected to lead to some modifications within those regions, probably including some consolidation of the lower-tier units. Finally, the provincial government can be expected to promote more amalgamation and consolidation of municipalities outside of regional governments as well, patterned on the creation in 1970 of the new City of Thunder Bay. This city was a consolidation of the former cities of Fort William and Port Arthur plus two neighbouring municipalities.

Manitoba

The one highly urbanized area in Manitoba has been the locale of an experiment which has excited widespread interest as well as some controversy. Developments in Winnipeg can be viewed as at least as innovative in 1972 as Metro Toronto was almost two decades earlier. Indeed, if one accepts the argument that Metro Toronto in 1954 was basically only an urban county, Unicity Winnipeg stands as Canada's only real innovation in urban municipal reorganization.

In 1960 Winnipeg became Canada's second city with metropolitan two-tier government, as a consequence of the report of the Greater Winnipeg Investigating Commission.[28] That report recommended that the existing municipalities in the urban area be reorganized somewhat along the lines of Metropolitan Toronto. The Commission had been established in 1955 by the provincial government to study the problems of the metropolitan Winnipeg area. What it found was a city that had experienced much suburban growth and expansion in the immediate post-World War II period, that was highly fragmented politically, that manifested considerable variations both in the levels of services provided and in the financial capacities of municipalities to provide services, that had its most highly developed unit (the City of Winnipeg, with a 1960 population of about 257,000) demanding total amalgamation while the second most populous unit (the City of St. Boniface with about 36,000 people) demanded retention of the status quo. Thus, although the metropolitan area's population was much smaller than that of the Toronto area in 1953, there were some strong parallels between the two cities. As the Cumming Report had done for Toronto, the Brodie Report recommended the formation of two-tier metropolitan government for the Winnipeg area. A total of nineteen municipalities were to be involved, ten of which would be wholly within the metro boundary, and parts of nine others would be included. But the commission went a step beyond the Cumming Report in that it recommended consolidation of the lower-tier units into eight cities. The metropolitan council was to be fairly small, composed of the mayors of the eight new cities plus a board of control of six directly elected members. The school boards were also to be reorganized, with each of the new cities having a board (two for St. Boniface), the chairmen of which would make up the metropolitan school board. The metropolitan council was to have responsibility for numerous services, the most important of which were regional planning, public transit, welfare, major roads, police and fire protection, and property assessment. Involved was an area of some 250 square miles with a 1960 population of 465,000. No clear explanation was given for the choice of the metropolitan boundary but the commission seems to have put emphasis on evidence that the people in that area constituted a single "community" defined in terms of inter-dependence of people within the area. Existing municipal boundaries were also taken into account.

While the provincial government accepted the commission's recommendation that two-tier metropolitan government be instituted for Greater Winnipeg, the legislation of 1960 did not involve consolidation of the existing municipalities. Nineteen municipalities in whole or in part were included, covering about the same area and population as had been recommended. The basis of representation was altered too, all ten metropolitan councillors being directly elected from ten electoral districts each of which included parts of at least two municipalities. There were no provisions for lower-tier councillors to sit on the metro council. As it turned out, the Metro council was not to have responsibility for welfare or for police and fire protection, and reform of the school system was omitted. For the purposes only of planning, Metro's boundaries were extended to include an "additional zone". The new Metro structure also absorbed three special-purpose area authorities that had been previously established to deal with transit, sewage disposal, and water supply. In sum, what was created in 1960 was, like Toronto in 1954, very clearly a compromise between the demands of the central city and the demands of the other municipalities in the area.

Greater Winnipeg's Metropolitan Corporation soon encountered severe problems that led to the provincial government creating, just two and a half years later, a study commission to examine the problems encountered in Winnipeg and to recommend solutions.[29] The commission was chaired by the same Mr. Cumming of Metro Toronto fame who was Deputy Minister of Municipal Affairs in Ontario in 1963. Some of the problems he saw related to the fact that nine of the member municipalities were only partly included in Metro Winnipeg. The "additional zone" appeared to be unnecessarily large. Of much importance was conflict between Metro Winnipeg's council and the member municipalities, in part due to the latter's loss of responsibilities, especially with regard to planning. The conflict was made worse by the system of representation, for there were still no members of the lower-tier municipal councils on the Metro council. There was thus little to encourage the local mayors and other councillors to try to make Metro work, for as Kaplan suggests, these people will not see themselves having a stake in the success of Metro.[30] Additionally, the first appointed chairman of the Metro council did not have the kind of commanding influence and drive like that of Metro Toronto's Mr. Gardiner. All in all, there seems to have been little political cohesion and a relatively low level of public support for Metro Winnipeg. On the other hand, the Metro council did succeed in improving the level of services provided and there were several active groups that supported Metro.

In view of the magnitude of the problems encountered so early by metropolitan government in Winnipeg, the Cumming Commission's rather strong endorsement of it is somewhat surprising. The Commission concluded that ". . . on the whole, the basic advantages of the local government system established [in 1960] have been demonstrated beyond question . . . we have found no justifiable grounds for criticism and no real defects . . . [and] no need for any change in the basic principles of the Statute."[31] Nevertheless, the commission recommended some changes, especially in Metro's outer boundaries. By provincial legislation of 1964, the area was reduced to about 170 square miles; five basically rural municipalities that had been only partly within Metro were withdrawn completely; and two other municipalities that had been partly included were now included in their entirety. While planning decisions taken by Metro became subject to appeal to the Manitoba Municipal Board and alterations were made in the business tax, the legislation of 1964 did little to resolve the serious problems faced by Metropolitan Winnipeg.

Two other commissions later made recommendations respecting Winnipeg but they were overtaken by the announcement of the Manitoba government's own plan of action.[32] In the provincial election of June 1969, the Progressive Conservative government was defeated by the New Democratic Party which had as one of its major campaign promises the reform of local government. The new government released a White Paper in December of 1970 in which it proposed to thoroughly reorganize Metro Winnipeg.[33] The proposals were made in light of several identified inadequacies in the existing arrangement—Metro Winnipeg's limited power to control development, fragmentation of services and excessive variations in the quality and level of services provided, a fragmented tax base, and the complexity and confused authority of a two-tier structure from the perspective of citizens.

The City of Winnipeg Act of July 1971, came into effect on January 1, 1972, and generally followed the proposals contained in the White Paper.[34] When Unicity Winnipeg (as it has come to be called) was created, its boundaries and territory were those of the former Metro Winnipeg with the addition of small bits of territory to the west and south. The total area remained at about 170 square miles, and the population in 1970 was about 520,000. As the word "Unicity" implies, the new arrangement was a unitary city, with no lower-tier municipalities. Hence the reorganization constituted a large scale amalgamation of the former twelve lower-tier municipalities. There was now no question of allocating powers and functions between multiple levels of municipal governments, and the new city was therefore endowed with the usual range of powers and functions.

The council is a large one by Canada's standards, with fifty aldermen plus a mayor elected at large, although the White Paper had proposed a forty-eight member council with the members choosing the mayor from among themselves. But what makes the Unicity experiment so unique and innovative is its network of "community committees" to which formalized "resident advisory groups" are attached. For the purposes of representation on council the city is divided into fifty wards, each with about ten thousand residents. Councillors from sets of between three and six wards constitute a community committee. Although their boundaries closely follow those of the former municipalities, the twelve community committees are not in any sense a new form of municipality. They have no power to raise taxes on their own and do not directly provide municipal services. They are really sub-committees of the city council.

The primary function for which the community committees were designed was one of communication between council and the citizenry, while at the same time fostering grass-roots involvement through the resident advisory groups. This novel system of political representation, with its built-in mechanism to encourage rather than to merely allow contact between elected representatives and their constituents, was one of the two major aims of the 1972 reorganization. It can certainly be argued that such an aim is characteristic of the New Democratic Party in Canada, but it also flows from Winnipeg's tradition of group activism in city politics, and perhaps also from the popularization in the late 1960s and early 1970s of "participatory democracy".

The Manitoba government's White Paper was initially received with little apparent public interest, but when the election for the first new council was held in October of 1971, interest picked up considerably and seemed to be sustained through the first series of meetings held to choose citizen advisors for the community committees. But at least one analyst, Lloyd Axworthy, was sceptical that the early citizen interest and activity would be more than transitory, for much would depend on the attitudes taken toward formalized citizen participation by elected and appointed city officials.[35] The new system was also a complex one, and therefore not easily comprehended by the general public. How the public would be able to mobilize the resources of expertise, time, money, and legitimacy needed to make the system work was not clear. In other words, developing structures and procedures to encourage close contact between officials and the public does not in itself ensure that close contact will result. Looking back after five years of Unicity Winnipeg, it appears that Axworthy's scepticism was well founded, for the community committee/resident advisory group structures have been only a qualified success.[36] Some city officials have not been enthusiastic or particularly receptive to citizen participation in civic affairs, and participation did fall off at least partly because of the powerlessness of the resident advisory groups (see Chapter 6).

The second main aim of the 1972 reorganization of Winnipeg was to rationalize and make more efficient the provision of services in the city. With amalgamation and therefore with a concentration of powers came a single tax base, standard levels of services, an end to competition among the former municipalities, and a single administrative structure. The outstanding and unique feature of the Unicity Winnipeg experiment is the coupling of this concentration with the decentralization of the decision-making processes through the community committees and resident advisory groups. It is this feature that makes the Winnipeg experiment one of international interest and certainly Canada's foremost innovation in municipal organization.

Alberta

Municipal reorganization in Alberta has been directed mainly toward the rural and less urbanized parts of the province rather than to its two major cities, and Alberta was a pioneer in this regard. School divisions had been consolidated as early as 1936 and consolidation of municipal districts began in 1942. With passage of the County Act in 1950 the province began the final stage of comprehensive rural municipal reorganization described briefly in Chapter 1.[37]

With the development of the petroleum industry after 1946, the population of Alberta swelled, particularly in and around Calgary and Edmonton. These two cities found their populations doubling between 1946 and 1956, and they faced serious burdens as a consequence. A provincial royal commission was appointed in 1954 to consider the questions of boundaries and structures of municipalities in these two major urban areas. Its report was presented in 1956 and recommended that existing municipalities in each of the two areas be amalgamated.[38] This would have had the effect of more than doubling the area of each city, in the case of Calgary from 49.5 square miles to 105 square miles. While the commission listed criteria to be taken into account in determining boundaries (such as the extent of the economic unity, topography, population density, sense of community, taxable capacity, and transportation and communication lines), little evidence that these criteria were actually used by the commission can be found in its proposed boundaries. Since two-tier government was not proposed, the commission was not confronted with questions of dividing powers or designing internal structures. Basically what was recommended seems to have been designed to enable the two cities to absorb fringe settlements and to give them room to develop for a period of fifteen years or so. That room to expand was chosen largely on a topographical basis. In the end, the territorial extents of both cities have been expanded several times so that the City of Calgary at the end of 1973 had a population of 425,000 in an area of 157 square miles, and the City of Edmonton had a population of 442,000 in an area of 122 square miles. Late in 1974 proposals were made for Calgary to annex another 125 square miles while Edmonton would annex 180 additional square miles.

It is of interest to note that the commission did consider alternative forms of organization including a two-tier metropolitan form of the Toronto and Winnipeg type. Such a form of organization was rejected by the commission on the grounds that the populations involved were not sufficiently large to justify such a structure, that it would be too costly, that the situations in Calgary and Edmonton were less complex than had been the case in Metropolitan Toronto, and that a two-tier structure would generally be too much of a compromise.[39] So Alberta's two major cities retain their long-standing structure, but cover increasingly larger populations and areas through annexation.

British Columbia

The major development respecting municipal reorganization in British Columbia was the introduction in 1965 of regional districts.[40] Implemented on a gradual basis, the regional districts were designed primarily to give that 99 per cent of the province's territory that had remained municipally unorganized some semblance of local government. The regional districts were to eventually cover almost all the territory of the province, both urban and rural. By the end of 1968 the program of regionalization was completed when the twenty-eighth region was created. There is also one, in the extreme northwest of the province, that is not incorporated. Only two of the regional districts are particularly urban, the remainder having populations in 1971 generally well below 80,000. In territorial terms most of the regions are large, the smallest one (Nanaimo) covering about 800 square miles and the largest (Peace River–Liard) covering over 80,000 square miles. The two that are most highly urbanized are the Capital Regional District which was created in 1966 and which had a 1971 population of 204,000 including the City of Victoria, and the Greater Vancouver Regional District. It was established in 1967 and had a population of 1,027,000 in 1971.[41]

Officially, the British Columbia government does not view the regional districts as a type of municipal government. "Regional districts were not conceived as a fourth level of government, but are a functional rather than a political amalgamation."[42] The districts were designed to be a mechanism for the joint provision of multiple services. In those areas that were municipally unorganized, the regional district board was to provide municipal services that otherwise would not be provided or that had been provided previously by the provincial government directly. It is extremely difficult to see just what it is about the regional districts that makes them something other than a unit of municipal government. Multiple functions are performed, they raise revenue, and they have councils (called "boards") that involve election by the public. In short they have the characteristics that are normally associated with municipal government. It has been suggested that the reluctance to refer to the regional districts as governments was a tactical move to head off any resistance to the reorganization, given the opposition with which regional government has sometimes been greeted elsewhere in Canada.[43]

The methods used for determining the size and boundaries of the regions have never been clearly stated, but factors that are said to have been taken into account include population size (desired minimum of 30,000), value of assessed property (desired minimum of forty million dollars), shape and extent of trading area, and suitability for provision of services.[44] In the case of the Greater Vancouver Regional District, fourteen municipalities are included as well as three municipally unorganized areas. It has never been made clear why the boundaries of the GVRD were determined to include those particular municipalities and unorganized areas. The same applies with regard to the seven municipalities and seven unorganized areas in the (Victoria) Capital Regional District. Boundaries are defined in the Letters Patent that are issued to create each individual regional district under the enabling legislation of the provincial government in 1965.

With regard to their internal organization, the two highly urbanized regional districts are each partly two-tier and partly unitary. This means that the member municipalities constitute a lower tier, with the councils of those municipalities selecting representatives from their councils to sit on the regional council. But for the municipally unorganized areas in the regional districts the district itself is the only form of municipal government there is. The residents in such areas directly elect representatives to the regional council.

The powers and functions exercised by the regional districts are not uniform across the province. They too are specified in the region's Letters Patent. There are some functions which all regions are obliged to perform by virtue of those letters, such as financing of hospitals and regional planning, plus other functions which are optional, depending on what it is that the member units as well as the regional council want the region to perform. There can also be contractual arrangements whereby services are provided by one level for the other level. In the case of the Greater Vancouver Regional District the functions performed include regional land-use planning, air pollution control, control of gatherings, senior citizens' housing, labour negotiations, regional parks, hospital construction, management of municipal debt, preparation of land use plans for member units, street lighting, building regulations, public housing, and provision to member units on a contract basis of water and sewage facilities. The list grows from time to time. In the 1965 legislation there was an opting-out provision, whereby a municipality or unincorporated area could decide not to participate in any designated function of the regional district. This provision applied to all regions but was repealed in 1970.

It should be noted that the Greater Vancouver Regional District was not the first metropolitan arrangement in the Vancouver area. There had been six special-purpose regional authorities dating from as far back as 1914, but all were ultimately absorbed by the GVRD. The special-purpose authorities had dealt with sewerage and drainage, planning, and health. Indeed it was the proliferation of such authorities that seems to have been an important consideration in the provincial government's deciding to create the multi-purpose regional districts.[45] Finally, it should also be noted that legislation was actually introduced in the provincial legislature in 1957 to enable the creation of real metropolitan government in the Vancouver area if later study showed that it was possible and desirable. Later study did recommend that metropolitan government be so introduced but no further action was taken.[46]

Overview

The recurrent theme that pervades virtually all of the instances of urban municipal reform in Canada beginning with Metropolitan Toronto in 1954 is that the process of urbanization severely strained the capabilities of any existing level of government to plan. The structures of municipal government were generally fragmented in the major cities so that none of them individually could shape their future growth. Even with their constitutional authority, provincial governments usually are reluctant to intervene in a continuous and forceful manner to control and plan urban development, for the tradition of relative autonomy of local governments is fairly strongly rooted in this country. But the development policies of the city municipalities were not always consistent with the overall development objectives of their provinces. Because of constitutional limitations the federal government could affect the growth of the cities in only a marginal way. It became commonly accepted that uncontrolled and unrestrained random growth of Canada's major cities was not desirable and must be prevented. It is no mere coincidence that the post-World War II acceleration of urbanization in Canada and the period of urban municipal reorganization correspond closely in time.

While the need for urban and regional planning was commonly accepted, the means by which it could or should be achieved was not. The two main means used prior to 1954 (and still used in some cities) were piecemeal annexation by the urban core municipalities, and special-purpose area planning boards. While the former mechanism has a certain desirable simplicity, it does mean bigness, and bigness runs counter to "grass roots" local self-government. A small council with jurisdiction over a large population, even in a fairly small area, is hard pressed to maintain or foster close contact between elected and appointed public officials on the one hand and the general public on the other. In any event, the elected officials of municipalities about to be annexed in part or amalgamated in whole to the core municipality will object. Special-purpose area planning boards were scarcely a better solution, for they present problems of accountability to the public, encounter the inevitability of inter-municipal competition for particular kinds of urban development (residential versus industrial/commercial, in the simplest terms), and possible incongruency of municipal zoning with area planning. If the municipalities in a major urban area are unable to come to grips with urban planning for the area satisfactorily, then the provincial government can be expected sooner or later to overcome its general reluctance to enter the scene by reorganizing municipal government in the city. Certainly the province can constitutionally do so, and it may also feel obliged to do so for economic reasons if it perceives municipalities as inefficient providers of services. This is so because substantial proportions of provincial expenditures are directed toward funding municipal

expenditures. One of the common features characteristic of urban municipal reorganization in Canada is that almost invariably the reorganization is conceived and implemented by provincial governments from up
above, rather than being initiated locally by all the municipalities themselves in a major urban area. Urban municipal politicians are rarely
afflicted by a suicide syndrome, so they are unlikely to initiate action
which would result in their losing their own positions and bases of power.
Unless circumstances are really dire, it is only the local politicians of the
highly urbanized core municipality who will push for reorganization.
Also unlikely except in extreme cases is support or demands from the
general public for reorganization that would fundamentally alter the
comfortable and familiar status quo. So the provincial governments have
been the primary agents of urban municipal reorganization, generally
supported by the major newspapers.

Proposals for and actual instances of urban municipal reorganization
involve two conflicting requisites of scale. On the one hand, the provision
of municipal services is generally facilitated and made more economical
when the area to be serviced is large, though the optimum area for one
service is not often the optimum area for all others. The requisite of large
scale applies particularly to planning functions, but it also tends to apply
to such services as water supply and sewage disposal, traffic control,
police and fire protection, and so on. Jurisdiction over an entire urban
area also mitigates against gross variations in the kinds and levels of
services provided and in the levels of taxation levied for the provision of
those services. Therefore the need for and desirability of large scale is
compelling from this perspective. But large scale is counter-productive
to the notion of grass-roots local government (this can be called the
representation requisite) as suggested above and as pursued in the following chapter. Therefore there is a tension between the two requisites of
scale, a tension which results in one of the two (generally the service one)
being given priority, or in a compromise between the two, or in an attempt
to develop new mechanisms designed to foster the representation requisite
but in a large-scale area of jurisdiction.[47] The technique of simple
amalgamation or annexation of additional area to urban-core municipalities as used in Calgary and Edmonton is indicative of the service
requisite being given priority. The technique of two-tier metropolitan or

regional government as used in Toronto, Vancouver, and other major cities especially in Ontario and Quebec is indicative of an attempt to find a compromise. In this case, the service requisite is more or less satisfied by having services that are better performed on an area-wide basis being the responsibility of the upper tier, and it is thought or assumed that the representation requisite is more or less satisfied by retaining the lower-tier municipalities. Unicity Winnipeg can be considered the only example in Canada of the third approach, an attempt to develop new mechanisms (large council, small wards, community committees, and resident advisory groups) designed to foster the representation requisite but in an area designed to satisfy the service requisite.

With increasing frequency and force, the earlier dominance of the service perspective in urban municipal reorganization is being questioned. One of the concerns is that power in cities is already too concentrated, and that to centralize political power further by urban municipal re-organization-through-consolidation will only further isolate and alienate a cynical and frustrated citizenry. The focus here is not so much on the legal power of municipalities, but on who exercises that power and on the processes involved. Thus it is thought that if municipal legal power is more concentrated by urban municipal consolidation and amalgamation, the exercise of the power will be further removed from the general citizenry, and democracy in the sense of power-sharing will be further eroded. Cities are not homogeneous social wholes. They are very hetero-geneous mixtures of all kinds of people who tend to sort themselves out into different geographical sectors of the city (see the following chapter). Few people now seriously question that there is some connection between the possession of economic power (as seen in some particular sectors of major cities) and the ability to exercise political power. The point is that if a major urban complex is reorganized only from the service perspective and in a way that would create only one or a very small number of large and populous municipalities in the urban area, political power will be more concentrated, thus enabling those with economic power to further dominate urban municipal politics. The conclusion that one would naturally draw from this is that power can most effectively be put in the hands of the general citizenry by decentralization; instead of creating a monolith, make urban government neighbourhood or community govern-ment—small-scale government with as many internal units as there are identifiable neighbourhoods or communities.

On the one hand, therefore, there are forces and apologists for a centralization approach to urban municipal reorganization, and there are also supporters of decentralization. It has been thought that the two cannot possibly be reconciled, and certainly there tend to be important ideological differences between the two schools of thought which mitigate against a reconciliation. Yet the Unicity Winnipeg experiment demonstrates some of the possibilities for harmony.

Urban municipal reorganization in Canada has involved considerations not only of scale but also of complexity. John Porter, though referring to the national context in Canada rather than to the municipal context, has written of the "hallowed nonsense" of federalism.[48] By this he meant that a federal form of government with its attendant division of powers and responsibilities becomes incomprehensible to the general citizenry. He might easily have made his comment with reference to the federated two-tiered structure of enlarged municipal government institutions in urban Canada with equal relevance and force. Aside from the complexity afforded by a plethora of quasi-independent special-purpose municipal bodies, by provincial-municipal and tri-level bodies and conferences, and by central-local relations, the increasingly common federated two-tier structure of municipal government with a division of powers and functions can be as confusing and complex to the public as the national context is. The question therefore arises of whether the reorganized urban municipalities are not only too large but their organization too complex to be consistent with principles of democracy. Such questions are pursued in the next chapter.

NOTES

1. Stewart Fyfe, "Local Government Reform: Some Canadian Experiences," (a paper presented to the annual meeting of the Canadian Political Science Association, 1971), pp. 2–3. See also Thomas J. Plunkett, "Structural Reform of Local Government in Canada," *Public Administration Review*, vol. 33, no. 1 (January/February, 1973), pp. 40–51; and Frank Smallwood, "Reshaping Local Government Abroad: Anglo-Canadian Experiments," *Public Administration Re-* *view*, vol. 30, no. 3 (September/October, 1970), pp. 521–30.

2. Newfoundland, Royal Commission on Municipal Government in Newfoundland and Labrador, *Report* (St. John's, 1974).

3. Ibid., p. 399.

4. St. John's Urban Region Study, *An Outline* (St. John's, 1973). The report was prepared by two firms of consultants.

5. Nova Scotia, Royal Commission on Education, Public Services and Provincial-Municipal Relations, *Report*, 4 volumes (Halifax, 1974).

Professor John Graham was the chairman.

6. Ibid., Volume II, Chapter 4, p. 20.
7. Ibid., Volume II, Chapter 5, p. 22.
8. Mr. F. Mooney, quoted in *The Mail-Star* (Halifax), June 12, 1975.
9. New Brunswick, Royal Commission on Finance and Municipal Taxation, *Report* (Fredericton, November, 1963). Mr. Edward Byrne, Q.C., was chairman. See also New Brunswick, *White Paper on the Responsibilities of Government* (Fredericton, 1965).
10. New Brunswick, Royal Commission on Metropolitan Saint John, *Report* (Fredericton, July, 1963).
11. Ralph R. Krueger, "The Provincial-Municipal Government Revolution in New Brunswick," *Canadian Public Administration*, vol. XIII (Spring, 1970), p. 51.
12. Montreal, Commission for the Study of the Metropolitan Problems of Montreal, *General and Final Report* (January, 1955). Judge Roland Paquette was chairman.
13. Quebec, Study Commission of Intermunicipal Problems on the Island of Montreal, *Report* (Quebec: Queen's Printer, December, 1964). M. Camille Blier, who was assistant deputy minister of municipal affairs for the province, was chairman of the Commission.
14. Québec, Commission d'étude sur les problèmes intermunicipaux de l'Ile Jésus, *Rapport*, two volumes (December, 1964). Judge Armand Sylvestre was chairman.
15. Québec, Ministre des Affaires Municipales, *Proposition de Réforme des Structures municipales* (Québec: l'Editeur officiel du Québec, March, 1971).
16. Ontario Municipal Board, *Decisions and Recommendations of the Board* (Toronto: Queen's Printer, January 20, 1953). Mr. Lorne Cumming was then chairman of the OMB. There are a number of good accounts of the origins and history of metropolitan government in Toronto such as Alfred Rose, *Governing Metro-*

politan Toronto: A Social and Political Analysis 1953–71 (Berkeley: University of California Press, 1972); Frank Smallwood, *Metro Toronto: A Decade Later* (Toronto: Bureau of Municipal Research, 1963); and Harold Kaplan, *Urban Political Systems: A Functional Analysis of Metro Toronto* (New York: Columbia University Press, 1967).
17. Smallwood, *Metro Toronto*, pp. 2–4.
18. Ontario, Metropolitan Toronto Commission of Inquiry, *First Report* (Toronto, March 14, 1953). No subsequent reports were ever made by this commission.
19. Ontario, Royal Commission on Metropolitan Toronto *Report* (Toronto, June 10, 1965).
20. Ontario, *Statement by the Honourable John Robarts, Prime Minister of Ontario, Re Report of the Royal Commission on Metropolitan Toronto* (Toronto, January 10, 1966).
21. For detail refer to Fyfe, "Local Government Reform: Some Canadian Experiences," pp. 25–40.
22. Ontario, Select Committee on the Municipal Act and Related Acts *Fourth and Final Report* (March, 1965), p. 168. Mr. Beckett was chairman.
23. Ontario, Committee on Taxation *Report*, 3 volumes (Toronto: Queen's Printer, 1967).
24. Ibid., Volume II, pp. 515–16.
25. Ontario, *Design for Development: Phase Two*, statement to the Ontario legislature by Municipal Affairs Minister D. McKeough, December 2, 1968, pp. 2–3.
26. Donald J. H. Higgins, "Community and Local Government: Boundary Determination" (unpublished PHD thesis, Carleton University, Ottawa, 1973), Chapter 2.
27. Quoted in the *Globe and Mail* (Toronto), February 12, 1975, p. 4.
28. Manitoba, Greater Winnipeg Investigating Commission *Report and Recommendations*, four volumes (Winnipeg: Queen's Printer, 1959). Mr. J. L. Brodie was Commission

chairman. For a description of the developments occurring in 1960 see S. George Rich, "Metropolitan Winnipeg: The First Ten Years," in Ralph R. Krueger and R. Charles Bryfogle, eds., *Urban Problems: A Canadian Reader* (Toronto: Holt, Rinehart and Winston, 1971).

29. Manitoba, Metropolitan Corporation of Greater Winnipeg Review Commission *Report and Recommendations* (Winnipeg, February, 1964).

30. Harold Kaplan, "The Integration of Metropolitan Federations: the Interaction of Political Theory and Urban Phenomena," in N. H. Lithwick and Gilles Paquet, eds., *Urban Studies: A Canadian Perspective* (Toronto: Methuen, 1968), p. 158.

31. Manitoba, Metropolitan Corporation of Greater Winnipeg Review Commission *Report and Recommendations*, p. 32.

32. Those two reports are Manitoba, Royal Commission on Local Government Organization and Finance *Report* (Winnipeg: Queen's Printer, 1964); and Manitoba, Local Government Boundaries Commission *Provisional Plan for Local Government Units in the Greater Winnipeg Area* (Winnipeg, September, 1970).

33. Manitoba, *Proposals for Urban Reorganization in the Greater Winnipeg Area* (Winnipeg, December, 1970). For a commentary on this White Paper see Gail C. A. Cook and Lionel D. Feldman, "Approaches to Local Government Reform in Canada: The Case of Winnipeg," *Canadian Tax Journal*, vol. xix (May–June, 1971), pp. 216–25.

34. For descriptions see P. H. Wichern, "Winnipeg's Unicity after Two Years: Evaluation of an Experiment in Urban Government," a paper given at the annual meeting of the Canadian Political Science Association, 1974; Dennis C. Hefferon, "Notes on Bill 36, the City of Winnipeg Act," in Lionel D. Feldman and Michael D. Goldrick, eds.,

Politics and Government of Urban Canada: Selected Readings, 2nd ed. (Toronto: Methuen, 1972), pp. 309–30; M. Brownstone and L. D. Feldman, "Innovation and City Government: Winnipeg, 1972," *The Canadian Forum*, vol. lii (May, 1972); and Lloyd Axworthy, "Winnipeg: An Experiment in Innovation," in L. Axworthy and James M. Gillies, eds., *The City: Canada's Prospects, Canada's Problems* (Toronto: Butterworths, 1973), pp. 276–83.

35. Axworthy, "Winnipeg: An Experiment in Innovation," p. 280.

36. Wichern, "Winnipeg's Unicity after Two Years: Evaluation of an Experiment in Urban Government," pp. 39–42.

37. See Eric J. Hanson, "The Changing Structure of Local Government in Alberta," *Canadian Public Administration*, vol. i, no. 3 (September, 1958).

38. Alberta, Royal Commission on the Metropolitan Development of Calgary and Edmonton *Report* (Edmonton: Queen's Printer, 1956). Dr. G. McNally was chairman.

39. Ibid., Chapter 13, p. 6.

40. See British Columbia, Department of Municipal Affairs *Regional Districts in British Columbia, 1971: General Review* (Victoria: Queen's Printer, 1972).

41. See Paul Tennant and Dave Zirnhelt, "The Emergence of Metropolitan Government in Greater Vancouver," a paper presented to the annual meeting of the Canadian Political Science Association, 1971.

42. British Columbia, Department of Municipal Affairs *Regional Districts in British Columbia, 1971: General Review*, op. cit., p. 6.

43. Tennant and Zirnhelt, "The Emergence of Metropolitan Government in Greater Vancouver," pp. 14–15 and 31.

44. Honourable Dan Campbell, *The Changing Face of Local Government, 1967* (Victoria: Queen's Printer, 1967), pp. 2–3; and Lower

Mainland Regional Planning Board, *Regional Districts: Proceedings of the Discussion on Bill 83, Regional Districts Legislation, as it Might Apply in the Lower Mainland Planning Area* (Vancouver, June, 1965), pp. 10–11.

45. Tennant and Zirnhelt, "The Emergence of Metropolitan Government in Greater Vancouver," pp. 7–9.

46. Metropolitan Joint Committee, *Final Report to the Minister of Municipal Affairs, British Columbia* (Vancouver, December, 1960). Mr. Hugo Ray was chairman of the committee which was composed mainly of local mayors, reeves and aldermen.

47. For a different way of classifying approaches to municipal reorganization see Smallwood, "Reshaping Local Government Abroad: Anglo-Canadian Experiments," p. 522. His method differs from that developed here mainly in that his does not deal with what is called the representation requisite.

48. John Porter, *The Vertical Mosaic: An Analysis of Social Class and Power in Canada* (Toronto: University of Toronto Press, 1965), p. 382.

Socio-Political Consequences

5

# of Urbanization:

The Setting For Urban Political Life

The previous four chapters have established the context of governmental institutions and relations within which urban political life takes place. Their importance lies in determining the parameters for the making of policies and decisions in Canada's major cities. What should now be clear is not only the complexity and scale of the institutional framework but also the fact that there are important constraints (legal, financial, and so on) on the kinds of policies and decisions that can be made by the cities themselves.

The glimpse given in the Introduction at the phenomenon of urbanization and the extent of it in Canada indicated that urbanization can be viewed as producing two kinds of issues that require or affect urban political decision-making. On the one hand there are urban problems such as transportation, planning, development, and housing. Such policy areas tend to be relatively concrete, public, and increasingly contentious. The other kind of issue produced by the process of urbanization is stress on the actual decision-making structures and processes of the major cities. It is with the political process issues that the following chapters are most concerned. These are issues that are often more abstract, generally considered outside the glare of publicity, but often as contentious (at least to the initiated few) as the other kind of issues. But there is another important aspect of urbanization too, one that is often neglected—it is that urbanization sets a socio-political framework or context for urban public decision-making. What is the socio-political nature of urban society? Whatever its nature, it clearly has important determinant effects on the decision-making processes of major cities as well as on the particular kinds of decisions that come out of those processes. It clearly has a bearing too on the kinds and sources of inputs to the process, on the ways in which those inputs are introduced, and on the relative chances of input demands from various sources being successful. And how can the nature of urban society be related to aspects of political theory, such as participation? These are the kinds of questions to which attention is directed in this chapter, and they centre around the concepts of community and integration, influence and participation, and the relationship between size and democracy. As should become apparent, these concepts are inter-related. Nevertheless they need clarification and are amenable to separate consideration.

Size and Democracy: "Grass Roots"

The process of urbanization produces demographically larger and socially more complex cities. The process of municipal reorganization in those urban areas generally produces geographically larger scale and organizationally more complex municipal government. Are these trends compatible with the notion of local self-government as "grass roots" democracy, or does that notion cease to be applicable to urban areas and urbanites? The term "grass roots" is highly value-laden and is frequently called into use for all sorts of purposes. In proposals for municipal reorganization the term is very often used by local elected officials to justify retention of the status quo on the grounds that annexation, amalgamation or boundary revisions will destroy the "grass roots" of the area and its inhabitants. Reformers frequently employ the term to justify their proposed reforms on the grounds that those reforms would return local politics and government to the "grass roots". Clearly what these two diverse groups of advocates mean by the term is not the same thing, and it is therefore necessary here to clarify the term.

"Grass roots" is not commonly used in academic literature, but in one such work Roscoe Martin (in a chapter titled "The Grass-roots Concept") notes that in its more responsible usage the term has at least five significant aspects.[1] One of these is that the term relates to government, more specifically to administrative decentralization, or to representativeness of the local legislature, or to local political action. Second, it symbolizes a spirit of community independence—local initiative, local autonomy, and local control of local affairs. He specifies next that the term has a personal or individual meaning—an expression of belief in the worth of the individual. Fourth, "grass roots" is almost always equated with democracy

—the expression of popular judgment on public questions. Finally, he notes that the term is normally used with a geographical connotation, more specifically that "grass roots" is non-metropolitan, even non-urban in character. This final aspect casts doubt on the possibility that "grass roots" is a concept applicable to urban areas and urbanites. In his book Martin equates "grass roots" with "little" government, and more accurately with rural local government. From this flows the logic that such government is direct, personal, intimate, informal, face-to-face, qualities that he seems to assume are not and cannot be found except in rural areas. These aspects can be subsumed under the word "closeness"— closeness of people to each other, and to the institutions, processes, and personalities of local government. Most usages of the term "grass roots" are compatible with this definition, but there is certainly not universal agreement that it is a notion applicable only to rural areas, rural residents, and rural local government. Such reformists as Alinsky[2] and Kotler[3] argue for what could be called "grass roots" local government especially in urban contexts.

If the notion of "grass roots" is taken to mean closeness as defined above, then it would seem questionable that the term has reference to evolving municipal government in Canada's majnr cities. Consider the geographical size of most of the reorganized urban municipalities— Metropolitan Toronto covers 243 square miles, the Montreal Urban Community covers some 180 square miles, Unicity Winnipeg covers about 170 square miles, the Greater Vancouver Regional District covers 1,005 square miles. Even most of the less populous reorganized urban municipalities are geographically large—the City of Saint John in New Brunswick has 104 square miles, the Outaouais (Hull) Regional Community in Quebec encompasses 908 square miles, the Regional Municipality of Sudbury has 1,088 square miles, and the City of Calgary covers 157 square miles. The fact that some of these municipalities (though not all) have within them a number of geographically smaller municipalities does not substantially detract from the generalization that a large proportion of the citizens of Canada's major urban centres are not very close, geographically, to their municipal institutions, for even in two-tier municipalities there is a degree of centralization of municipal power. Whatever feeling of closeness they may feel could only be psychological, for it can scarcely be physical. One could restate the populations of Canada's urban municipalities, and conclude that whatever closeness the citizens have to their city society as a whole must again be psychological, for it can scarcely be social. How does one feel close to one's hundred thousand fellow citizens, or to one's million fellow citizens? Of course one cannot feel close to all of them, only to a tiny proportion of them. Finally, one could restate the size of the municipal councils in most of Canada's major cities, relate that to population, and question whether there can really be "grass roots" closeness between the public and elected representatives.

The previous chapter raised the question of size and scale, both in terms of geography and population, and noted that the question is one which has confronted those who have been responsible for formulating the schemes of urban municipal reorganization. Here the concern is focused on what was earlier called the representation requisite of scale. Only a very few of the studies and reports relating to urban municipal reorganization have taken up the question of size from the perspective of the relationship (actual or desired) between the citizen and the institutions, personalities, and processes of his municipal government. The Ontario Committee on Taxation's report is one of that small handful. In that report the Committee identified what it considered to be two prime values ". . . for whose fulfilment local government exists in a constitutional democracy. . . ."[4] Those two identified values it called *access* and *service*. These can be viewed as synonyms for what in the previous chapter were called the representation and service requisites of scale respectively.

By *service* we mean not only the economical discharge of public functions, but the achievement of technical adequacy in due alignment with public needs and desires.

. . . Were service the only value to be maximized, each separate function of government might claim a territorial jurisdiction of its own, whose size would be tailored exactly to the area in which the service in question could be discharged most efficiently. Furthermore, with such a multiplicity of service areas, efficiency could only be maintained through a technocracy prepared to function without awaiting direction from a confused and faltering public. In such circumstances, access would be virtually non-existent.[5]

But, as the committee pointed out, government at whatever level must be more than a mechanism for maximizing the provision of services:

By *access* we mean the most widespread participation possible on the part of all or virtually all individual citizens. Access to government, in terms of capacity to influence public policy decisions and to enforce responsive and responsible administration is, of course, fundamental to any democratic government. But that local government is peculiarly conducive to the realization of the access value has been recognized by political philosophers at least since the time of Plato. The central reason is that the capacity of government to promote access is in part an inverse function of size. The local government that is sufficiently small to enable all citizens to participate directly in public affairs—in short, the town-meeting government—is that local government which is capable of realizing the access value most fully.[6]

If, as suggested earlier, the two values cannot be reconciled with respect to their optimum size requirements, which value should receive the greater attention? In more or less autocratic/totalitarian political systems the answer would be clear—emphasize efficiency and economy of service at the expense of access. But Canadians generally view the political system as democratic, in which case the access value should not easily be sacrificed to the exigencies of the service value. Since these two values appear to be inherently conflictive with respect to the optimum area of the municipal units, it would seem that either some compromise is required, or one value must be sacrificed. To determine which value *should* be sacrificed is far more difficult than determining which value *is* usually sacrificed. Perusal of the studies and reports leading to urban municipal reorganization in Canada shows that it is almost without exception the access value that is surrendered.[7] The usual boundary determinants used relate to the provision of municipal services, taking into account topographical features, adequacy of tax base, geographical size as related to services, population size as related to provision of services and to ability to pay for those services, and the like.

The principal exception to this generalization is of course the Winnipeg experiment which was in considerable measure based on political/philosophical considerations about size and democracy, concerned with size as it affects the relations between the citizen and the citizen's municipal institutions. In the Manitoba government's white paper that became the basis for the Unicity experiment in Winnipeg, repeated reference was made to what could be described as the access value. A couple of sentences illustrate that concern:

Introduction of a second tier of government in 1960 effected major improvements in the quality of certain services administered on an area-wide basis. Regrettably, it also aggravated a much more fundamental and critical problem—the individual's sense of frustration with, and alienation from, the governments supposedly in existence to serve him.[8]

And the white paper approvingly quoted a passage from the Royal Commission on Local Government in England:

. . . We had become increasingly convinced by those who emphasized the need for an organ of community at the grass roots level. Our first firm conclusion was that any new pattern of democratic government must include elected "local councils", not to provide main services, but to promote and watch over the particular interests of communities in city, town and village. . . .[9]

Yet the Manitoba government disbanded twelve smaller municipalities to create one single larger one. Was the concern expressed in the white paper over the access value just window-dressing which ended up being sacrificed to the service value? Although it does seem that this has been the eventual outcome, such was clearly not the intention, for the large council, small wards, community committees, and resident advisory groups, to which reference has been made in Chapter 4, were intended to satisfy the access value.

Unicity Winnipeg is more an exercise in deconcentration than in devolution. The former term means simply that there is a delegation of authority for the discharge of certain functions to staff of a city department who are situated outside the headquarters, while devolution means that legal powers to perform specific functions are conferred on formally constituted local authorities. Decentralization is a combination of deconcentration and devolution.[10] The community committees and their associated resident advisory groups did not really have legal powers delegated to them; they were to be basically advisory and agencies of communications. Indeed one objection that could be made about the community committees is that they do not work as intended because they cannot *do* anything significant, and that there is as a consequence too little incentive for the citizenry to use them as points of access. If this point is accepted, one would be tempted to suggest that community committees, or whatever one wants to call them, be delegated more substantial decision-making powers. To beef up such committees in this way, though, could produce the same kinds of problems typical of two-tier federated municipal government. However, it should not prove impossible to buttress the community committee type of mechanism without producing virtual two-tier municipal government. For example, committees could conceivably be retained with a largely advisory function but connected to a more deconcentrated city administration, rather along the lines of police precinct stations of the past (something like little city halls); those area offices could be concerned with as many functions or services as possible rather than with only one or a few functions.[11] Having a large municipal council with a large number of small wards (such as Winnipeg has) can also go some way to bringing urban municipal government in Canada back to the "grass roots".

It could be argued that two-tier federated municipal government of the sort that has evolved in most Canadian provinces represents an attempt to combine the access and service values, and indeed it may even be the case that it works to some extent, although there is scant evidence to indicate that such has been the rationale for retaining a lower tier. There are few exceptions to the generalization that lower-tier municipalities were intended to perform localized *services*—services that could best be performed in areas smaller than that of the metropolitan/regional municipality as a whole. Further, if retention of lower-tier municipalities was intended to satisfy the access function, then one wonders why it is that there is a tendency to *consolidate* them (see, for example, Table 4:1 in Chapter 4 on regional government in Ontario) either at the same time that metropolitan/regional government is created, or after it is created. The conclusion seems inescapable that in so far as lower-tier municipalities do go some way to satisfying the access value, it is coincidental.

Some would argue that most lower-tier municipalities are far too large to promote the access value, and that what is needed is what is often called "neighbourhood" government.[12] As the word "neighbourhood" implies, the scale here would be very small (small enough to permit direct democracy rather than requiring representative government), and as the word "government" implies, they would have legal powers conferred upon them. It is maintained that such governments would promote a sense of community within the neighbourhood, would overcome feelings of helplessness and powerlessness, would encourage participation in more than just the sense of mobilizing support for governmental institutions and policies, and would generally promote democracy because they would ensure that there is local control over decisions and decision making. Neighbourhood governments can be seen as a replication of the ancient Greek city-states, but in a highly urban and highly technological environment. Critics tend to dismiss such a concept as nostalgic nonsense, but the philosophical underpinnings of neighbourhood government are attractive (although the ideological militancy associated with it may be less so). Rather than being dismissed as mere nostalgia, they can more properly be dismissed as unlikely in Canada. This sort of local government structure (which would presumably be the lowest of a multi-tier system of municipal government) does have practical and political difficulties. To decentralize local government to this extent would necessarily decrease the power of the city's government, so no city councils are likely to press for neighbourhood government. Additionally, neighbourhood governments would presumably have a call on local finance, which would be seen as weakening the finances of the city's government. Finally, it is worth asking what kinds of powers neighbourhood government might have, for their scale would be so small as to make it impractical, if not impossible for them to exercise many powers or to provide a reasonably wide range of services. There are as yet few working examples of formal neighbourhood government, and none in Canada. In the United States, the principle was instituted in a couple of cities (notably New York and Detroit) in the early 1970s, but in only one area of policy—schools.[13] Not being multi-functional, they cannot properly be considered as governments.

How, then, is size or scale connected to democracy? Some analysts deny, contrary to popular assumption, that democracy is furthered by

local self-government, and especially by small-scale local self-government. In arguing that there is a "fundamental contradiction" between
local government and democracy, Georges Langrod[14] stands in sharp
contrast to the general body of opinion. It would seem that he has a
different operating definition of both local government and democracy
than Hampton, for example, who argues that there is a direct connection
between the two concepts, and that the connection is stronger when the
size and scale of local government is small.[15] By "democracy" he means
basically that democracy necessitates open government, popular knowledge of and interest in public decisions, and popular control of and
participation in government. In other words, power must be pluralized
so that the public can control the making and makers of decisions. As
Dahl and others suggest, the ability for a public to maintain such control
increases in difficulty as the size or scale of government increases.[16]
Hence closeness tends to increase popular control.

The problem of relating size and democracy, of relating governmental
institutions to the citizenry, is a problem not unique to urban municipal
government. The problem is equally important at other levels of government such as the nation state. Dahl and Tufte deal with the problem of
size and democracy in government generally, not just cities, but it is
remarkable how well their argument holds when one reads it with cities
in mind.[17] Although the problem is not unique to cities, the municipal
level of government seems to be where the problem is most easily subject
to resolution because it is at that level that institutions are most easily, or
at least most often, changed in Canada. Further, if local self-government
is the cornerstone of democracy, as is so often suggested,[18] then it seems
especially appropriate that the problem of size and its effects on the
relations between citizens on the one hand and the institutions, personalities, and processes of government on the other, be first resolved at the
municipal level.

The Concept of Integration and the Decline of Community

It was suggested above that the notion of "grass roots" local self-government is sometimes thought to be a relic in terms of its application to
urban areas and urbanites. Perhaps the same kind of statement can be

made regarding the notion of community. What is certainly clear is that there is no *one* concept of "community". One attempt to perform a conceptual analysis of the word, by examining ninety-four definitions of community, yielded sixteen different concepts, among which the only element of agreement was that community somehow involves people![19] The necessity of social interaction of the people was specifically denied as an essential feature of community in several of the definitions examined, and there was even less agreement on a geographical area locus as an essential feature of community.

Probably the most common usage of the word community is simply "people in a place". But that usage is not helpful because it lacks precision. Which people? What place? How many people? How large (or small) a place? *All* the people in a place, or only some of them? What connections must there be among those people? The literature on community yields several schools of thought or approaches which have been influential in guiding research. These can be labelled for convenience the objective approach and the subjective approach.

The objective approach to the study of community is concerned with inter-relationships, or interdependent interactions, among people by which those people meet their frequent and regular requirements.[20] Nowhere are individuals absolutely self-sufficient and independent of others. Their daily needs require some degree of interaction with others if those needs are to be satisfied. Therefore this approach holds that if one starts by focusing on one small geographical place and examines the space involved in people's interactions in meeting their frequent requirements, one has identified the territorial extent of a community. That territorial extent is likely to be larger than the initial geographical focus. Presumably all the people in that territory constitute a *single* community, although this point is not usually made explicitly in the literature. The kinds of interactions with which this approach is most interested are economic relationships such as employment, grocery shopping, banking, and so on, and what the researcher of objective community looks for is spatial patterns of interaction. To illustrate, Charles Galpin's method of determining the territorial extent of a community was what has come to be known as the "ruts in the road" method, by which the researcher simply travelled around the countryside noting in which direction wheel ruts from farmyards turned.[21] Assuming that wheel ruts indicate travel and that travel indicates interaction, the idea was that one travelled along a road noting the point at which wheel ruts begin to turn right rather than left on to that road. That point marked one boundary of a community. Then one went out in other directions from the same starting point looking for other such boundary points, until one had mapped out a community.

The methodology of identifying this sort of community has been much refined since Galpin's pioneering work in the early part of this century, but the fundamental point remains: that the identification of communities lies in determining the spatial patterns and extent of movements of people to interact with other people, or movements of messages among people. The kind of techniques now used include mapping travel patterns from people's place of residence to the places where they work, shop, visit, and engage in other frequent interaction, examining places of origin and

Figure 5:1   The Ruts-in-the-road Method of Locating Objective Community

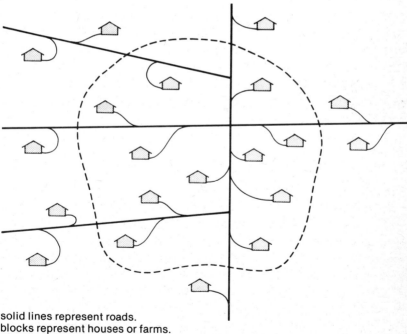

solid lines represent roads.
blocks represent houses or farms.
the dotted line represents the boundary of the identified community.

destination of telephone calls, places where a particular newspaper is circulated, viewing areas of television stations, and listening areas of radio stations. As Hawley stated,

. . . The boundary of every community is determined in the same manner. It is fixed by the maximum radius of routine daily movement to and from a center. Thus the community includes the area the population of which, however widely distributed, regularly turns to a common center for the satisfaction of all or a major part of its needs. That distance may differ considerably, depending on the kind of transportation facility in use. Where human locomotion or animal carriage is the prevailing mode of transportation and communication, the distance from center to periphery seldom exceeds five miles, but the use of mechanically powered agencies of movement enlarges the radial distance to twenty or more miles.[22]

Just as the methods of locating communities in this objective sense of the word have been refined over the ruts-in-the-road method of Galpin, so has this objective notion itself. As researchers find, the boundaries are not as sharp as the diagram shows, for some people go not to just one centre for all purposes but to different centres depending on the purpose. For example, where an individual goes to shop is not necessarily the same place that he goes to work. So the community's boundaries need not coincide for all purposes of frequent and regular interaction. What has been done is to distinguish between primary communities (based on daily movements and interactions) and secondary communities (based on regular but less frequent movements and interactions).[23]

This objective notion of community is relatively easy to research, for data can fairly easily be obtained on spatial patterns of movement and interaction. However, the relative ease of identifying such communities does not overcome problems in the notion itself. How can objective community be related to urban areas? In other words, does it not seem likely that this notion of community is basically applicable only to non-urban areas? The patterns of movements and communication in cities seem far too complex to be much use at all as indicators of community, primarily because the *choices* are so much more numerous in the setting of a major city. A person wanting to go grocery shopping is not limited to just the corner store. A resident in a major city normally has numerous corner stores as well as numerous shopping centres from which to choose, and may go one week to one store nearby, the next week to a different store, and the third week to a shopping centre to take advantage of a particularly good buy. No one store or office is likely to have a monopoly on its goods or services, and therefore cannot monopolize a particular clientele. In other words the frequency of grocery shopping is not a particularly important matter, and movements or interactions even for this one purpose need not follow any regular pattern.

If what the analyst is concerned with is interdependencies (which is what this objective approach to community is concerned with), then one really ends up defining virtually a whole metropolis, a whole province, a whole country, a whole continent, or even the whole world as a single community. There may be merit to this, but it does make this notion of community extremely difficult, if not impossible, to apply in the context of a city. It therefore has little relevance to the structures and processes of urban government.

The most obvious omission in this approach to community is any attention being given to people's attitudes, sentiments, and motivations. Why do they interact the way they do, and are there any political and social consequences of that interaction? This omission has not escaped the attention of such people as Hawley, but he stated that these are omitted not because they are considered to be unimportant but because the assumptions and point of view of this approach are not adapted to their treatment.[24] The point is that people interact with other people not only just to satisfy their daily physical requirements (especially requirements involving economic relationships with which this approach is primarily concerned) but to satisfy needs for friendship, as an example, and for such non-economic reasons as loyalty. Regular interaction may lead to loyalties and friendships, but it may become nothing more than an economic relationship. The inability of the objective approach to community to take into account such things, and its questionable applicability to city life, brings us to the other approach to community.

The subjective approach to the study of community can be said to focus on a sense of "we-feeling", a sense of "belonging", a feeling of common interest—the sort of thing to which Ferdinand Tönnies referred by the word *Gemeinschaft* (which is translated appropriately enough as "community").[25] What is important to note is that this approach is basically a psychological approach—what people feel, rather than how they behave. Tönnies held that the notion of community has three central aspects: blood (kinship), place or land (neighbourhood), and mind (friendship). In other words community is a sense of identification with or caring about other people in some particular geographical area. Identification is a function not only of common residence but of family and friendships. What Tönnies rejected was that relationships for rational economic purposes necessarily lead to people's acquiring a sense of identification or "we-feeling" with each other.

The subjective and objective approaches to the study of community are therefore far apart; the objective approach focuses on patterns of interaction for economic purposes mainly (though not exclusively) and it is sometimes assumed that such interaction is conditioned by or results in mutual identification, while the subjective approach doubts the relevance of such interactive behaviour to the acquiring of a sense of identification. And Tönnies, as an advocate of the latter approach, is particularly concerned with attitudes, sentiments, motivations—just the sort of thing which those who utilize the objective approach do not take into account.

How would one go about locating geographical boundaries of communities in this subjective sense of the word? Here the subjective approach runs into considerable difficulty, for there is a lack of available data as well as lack of agreement on what kinds of indicators of identification one could use. Furthermore, to measure people's sense of belonging or identification with others clearly requires that some kind of interview technique be used, a research technique that is expensive and time-consuming. What measures or indicators one might use are not immediately apparent. A number of attempts have been made (though few in Canada[26]) to study the territorial extent of people's identifications, but these must be viewed as experiments requiring refinement, for many of the attitudinal scales used either do not work well as scales, or assume things that should not be assumed. Probably the most successful experiment is that done for the royal commissions on local government in Scotland and in England, where people were first asked whether there was an area around where they lived to which they could say they "belonged" and where they felt "at home".[27] If they answered in the affirmative (which more than three-quarters of the respondents did), an attempt was made to determine the territorial extent of the "home area". What was found was that most people thought of their home area in very small territorial terms, rarely extending to a whole city for example, although the use of the term "home area" may have compelled people to think in terms of small areas.[28] Almost two-thirds of the English respondents defined their home area in terms that were smaller than a ward, and only one person in twenty defined it in terms equal to or larger than the area of the unit of local government in which they resided. While one can legitimately question whether a researcher would find similar results in Canada's major cities, the likelihood is that urban Canadians would consider themselves belonging to fairly small communities, with areas and populations that are very much less than the entire territory and population of their city.

A major city is highly unlikely to comprise one single complete community, either in the objective sense or in the subjective sense of the word. Not only is a city too big in territory and population but it is too socially diverse to be able to constitute a single community in the subjective sense, and it is probably too small to be a complete community in the objective sense. Non-urban areas tend to be much more socially homogeneous than cities, and on the whole it seems probable that in so far as people do identify with other people, they do so largely with those who are most like themselves in terms of socio-economic class, ethnicity, language, religion, and other such factors. So each city can best be considered a complex of communities in the subjective sense and only part of a community in the objective sense.

The kind of land-use planning that has typified Canada's cities, whereby areas of multiple-family dwellings are usually segregated from areas of single-family dwellings, and where different types of multi-family dwellings are themselves segregated (such as areas for duplexes from areas for large apartment buildings), accounts in part for the social fragmentation of cities. But social fragmentation in areal terms is only partly a consequence of land-use planning; more importantly it is a reflection of a natural desire of people to live in areas where they will feel most comfortable, which is to say areas where others like themselves live. Hence younger middle-class families with small children usually choose to live in suburbs because that is where other families like themselves live, and a new immigrant from the West Indies will probably move to an area where other immigrants from the West Indies live. In other words, strong subjective communities are most likely to be found in small areas that are socially homogeneous.

These few examples should suffice to illustrate the socially fragmented character of cities, and therefore the multiplicity of subjective communities in each such city. The phenomenon is of course most obvious in the three Canadian supercities, but even those at or even under the Census Metropolitan Area criteria of Statistics Canada exhibit social fragmentation to some extent. Major cities tend not only to be somewhat "ghetto-ized", in the sense of areas of residence reflecting social fragmentation, but within any one city there tend to be multiple areas that are socially similar but not geographically contiguous. The importance of this point is that if it is the case that people are most likely to identify with other people who are socially similar to themselves, and that such people tend to cluster in distinctive residential areas, feelings of belonging (community in the subjective sense) may involve not just one area, but multiple areas that are not adjacent to each other, as Figure 5:2 illustrates in a simplified way.

Twelve separate communities are shown, and there are two areas in the city for each of six groups of people identified by socio-economic class and language/ethnicity. For example, working-class people whose main language is English are clustered in areas 10 and 12. What is likely is that people within area 10 would identify well with each other and therefore constitute a community, as would those within area 12. In addition, though, the people in area 10 might be expected to identify with residents of area 12, at least more so than they would with those in any other area, because the people in area 12 are socially close to them even though geographically distant. Therefore one could say that people in areas 10 and 12 *together* could constitute a subjective community, although the geographical distance may result in feelings of identification that are less intense than is the case within either area on its own. Perhaps, then, there are not simply multiple communities within a city, but multiple *levels* of community—high-level communities within areas, and lower-level communities involving sets of socially similar areas.

Given the relatively high physical mobility of city dwellers, coupled with the availability of such means of communication as the telephone, it seems likely that socially similar but geographically distant areas of

Figure 5:2   Socio-economic Spatial Fragmentation of a City

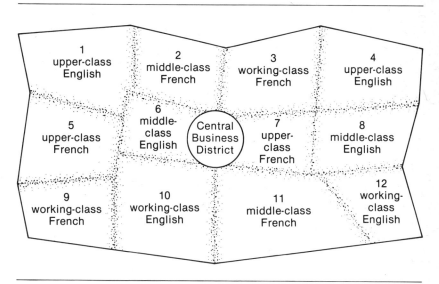

people will not only identify with each other (subjective community), but will interact socially with each other as well (objective community). Such social interaction is less likely to occur between geographically near but socially distant groups. What all of this suggests is that the notion of community in either the objective or subjective senses, with a territorial reference point, may not be very applicable to highly urbanized settings. In this connection, it is worth noting that Warren[29] carefully distinguishes rural community studies from urban community studies, saying that the two are each studied by a different type of sociologist, with a consequent isolation of the two approaches. This dichotomy echoes Hillery's analysis, in which he suggested that ". . . the rural sociologists have somehow been closer [than have urban sociologists] to the actual core of the community concept, and that community is perhaps a phenomenon more easily recognized in rural areas."[30] Perhaps what is closer to the truth is that what they are trying to study is fundamentally different—that urban community is not comparable to non-urban community.

There is no question that urban residents are highly interdependent in terms of satisfying their regular requirements, for no one in the city is completely self-sufficient. It is therefore the case that the web of inter-actions (movements of goods, people, and messages for the satisfaction of regular requirements) is extremely complex. To some extent almost everyone in a city is somehow interdependent, however remotely, with everyone else. It can thus be concluded that people in a city are highly integrated functionally. Theory of integration has perhaps been most highly developed in the context of international relations rather than at the local level, but some analysts and theoreticians have considered that integration theory can be applied in local contexts as well, using trans-action (or interaction) analysis.[31] The functionalist view of integration generally posits that interaction (objective community) leads to identi-fication (subjective community) among those engaged in the interactions, provided that the interactions are frequent enough and involve a wide enough range of purposes or functions. Not all analysts are agreed that interaction is necessarily integrative in the sense of giving rise to feelings of identity and cohesiveness. But the generally accepted assumption is that interactions are, by and large, integrative in this sense even though "familiarity sometimes breeds contempt".

The assumption is neither logically compelling nor supported by much evidence. What logic is there to the idea that people who go through a check-out counter in a supermarket will strike up continuing and socially significant relationships with the cashier or with the other people in line at the counter? This type of interaction/transaction is too mechanical, too specifically economic, to have any important effect on the social and spatial fragmentation of major cities. If it is unlikely to have social consequences, it is even more unlikely to have political consequences. Although social groupings do not necessarily engage in political activity, such activity is to some extent contingent on prior social groupings. Group theory of politics does go some distance in explaining why people become politically active, how they are active, and even the relative success of their activity, even though critics of the theory correctly point out that some political action is more a function of personality than of group associations.[32] The connection between this and the foregoing is that community in the subjective sense is a type of group association, a type which is especially likely to have political significance if the struc-tures and processes of city government are designed to reflect and perhaps buttress prior perceptions people in an area of a city have of "belonging" to that area and to the other people in it.

But it was suggested earlier that any strong perceptions people have of subjective community tend to be confined to very small areas (neighbourhoods) in major cities. Therefore if it is accepted that there is a connection between community and democracy and between democracy and local government, and if it is accepted that institutions and processes of local government should reflect and support perceived communities, then those institutions and processes must themselves become rather fragmented through decentralization within cities. This recalls the notion of neighbourhood government, to which reference was made above.

If perceived communities are generally so small and the size (area and population) of Canada's major cities is so large, then it clearly follows that units of urban local government do not reflect existing communities. They may once have, but since urban local government boundaries have tended to expand and areas of perceived communities are subject to change, any possible connection now between urban units of local government and perceived communities is entirely accidental (with the possible exception of Unicity Winnipeg). Nor does there seem to be any evidence that city boundaries can create perceived communities.

What this section suggests is that people in cities are highly integrated with respect to the web of interactions but that the bulk of those interactions do not progress beyond mere civility or common courtesy to levels of friendship, respect, loyalty—in short, to a sense of belonging or "we-feeling". Hence cities tend to be economic units and to have a degree of unity in their formal structures and processes of government, but are characterized by social fragmentation and a multiplicity of small perceived communities. Since these communities almost never receive formal governmental recognition in cities, their potential for organizing members for participation in city politics is not fulfilled. The politically valuable resource which they most lack is legitimacy in the eyes of elected and appointed city officials. Therefore whatever politically valuable resources members have are dissipated in trying to acquire legitimacy, or those resources must be utilized through other channels of political participation, or the resources are so dispersed that other participants in city politics are able to dominate the decision-making processes and outcomes in the city.

Participation and Influence

It is axiomatic that people in cities are more likely to identify with their city's governmental institutions, political personalities, and processes if or when those institutions, personalities and processes reflect people's perceived spatial communities; that is, if external (and internal) boundaries of municipalities are drawn so as to correspond to boundaries of communities, and altered as community boundaries alter.

The consequences of people's identification with their governmental units seem to be largely self-evident. Such identification is likely to increase knowledge of, interest in, and therefore perhaps also participation in the affairs of governmental units. Such consequences of identification with governmental units are really pre-conditions of democratic government and are therefore normatively valued. Further, when individual members of communities are readily able to identify with their governmental units and to participate in the affairs of those governments, it seems likely that their elected representatives (presuming that the city has representative rather than direct democracy) on council will be more conscious of their responsibility and accountability to their respective electorate, and therefore more responsive to the interests and demands of that electorate. Otherwise, the electorate is likely to assume a collective role at best approximating that of small-scale shareholders in a big corporation who participate (if at all) only in the minimal sense of electing the board of directors and ratifying recommendations from the board. In such circumstances the board (council) members' accountability to them is nominal, a matter of form rather than of fact. To extend the simile, a small proportion of the elector/shareholders who feel they have a particularly strong vested interest in the business of the municipality/corporation can, if they so wish, maximize their personal benefit by dominating and manipulating the municipality/corporation. The point here is that there is an important linkage between the extent to which cities reflect perceived communities and the extent to which they are, or can be, democratic governments—not in terms of nominal and ritualistic participation (epitomized by such exhortations as "Vote for whomever you like, *but vote!*"), but in terms of thoughtful and meaningful participation that tends to be more critical about the status quo. When the latter kind of participation in city affairs is weak or absent, the possibility of city affairs being dominated by minorities is increased.

Dahl and Tufte note the lamentable paucity of evidence on the relationship between size (especially in terms of population) of units of local government and participation, and their lament applies to Canada, for any such relationship has never been systematically explored in this country. They cite data from a study in Sweden begun in 1966, and while one ought not to assume that similar research in Canada would necessarily yield the same results, the study is instructive. It involved thirty-six municipalities of different population sizes and densities. Although the three largest cities, with populations of from 260,000 to 800,000 people, were excluded from the study, some data were available for them too. The thirty-six communes were grouped into three population size categories: those with under 8000 people, those with populations of between 8000 and 30,000, and those with over 30,000 people. As Dahl and Tufte state, "The major finding of the study is that in Sweden the values of *participation and effectiveness are best achieved in densely populated communes with populations under 8,000.*"[33] The trend was strong and consistent—participation was highest in the smallest population category, next highest in the middle range, and lowest in the most populous communes. Membership in organizations, acquaintance with local representatives, knowledge of politics, and frequency of discussion of local problems were all variables connected inversely to population size. It should be noted that this study also indicated that in the smaller, more densely populated communes the elected officials were more representative of characteristics and attitudes of their constituents than was the case in larger communes.[34] These findings tend to be supported by other studies.[35]

The most obvious critical reaction to these findings and their implications is that one cannot depopulate the cities, at least not in a political system where people can live where they wish to live. But what can be done is to look more closely *inside* cities (as the Unicity Winnipeg experiment tried to do) and in effect try to simulate small municipalities. The delineation of ward boundaries and boundaries for deconcentration of city administration can be done in such a way that relatively small numbers of people are included in those boundaries, and that those boundaries reflect perceived communities. To have continuing effect, such an attempt would also require periodic review and probably periodic redrawing of the boundaries since spatial perceptions of community are as likely to change as the population composition in each area is likely to change over time.

In so far as people participate at all in politics, they do so in reaction to political stimuli. But not everyone reacts in the same way to the same political stimuli, and the differences are accounted for by a variety of personality factors. Researchers into political participation are generally agreed that such personal factors as level of interest in politics, level of knowledge about government and politics, and such attitudes as a sense of civic duty and of political efficacy (feeling that political change can be effected and that one is personally able to have some effect on the decision-making process) are important determinants of not only whether a person will participate but how actively a person will participate, how often, and perhaps also with what effect.[36]

The scale of the government unit seems also likely to be related to citizen participation in the decision-making process. Verba argues that the payoff for any individual to participate decreases as the scale of the governmental unit increases, for the amount of contribution one person can make in decisions is likely to be higher when the total number of people (and the number of competitors) involved is small.[37] It should be pointed out, however, that Verba is referring to *successful* participation rather than to any and all participation, for he points out that small-scale governmental units may have effects that impede opportunities to participate.[38] It is possible, for example, that a particular faction so monopolizes the decision-making processes in small-scale governmental units that there are real disincentives for others to even try to participate.

As chapters 6 and 7 explain, participation in urban politics is not merely electoral, either in the sense of contesting a seat on council, or just casting a vote in municipal elections. There are other avenues of participation as well for people, both as individuals and in groups. In particular it is group forms of non-electoral participation that have become such a significant feature of urban politics in Canada recently.

Virtually all elected and appointed city officials affirm their belief in citizen participation, but such officials do not always have in mind the same thing when they use the term. A number of typologies or hierarchies of political participation have been developed.[39] Except for participation through political parties, most such hierarchies are applicable not only to the federal and provincial levels of government but in a general way to urban politics as well. But because of the smaller scale of politics in cities compared to federal and provincial politics, the possibilities, especially for group participation, are greater at the urban level. The Toronto-based Bureau of Municipal Research specified in one study four concepts or levels of participation.[40] From the lowest to the highest level they were termed the information, consultation, partnership, and citizen-control concepts. The first of these involves the objective of creating a better informed electorate but does not promote sharing in decision-making. In the consultation concept, citizens are encouraged not only to obtain information but to comment on issues and to assist in the development of alternative solutions to questions of policy. The partnership concept goes beyond that to the extent that citizens are permitted a share of decision-making power through such mechanisms as planning committees on which groups are directly represented. Finally, the control concept gives citizens controlling influence on the decision-making process so that councillors function mainly as delegates or spokesmen for groups. This last type would seem to be limited in its applicability to small-scale neighbourhood government rather than to major cities as a whole or to senior levels of government.

To participate in politics is to attempt to exercise influence on the structures, personalities, and processes of government in order to produce new decisions, reverse previous decisions, or alter the decision-making processes themselves. But participation is not always successful. In major cities political participants (excluding for the moment elected and appointed public officials) generally encounter opposing participants, and the larger the city the greater the likelihood is of there being competition on any one issue. Aside from the presence or absence of competition, the success of attempts to exercise political influence depends on the amount of politically valuable resources available to the participants, and the value of particular political resources that a participant (individual or group) has can vary depending upon the issue at hand. For example, the number of people that can be mobilized by a group on a non-technical issue may be the deciding factor in that group's success at exerting influence, but on a more technical issue the amount of expertise available to the group may be rather more important than numbers of supporters. We have already seen that cities are not socially homogeneous; instead they are socially heterogeneous and fragmented. Not only are people in cities socially differentiated but they are politically differentiated too, in that resources available to individuals and groups to exert influence in cities are not distributed equally. Some people have more politically valuable resources than do others—wealth, contacts, social standing, legitimacy, time, cohesion of membership, incumbency in a political office, specialized knowledge, and popularity in terms of the numbers of other people they are able to mobilize. Therefore it is unlikely that, in its actual exercise, influence is equally distributed.

Considerable research has been conducted, especially in the United States, into what have become known as "community power structures" (the word "community" in this context is generally used only in the minimal sense of people in places), to attempt to determine who governs in cities. Such studies were particularly popular after the early 1950s, notably the work of Floyd Hunter and Robert Dahl among a number of others.[41]

Basically, there have been two main approaches to the study of community power, and two main kinds of findings. The *positional/reputational* approach (for example, Hunter's study of Atlanta, Georgia) involves compiling a list of people who can be called the top influentials in the city. Such lists are drawn up either by the researcher after looking at which people occupy offices or formal positions that are presumed to have political power (such as the mayor, members of council, and senior civic bureaucrats), or by soliciting names of reputedly influential people from others who are presumed to be knowledgeable about affairs in the city. The conclusion at which studies using this approach almost invariably arrive is that political power is *stratified*, which means that power is not widely distributed but is concentrated and monopolized in the hands of a few people who constitute an *elite*. For example, Hunter's conclusion was that policy-making was done mainly by a fairly small group of economically important people who had close connections with the top-ranking public officials who implemented those policies. The other approach (for example, Dahl's study of New Haven, Connecticut) is the *decisional/immersion* approach, where the researcher or a team of researchers often spends a lengthy period of time in the city to observe the daily life in the area, and more specifically to see who is actually involved in making decisions. What the researcher does is to look at a number of issues that arise and to see who exercises influence on those issues. Here, the researcher does not assume that those who hold formal political office necessarily monopolize political power—non-office holders too may possess political influence. The conclusion generally reached in such studies is that political influence is *pluralized*—no one elite dominates all political decision making but numerous individuals and groups of people have influence, the influence of each person or group being greater on some kinds of decisions than on other issue areas. It is to this phenomenon that Dahl attached the term "dispersed inequalities" of politically valuable resources.[42]

Since there tends to be a strong connection between the research approach used and the conclusions reached regarding the distribution or concentration of political influence in the city, the analysis of community power structures has come in for some heavy and persuasive criticism, for it is thought that the research methodology chosen largely predetermines the findings.[43] The pluralists are faulted for not taking into account the possibility that political power may often be exercised by confining the scope of decision making to relatively safe or non-contentious matters, and for their choice of which decisions or issues to examine (that is, to distinguish between important and unimportant issues). It is argued that political influence may successfully be exercised to persuade decision-makers to drop an issue before it really becomes an issue. The elitists are subject to more serious objections, especially their assumption that there *is* a stratified power structure which they then set about to identify, presuming that the stratified power structure is stable (unchanging over time and according to issue area), and equating reputed political influence with actual political influence. Thus the reputational approach predetermines its elitist conclusions because important offices are by definition few in number, and it is easy to call those few people who occupy those few reputedly influential offices an elite.

The most useful approach to the study of political influence in a city would seem to be one based largely on the decisional/immersion approach but examining a much larger number and broader range of issues than the three or four that Dahl examined, as well as what can be called "non-decisions"; that is, the filtering out of potentially contentious matters from the decision-making process.[44] Such filtering out does seem to characterize decision-making in most Canadian cities, and is worthy of examination. Finally, it seems to be imperative that if one is to be able to generalize from one's findings, those findings must be based not just on one city for one period of time but on multiple cities over an extended period of time. One cannot legitimately assume that city politics in Atlanta, Georgia are (or were) the same as city politics in New Haven, Connecticut, or that politics in St. John's are (or will be) the same as politics in Saskatoon. Even disregarding the tendency of the approach used to predetermine their findings, it is entirely possible that both Dahl and Hunter were correct—that political influence in Atlanta was stratified and monopolized by an elite at the time, whereas in New Haven political influence was pluralized at the time, with different elites being dominant over certain kinds of issues. But we can never know if they were both correct, for each researcher examined only one city.

What is proposed above is of course an impossible research strategy. To embark on a study using the decisional/immersion approach over an extended period of time in even a selection of Canadian cities would require research resources on a scale not available even to royal commissions, let alone to universities or independent researchers. What is important, though, is to be cautious in assuming that what was done and found in one American city can be generalized to apply to other American cities, or to Canadian cities. Further, it is extremely important to get away from the common presumption that political influence is monopolized by those who hold formal governmental office, whether elected or appointed, in Canada's cities.

The body of literature on the structure of community power and influence in Canadian cities is not extensive. The major work in this area of research is Kaplan's study of Metro Toronto, although his concerns and methods were not entirely parallel to those of the community power structure studies in American cities.[45] He examined fifty-five major issues that came before Metro Council in Toronto between 1953 and 1965, looking for the effect that councillors, groups of assorted types, the media, and others had on those issues. Briefly, he found that Metro was elitist in some ways, pluralist in other ways, and had aspects that could not be described in either elitist or pluralist terms.[46] He described Metro Toronto as being an "executive-centred" political system, meaning that the executive committee of the Metro Toronto council dominated the initiation and definition of matters brought before council. Forty-seven of the fifty-five issues were initiated and defined by either the chairman of the Metro Council, Metro department heads, or such bodies as the Toronto Transit Commission.[47] Hence Kaplan's "executive-centred" conclusion:

The most politically influential people in Metro were the appointed and elected officials—in contrast to both the business elite and broker leadership systems. These public officials, moreover, made their decisions in a low-pressure environment. The creation, agitation and resolution of issues occurred within the formal institutions of government. Interaction among public officials was far more significant for the outcome of issues than interaction between officials and private actors. The Metro councilor, far from viewing himself as an interest group spokesman or as a mediator of group demands, often seemed unaware of what the groups wanted in particular cases.[48]

In other words, Kaplan found that in so far as there was a dominant elite, that elite was composed of elected and appointed officials of Metro itself. Lest one assume from this that no other groups were ever involved, it should be pointed out that other groups were occasionally but selectively involved, depending on the nature of particular issues, rather than across the spectrum of issues, and that their involvement was infrequently decisive. Among the number of reasons that Kaplan cited as depressing group involvement in Metro was the fact that most issues that directly affected grass-roots groups were dealt with by the councils of the member municipalities of Metro Toronto rather than by Metro Council itself. Several points emerge from this. First, Kaplan dealt with only one part of the decision-making apparatus in only one city. Hence the question of the extent to which his findings have applicability to lower-tier municipalities and to cities other than Toronto cannot be answered. Second, his analysis pre-dated the reorganization of Metro Toronto in 1967, when not only were the number of member municipalities consolidated from thirteen to six, but the powers and functions of the upper tier were increased to include welfare. This change of scale may have had subsequent effects on the exercise of political influence. Therefore, were his study to be replicated in Metro Toronto now, his conclusions could be somewhat different, even though Kaplan speculated that "These reforms are not likely to change any basic features of the executive-directed system".[49] Finally, Kaplan's analysis largely pre-dates a shift in the nature and activities of group actors in city politics, as well as the phenomenon of "reform" blocs of councillors that, at least in public, commit themselves to being the spokesmen of the new advocacy groups. It is with such developments that the remaining chapters are concerned.

NOTES

1. Roscoe C. Martin, *Grass Roots*, 2nd ed. (New York: Harper and Row, 1965), pp. 1–20.
2. Saul Alinsky, *Rules for Radicals: A Practical Primer for Realistic Radicals* (New York: Random House, 1971).
3. Milton Kotler, *Neighborhood Government: The Local Foundations of Political Life* (Indianapolis: Bobbs-Merrill, 1969).
4. Ontario, Committee on Taxation *Report*, 3 volumes (Toronto: Queen's Printer, 1967), Volume II, p. 503.
5. Ibid., pp. 503–04.
6. Ibid.
7. See Donald J. H. Higgins, "Community and Local Government: Boundary Determination" (unpublished PHD thesis, Carleton University, Ottawa, 1973), Part Two.
8. Manitoba, *Proposals for Urban Reorganization in the Greater Winnipeg Area* (Winnipeg, September, 1970), p. 2.
9. Ibid., p. 7, quoting Great Britain, Royal Commission on Local Government in England *Report*, 3 volumes (London: Her Majesty's Stationery Office, 1969), Volume I, p. 5.
10. These definitions are derived from Henry Maddick, *Democracy, Decentralization and Development* (Bombay: Asia Publishing House, 1963), p. 23.
11. A similar proposal is made by William Hampton, "Local Government and Community," *The Political Quarterly*, vol. 40, no. 2 (April-June, 1969), pp. 151–62.
12. See for example Kotler, *Neighborhood Government: The Local Foundations of Political Life*; and Joseph Zimmerman, "Community Building in Larger Cities," in L. Axworthy and James M. Gillies, eds., *The City: Canada's Prospects, Canada's Problems* (Toronto: Butterworths, 1973), pp. 267–75.
13. Zimmerman, "Community Building in Larger Cities," p. 274.
14. Georges Langrod, "Local Government and Democracy," *Public Administration*, vol. XXXI (Spring, 1953), pp. 25–33.
15. William Hampton, *Democracy and Community: A Study of Politics in Sheffield* (London: Oxford University Press, 1970), especially Chapter 1.
16. Robert A. Dahl, *After the Revolution? Authority in the Good Society* (New Haven: Yale University Press, 1970). See also his article "The City in the Future of Democracy," *American Political Science Review*, vol. LXI, no. 4 (December, 1967), pp. 53–70.
17. Robert A. Dahl and Edward R. Tufte, *Size and Democracy* (Stanford: Stanford University Press, 1973).
18. See for example, Alexis de Tocqueville, *Democracy in America* (New York: Vintage Books, 1963), Volume I, Chapter 5.
19. George A. Hillery, "Definitions of Community: Areas of Agreement," *Rural Sociology*, vol. 20 (March, 1955), pp. 111–23. For a consideration of concepts of community see Donald J. H. Higgins, "Community and Local Government: Boundary Determination," Part One.
20. Examples of this approach are the work of Amos Hawley, *Human Ecology: A Theory of Community Structure* (New York: Ronald Press, 1950); Robert E. Park, *Human Communities* (New York: Free Press, 1950); and R. D. McKenzie, *On Human Ecology* (Chicago: University of Chicago Press, 1968).
21. Charles Galpin, *The Social Anatomy of an Agricultural Community*, Research Bulletin 34 (Madison: University of Wisconsin Agricultural Experiment Station, 1915).
22. Hawley, *Human Ecology: A Theory of Community Structure*, p. 246.
23. Ibid., p. 46.
24. Ibid., p. 180.

25. Ferdinand Tönnies, *Community and Association*, trans. C. P. Loomis (London: Routledge and Kegan Paul, 1955).

26. The two main attempts that were sponsored by governments are Earl Berger Limited, *Local Orientation and Identification Study*, 3 volumes (Toronto: Department of Municipal Affairs, 1971)—a study done preparatory to the introduction of regional government in Haldimand and Norfolk counties in Ontario; and Newfoundland, Royal Commission on Municipal Government in Newfoundland and Labrador *Report* (St. John's, 1974), Chapter 4 (the aggregate results of the Citizen Attitude Survey were published separately as Appendix F to the Report). See also Higgins, "Community and Local Government: Boundary Determination", Part Three.

27. Great Britain, Royal Commission on Local Government in Scotland, *Research Studies 2: Community Survey: Scotland* (Edinburgh: Her Majesty's Stationery Office, 1969); and Royal Commission on Local Government in England, *Research Studies 9: Community Attitudes Survey: England* (London: Her Majesty's Stationery Office, 1969).

28. This point is also made by Hampton, *Democracy and Community: A Study of Politics in Sheffield*, p. 100. He conducted a study in Sheffield replicating the larger study by the Royal Commission on Local Government in England and found (p. 106) that the size of this "home area" perceived by his respondents was even smaller than the larger survey found.

29. Roland L. Warren, *The Community in America*, 2nd ed. (Chicago: Rand McNally, 1972), p. 25.

30. Hillery, "Definitions of Community: Areas of Agreement," p. 119.

31. See, for example, the articles by Toscano and Wheaton in Philip E. Jacob and James V. Toscano, eds., *The Integration of Political Com-munities* (Philadelphia: Lippincott, 1964), pp. 98–142.

32. Classic formulations of group theory of politics are Earl Latham, *The Group Basis of Politics: A Study in Basing-Point Legislation* (New York: Octagon Books, 1965); Arthur F. Bentley, *The Process of Government*, ed. Peter H. Odegard (Cambridge: The Belknap Press of Harvard University, 1967); and D. B. Truman, *The Governmental Process* (New York: Knopf, 1951).

33. Dahl and Tufte, *Size and Democracy*, p. 63 (emphasis their's).

34. Ibid., pp. 64 and 84–6.

35. See, for example, M. Cohen, "Community Size and Participation by Lawyers in Community Politics," *Journal of Politics*, vol. 31, no. 4 (November, 1969), p. 1109. By "participation" Cohen means holding or ever having held elective or appointive public office.

36. See, for example, Lester W. Milbrath, *Political Participation: How and Why do People Get Involved in Politics?* (Chicago: Rand McNally, 1965). See also Ada W. Finifter and Paul R. Abramson, "City Size and Feelings of Political Competence", *Public Opinion Quarterly*, vol. XXXIX, no. 2 (Summer, 1975), pp. 189–98.

37. Sidney Verba, "Democratic Participation," in Bertram M. Gross, ed., *Social Intelligence for America's Future* (Boston: Allyn and Bacon, 1969), p. 153.

38. Ibid., p. 154.

39. For example see Richard J. Van Loon and Michael S. Whittington, *The Canadian Political System: Environment, Structure and Process*, 2nd ed. (Toronto: McGraw-Hill Ryerson, 1976), pp. 108–09.

40. Bureau of Municipal Research, *Citizen Participation in Metro Toronto: Climate for Cooperation?* (Toronto: Bureau of Municipal Research, 1975), p. 46.

41. Floyd Hunter, *Community Power Structure: A Study of Decision Makers* (Chapel Hill: University of

North Carolina Press, 1953); and Robert A. Dahl, *Who Governs? Democracy and Power in an American City* (New Haven: Yale University Press, 1961). For an extensive bibliography of such studies see Nelson W. Polsby, "Community: The Study of Community Power," in *International Encyclopaedia of the Social Sciences* (New York: Macmillan and the Free Press, 1968), Volume 3, pp. 157–63. See also Nelson W. Polsby, *Community Power and Political Theory* (New Haven: Yale University Press, 1963).

42. Dahl, *Who Governs? Democracy and Power in an American City*, p. 85.

43. See especially Peter Bachrach and Morton Baratz, "Two Faces of Power," *American Political Science Review*, vol. 56 (1962), pp. 947–52.

44. A more recent and particularly interesting study that used a combination of approaches is Hampton, *Democracy and Community: A Study of Politics in Sheffield*.

45. Harold Kaplan, *Urban Political Systems: A Functional Analysis of Metro Toronto* (New York: Columbia University Press, 1967), especially chapters 6 and 7. Some other published Canadian studies relating to community power structure include: William D. Knill, "Community Decision-Making in Education," *The Canadian Administrator*, vol. VI (February, 1967), pp. 29–32; and Neville O. Matthews, "Decision-Making in Two Alberta School Boards," in Lionel D. Feldman and Michael D. Goldrick, eds., *Politics and Government of Urban Canada: Selected Readings*, 2nd ed. (Toronto: Methuen, 1972), pp. 112–31. See also John B. Hawley, "Comparative Study of Four Community Councils in Rural Saskatchewan," *International Journal of Comparative Sociology*, vol. 9, no. 2 (June, 1968), pp. 121–9.

46. Kaplan, ibid., p. 31.

47. Ibid., pp. 65–6.

48. Ibid., pp. 157–8.

49. Ibid., p. 262.

Participation in Urban Politics:

6

Group Actors

Urbanization results in more people living in more and bigger cities, increases the heterogeneity of the population within cities, magnifies the tendency of people to segregate themselves into areas that are socially similar, and produces a broader range of problems. One might expect that each of these factors would increase participation in city politics, for there are more potential participants and more things to stimulate them to participate. On the other hand, each of these factors can impede participation—more people mean more (and perhaps) better competition so that people feel like very small cogs in a very big machine; increasing heterogeneity produces a wider variety of viewpoints on issues, a variety that can make it difficult to reach acceptable compromises so that people see their participation as having little worthwhile payoff; areal or social segregation increases the difficulty of wide-scale organization for political action; and the broadening range of problems can seem so daunting that political action seems pointless.

Defining participation as attempts of people as individuals or in groups to exercise influence on outputs of the decision-making process or on the process itself, the level of citizen participation in city politics has generally been considered to be low compared to participation in provincial and federal politics. Election turnout is the indicator most often cited, which does show comparatively low participation in municipal politics (see the next chapter on electoral participation). The same conclusion can be reached by examining such other forms of electoral participation as degree of competition in municipal elections. A number of reasons besides those associated with the process of urbanization can be cited as possible explanations for the comparatively low level of electoral participation (both by citizens as individuals and citizens in groups) in city politics. One reason suggested in the previous chapter and pursued below is that there is a linkage between participation and perceptions of community, but a lack of linkage between city boundaries and community boundaries.

Other possible reasons relate to the structures of decision making in municipalities, such as the fact that so many of Canada's smaller cities (and a few of the larger ones too) have a council/city manager structure, patterned on that of business corporations. This tends to de-politicize civic affairs and thus probably tends to make city politics less stimulating and less interesting to many people than provincial or federal politics. As a consequence the citizenry is less motivated to take much of an active input role in city affairs. Another structural aspect often thought to have a bearing on citizen participation in city elections is the timing of those elections. Typically they are held in the late fall or early winter, times when the weather is likely to be inclement and a possible deterrent to a high turnout of voters. The predilection of many municipal councils to hive off some of their functions onto semi-autonomous *ad hoc* bodies and committees, and to hold council meetings "in camera" are other structural features that may depress citizen participation. Since these tend to deal with municipal matters outside the glare of publicity, the citizenry remain less informed than they could be, and level of information is one determinant of participation. Another factor that should not be treated lightly is to be found in the size of city councils. As noted before, the tradition in Canada has been one of small councils, with a consequently high ratio of citizens to elected councillors. Hence the points and avenues of access available for the citizenry to introduce inputs to the city's decision-making process are fewer than they could be.

Another important structural explanation can be found in the kinds of powers and functions in which cities are involved compared to those of the provincial and federal governments. Municipalities in Canada have traditionally been typed as performing functions and providing services of a different class than those of other governments, the municipalities being largely concerned with non-controversial "house-keeping" roles to a much greater extent than senior governments. No one argues that pot-holes in city streets should not be filled or that garbage should not be collected. Nor are such matters, though close to home, of high salience (perceived prominence or importance) to the citizenry, and participation certainly can be connected to level of salience. A useful distinction can therefore be made between *decisions* and *policies*, the former being applicable to house-keeping matters of relatively immediate importance and, basically, of non-conflictive common sense. In contrast, policies affect the longer term and involve questions of judgment, preference, and perhaps ideological orientation. As such, policy issues are divisive and controversial. While it is obviously the case that the federal and provincial governments have always been involved to some extent in making decisions and that cities have always been involved to some extent in making policies, it is true that cities have traditionally been preoccupied with powers and functions that are more of the decision type than of the policy type. Because they are less controversial and generate less conflict and cleavage than policies, decisions are less likely to stimulate the citizenry into political action.

The level of participation engaged in by citizens as individuals or in groups is affected not only by structural and urbanization features. To participate or not, or to participate more or less actively and more or less frequently in city politics is also a function of the dominant norms, values, and beliefs of society. In political systems that are identified as democratic, citizen participation in the governmental process is valued, encouraged, and considered essential to maintenance of the democracy. To encourage citizen participation, assorted measures are taken such as extending the franchise to a large proportion of the citizenry, permitting open and free competition, minimizing the costs required to participate, and so on. Without getting enmeshed here in definitional problems of "democracy", it can be taken as fact that Canadians perceive the political system as largely democratic, and it can therefore be assumed that one of the values of the Canadian political culture is participation in the governmental process, at whatever level. At the municipal level, though, citizen participation does seem to be less valued than it is at other levels of government, at least in terms of electoral participation. For example, the franchise for municipal elections has traditionally been more restricted than at the other two levels of government, and in many municipalities only owners of property are allowed to vote on money by-law plebiscites. The subject of franchise is pursued in the following chapter. It is sufficient to note here the fact that in a large proportion of Canada's cities the vote for election of councillors has been at one time or another limited to people who have been able to meet some sort of property qualification, which effectively disenfranchises all non-owners of property. All of Canada's major cities have now abolished property qualifications for voters and for candidates in city elections, but there are places in Canada that retain a provision whereby property owners who are not residents of the city can vote. A residence qualification (often one year) is commonly required for city elections. Another aspect of the societal context is what Kaplan found in Metro Toronto to be an attitude of deference toward leadership and authority, an attitude not supportive of intense participation.[1] Long-term residence in a city, especially when coupled with ownership of substantial property, is sometimes viewed as endowing members of "old families" with a degree of authority to which deference is due in the eyes of working-class people and members of minority ethnic groups. In consequence, they have not tended until recently to be very active politically.

In addition to effects of urbanization, the structure of decision making, and societal norms and values, participation is a function of personal attitudes and characteristics. The degree to which individuals are informed about city affairs, the salience of city affairs relative to other concerns in the minds of individuals, people's sense of political competence/efficacy, and of course their level of interest in city affairs are all personal factors that help determine whether a person will participate or not. They also help determine at what level and with what degree of intensity they will participate. A national survey conducted in 1965 offered some indication of the relative salience of our three levels of government. People were asked which election (local, provincial, or national) they would consider more important if they were not able to vote in all elections. Thirty-four per cent of the respondents replied that national elections were most important, 18 per cent said provincial elections were most important, and only 7 per cent singled out local elections as most important (31 per cent

Table 6:1 Perceived Importance of Civic Government and Other Government (%)

government	very important	somewhat important	not very important	no answer
provincial	73	21	2	4
federal	80	14	3	3
city (Calgary)	56	32	8	4
U.S.A.	46	22	27	5

replied that all three were equally important).[2] In a study in Calgary in 1972 respondents were asked how important they thought their civic government was for themselves and their interests compared to the other two levels of government and compared to the government of the United States.[3] (See Table 6:1.)

Woods also asked people to compare the interest they took in various kinds of news, and found that news about civic affairs was said by 28 per cent of those responding to be "very interesting", compared to 46 per cent for national news, 54 per cent for international news, and 27 per cent for news about provincial affairs. If the Calgary findings are at all representative of the situation in other Canadian cities, the place of city affairs in the minds of citizens is comparatively low.

People participate politically (if at all) either as individual citizens or in groups. Some aspects of individual participation are examined in the following chapter; the rest of this chapter is concerned with group actors in city politics, except for political parties which constitute a special kind of group and are considered in Chapter 7. Of concern here are *organized* groups which are exclusively or frequently involved with city politics, such as some corporations, the media, community associations, and chambers of commerce.

Since the middle 1960s, the relative tranquillity of city politics has been shattered, or at least dented, for the past decade has borne witness to what in some Canadian cities amounts almost to a wave of group activism. Whether this wave will be sustained or not cannot be predicted, but there are some signs of it waning in those cities (such as Toronto) where it hit earliest. The phenomenon of group participation in city politics is not new in Canada. For at least five decades some kinds of organized groups have been at least sporadically active in city politics but there are some new dimensions to the phenomenon, most notably its magnitude.

What factors seem to account for the recent upsurge of group activism in city politics? In addition to aspects of urbanization noted earlier, it is possible again to categorize factors into those related to structures, to societal values and beliefs, and to personal attitudes and characteristics.

The tendency for people to segregate themselves socially into identifiable areas is most obvious in the largest cities, where the wave of group activism was first manifest. As clusters of socially similar people grow in size, the people therein can be expected to become increasingly aware of common problems, needs, and desires, and of the fact that if they organize themselves they may be able to exercise political influence in the city. Nothing can be better calculated to produce group activism, as a protective reaction, than proposals to construct a new major roadway, for example, in a city. Vancouver's Chinatown freeway, Ottawa's Vanier arterial, Toronto's Spadina expressway, Halifax's Harbour Drive—virtually all such proposals stimulate group activism.[4]

It seems more than merely coincidental that the widespread emergence of organized groups active in Canadian city politics corresponds in time to the period of widespread municipal reorganization. The governmental structures were changing, often in quite fundamental ways, and that structural change may be related to the new wave of active citizen groups. Metro Toronto was reorganized in 1967, Montreal in 1960 and again in 1970, Ottawa in 1969, Winnipeg in 1960 and again in 1971, and regional district government came to Vancouver in 1967. Whether structural changes were a cause or were a consequence of increased activity by organized citizen groups cannot really be determined, but the two phenomena seem to be related.

An important aspect of changes in municipal structures relates to the fact that in relatively recent times there has been a detectable trend in which municipal decision-making powers and functions have been transformed into policy-making powers and functions. For example, maintenance and construction of city streets has been transformed from a matter of non-controversial decision making to a policy-making matter intimately connected to public transportation. People in cities do not usually argue among themselves about the desirability of maintaining existing streets, but they can and do argue about public transportation (versus the private automobile), so street decisions have tended to become expanded into questions of transportation policy involving long-term consequences for the nature of the city. Much the same can be said of sewage disposal—people do not argue that sewage should be collected and treated, but they do argue about physical environmental policy, involving questions of economics and jobs versus the ecology of the city. Zoning too has ceased to be mainly a decision-making matter, instead being broadened into land-use planning policy. Hence, even within their relatively restricted powers and functions, Canada's cities have quite recently become frequently and intensely involved in longer-term matters of policy—public housing, transportation, development and urban renewal, environmental control, etc.

Such issues can arouse and impassion people, and this seems a particularly important reason accounting for heightened interest in city politics, new avenues of participation, and new kinds of actors in city politics. In short, the old stereotype of municipalities being mainly decision-making, non-political managers is rapidly being eroded, the cities becoming the loci of heated political debate based on conflicting competitive views (that sometimes take on ideological stances) over the purpose, nature, and form of cities. The structural changes in terms of municipal reorganization, and probably more importantly in terms of the shift toward controversial policy-making, have had the effect of heightening the perceived salience of city affairs.

The 1968 federal election campaign, with Pierre Trudeau's popularization of the slogan "participatory democracy", can be assumed to have some relation to politics at the city level, and this is an additional factor that can therefore account in some measure for the wave of group activism in city politics. The term "participatory democracy" is more value-laden than the term "public participation", and may therefore have awakened or strengthened not only people's sense of civic duty or obligation to participate in city politics but their awareness of the possible payoffs that can sometimes be gained by participation. Even if the specific outcomes desired are not achieved, people may see a payoff in their participation in the sense that promoters of projects will proceed more cautiously next time. Perhaps this also indicates a diminished level of deference to authority and leadership than Kaplan thought was the case in Toronto up to 1967.

Several typologies of citizen group actors in Canadian urban politics have been constructed. Betts, for example, says that such groups may be classified by the functions they perform, and identifies several types such as neighbourhood groups, ratepayer groups, welfare groups, urban renewal groups, low-income groups, and education groups.[5] The Bureau of Municipal Research developed a classification less of groups than of the methods or techniques of participation, such as use of task forces, plebiscites, working committees, public meetings, and so on.[6] Organized groups in city politics can also be differentiated according to the size of the area in which they are organized, such as Kaplan's distinction between neighbourhood groups and region-wide (or general-purpose) groups.[7]

For the present purposes it is useful to categorize group actors in urban politics according to this classification:

1) "official" groups
   a. the usual type
   b. Unicity Winnipeg
2) citizen associations
   a. the old style
   b. the new style
3) non-corporate specific-interest groups
4) corporate groups
5) the media of mass communication
   a. the "establishment" media
   b. the "alternate" media
6) parties
   a. civic parties
   b. local branches of the major national/provincial parties

The "party" category is dealt with in Chapter 7.

These various kinds of groups tend to differ according to the way in which they act as participants in city politics. As explained below, some groups such as ratepayer associations and the "establishment" media tend to behave in a largely protective/reactive way, while such other groups as community associations and corporate groups tend to behave more as initiators/advocates. All group actors in city politics to some extent take positions in response or in reaction to decisions and proposals from city hall, these responses typically being protective of the group actor's perceived interests. All group actors also respond to some extent to decisions and proposals made by other groups, the responses again tending to be protective. Reactions normally are directed toward the city's decision-making apparatus. For example, a residents' association will almost certainly respond to a decision or proposal of the city to rezone land from residential to industrial or commercial purposes in their neighbourhood, and the response will be based on the interest of the group in protecting the existing character of the neighbourhood. Similarly, a residents' group will react to a decision or proposal of a land developer to erect a large complex in the neighbourhood (such as the Quinpool Road case in

Halifax)[8] and again the response is likely to be a protective one directed more toward city hall than to the initiator of the scheme. While all group actors in urban politics will at times behave in a protective/reactive way (some group actors may behave only in that fashion), some groups are active on what could be termed a second level of participation too. By this it is meant that the group actor takes initiatives in proposing or advocating a course of action that necessitates some involvement by city hall. Examples include advocating a development plan for an area, provision of recreational facilities, banning of through traffic in an area, and upgrading public transportation facilities and services. In the discussion that follows it is also useful to consider the techniques of participation that are likely to be used, for the various categories of group actors differ in this regard. Those techniques are to some extent contingent on variations in the resources available to the particular group actor.

"Official" Group Actors

THE USUAL TYPE

Some group actors are institutionalized, which means that they have some official designation, some formal recognition as adjuncts of the decision-making structure of the city. The kinds of groups included in this category are boards, committees, and commissions—special-purpose bodies of the sort described in Chapter 3 that are officially connected to city councils. The members of such groups are not publicly elected and may not possess formal office within the city administrative structure. Occasionally members of such groups are nominated by other group actors such as chambers of commerce.

As Wichern notes, such actors are the most common form of citizen participation in cities, though the most neglected in the literature.[9] Although there is little data available on the extent of such participation, he estimates that between 25,000 and 50,000 Canadians are involved in this way. Virtually all cities have several such bodies that have an advisory function, and some such group actors are endowed by the city with specific and limited delegated power. Examples are city task forces to investigate particular issues; advisory committees on recreation and planning; and boards dealing with hospitals, cultural and sports facilities, libraries, tourist promotion, and civic festivals. Often the membership of such groups is a mixture of appointed private citizens and elected or appointed officials of the city. In Nova Scotia, for example, boards of education are composed of some municipal councillors plus some private individuals appointed to sit as members on the board.

On the whole, this category of group actors tends to be largely reactive and deals with matters referred to it for investigation or advice by city council. Somewhat less frequently are these advisory boards and committees active in the sense of advocating action to be taken by council. They tend not to be particularly visible to the public, and this reflects the fact that controversy seldom surrounds official advisory groups. They constitute adjuncts of the decision-making "establishment", and an examination of the kinds of people who are selected by city councils for membership on this kind of group would no doubt bear out the generalization that the citizen members too are "establishment". They tend to be chosen not on the basis of a reputation for political activism but for their technical or professional expertise in the subject matter, or because they are nominated by other group actors.

The methods of participation employed by this kind of group follow from their official status, which gives them ready access to the formal decision-makers of the city. Submission of reports to council and personal contact with councillors and/or appointed officials in city hall are the two techniques most likely to be used. Because of their official status, which is a particularly valuable political resource, they have little or no need to employ such tactics as the circulation of petitions, seeking publicity, making deputations, holding demonstrations, or generally trying to mobilize the public. Their other main political resource is the group's expertise and the associated information which is available to the group, supplemented with information from the city administration. All these factors tend to make this the most successful type of group actor in urban politics, successful in the sense of having inputs translated directly and expeditiously into decision outcomes.

UNICITY WINNIPEG

Passing reference was made earlier to the resident advisory groups (RAGS) that were first created when Winnipeg was municipally reorganized in 1971.[10] The RAGs were intended to constitute an important aspect of the

Unicity Winnipeg experiment. They were to be associated with the community committees (originally thirteen of them, reduced to twelve in 1974, each of which is composed of between three and six members of city council), and were institutionalized by provision being made for them in the City of Winnipeg Act by which the Manitoba government reorganized municipal government in the Winnipeg area.

The official function of the RAGs was to be an advisory one, and to generally "assist" the respective community committee, but the legislation specified little else. The number of advisors to be elected and the method of electing them was to be determined by a meeting of residents of the area, and that meeting was also to elect the advisors from among those residents in attendance. A provision by which elected advisors would be subject to recall at any time by residents present at a community conference was also written into the Act.

The innovation was initially greeted with considerable interest and enthusiasm by residents in Winnipeg as well as by some analysts.[11] The turnout of residents at some of the initial meetings was impressive, with attendance approaching five hundred residents at the initial meeting of the St. Boniface community conference. Almost five hundred advisors in all were elected at the initial meetings for the thirteen RAGs, the number of advisors in each group ranging from twelve to 146. The election of advisors was based on wards within each community committee. In some RAGs everyone who was interested was elected as an advisor while in others the number of people who could be elected was limited. The Act was also silent with regard to the way that RAGs organized themselves. Most formed a number of sub-committees dealing with particular areas of civic administration.

Initially, many RAGs went beyond simply reacting and responding to matters referred to them by city council through the community committee, so that they were actively involved in initiating action, such as neighbourhood development plans. However the RAGs have become inundated with a torrent of matters referred to them for a response, often including highly complex and detailed matters to which responses have had to be made quickly with insufficient time to enable making the best responses possible. Hence little time has been left to the RAGs to engage in the second level of participation and as a consequence they have tended to become more reactive and protective than before.

With regard to techniques of exercising influence, the Resident Advisory Groups are in direct contact with their respective community committee. However, the community committees are composed of between only three and six of the fifty-one members of city council; therefore each RAG is limited in its ability to influence city council as a whole. Nor can they necessarily count on the support of even those few councillors on their community committee, for there is a good deal of scepticism and ambivalence in the attitudes of city councillors toward the RAGS and toward citizen participation in general. During the transition period of Unicity, before the administration of the city became almost totally centralized, the Resident Advisory Groups were in a position to deal directly with some appointed city personnel. However, centralization diminished the possibilities of direct contact with appointed personnel. In any case, senior administrators of the city have been generally indifferent and sometimes hostile to these groups.

The techniques of participation are of course highly dependent on the resources available to the RAGS.[12] They do not have any more or less permanent staff of their own, although some have occasionally succeeded in getting Local Initiative Program (LIP) grants and the like which have enabled them to hire staff occasionally but temporarily. An attempt begun in late 1972 to get a grant of $230,000 from the federal Ministry of State for Urban Affairs to enable an association of the RAGS to engage personnel and to conduct research has been held up for years by the city council. Hence the groups have not had the resources to hire professional staff that could help them deal adequately and quickly with matters to which they are expected to respond. By and large they have been left to rely on their own devices. Such was the initial interest and enthusiasm for the RAGS that some were able to attract residents unusually well qualified to comment on technical matters, but again constraints of time have been important. A few have been successful in getting assistance from various service agencies, but the shortage of funds has restricted their ability to conduct research and to publicize their actions. As a consequence the reputation of the Resident Advisory Groups has suffered because they have lacked the time, personnel, and money required to present well-substantiated positions.

Whether the resident advisory groups have been a successful innovation is open to interpretation. Their primary purpose was to increase citizen involvement in city politics in Winnipeg, and in this sense they can be considered a success. However, some 80 per cent of the resident advisors were found to have been involved in community affairs prior to creation of the RAGS[13] so it can be maintained that most of those who are involved would have been involved anyway because they are activists. Also, the number of people involved as advisors has diminished somewhat over time. In terms of being able to exercise effective influence on both elected councillors and appointed city administrators, RAGS' success is somewhat qualified. Although there are exceptions, some councillors and senior appointed personnel view them with indifference or as a nuisance. City council has taken actions that were opposed by the RAGS, and some groups have been beset by internal dissension over such basic matters as who should be members. Several of them have membership limited only to those people who are eligible to vote, and others have made non-owners of property unwelcome as members even though the City of Winnipeg Act made no such distinctions. The turnover of membership in the RAGS has been high and turnout at meetings has been sporadic. As a consequence there are problems of maintaining the momentum of some RAGS. It has been calculated that only about 14 per cent of the resident advisors in 1975 had been resident advisors in 1972.[14] While the high turnover can be interpreted as indicating that large numbers of people have been involved in the groups at one time or another, the turnover can also be interpreted as an indication of some disillusionment and dissatisfaction with them as a vehicle for citizen participation.

Many of the problems faced by RAGS stem from problems faced by the community committees, for the formal function of the Resident Advisory Groups is to "advise" and "assist" the committees. RAGS themselves can be faulted for becoming overly formal and for displaying a lack of initiative, but an important problem lies in the fact that the community committees really have a very modest formal role in Winnipeg's governmental structures. As noted in Chapter 4, the committees were to be not only a channel of communication between city council and the public, but by virtue of the act by which the provincial government reorganized Winnipeg they were to be responsible for supervising the delivery of local services. The word "supervise" presented problems of interpretation and was changed in 1972 to the phrase "to watch, observe, and make qualitative assessment" of the delivery of local services. In other words the community committees were divested of any administrative functions. As a result the Resident Advisory Groups lack a substantial and clearly defined role in the overall structure of Winnipeg's government.

Citizen Associations[15]

There are two basic types of citizen associations, the differences between them lying most obviously in the times of their origination. The terms "old" and "new" style are not intended to imply that the "old" are no longer with us, or even that they are necessarily dying out. They *are* still with us, but their roots are much more historical than those of the "new" style.

THE OLD STYLE

Ratepayer associations are the more historically rooted version of citizen associations, having developed at least as far back as the early part of this century in many municipalities, both large and small, in Canada. The emergence of this type of group actor in urban politics and government corresponds roughly in time to two other developments, and while these developments do not constitute a total explanation of why ratepayer groups did arise, some causal significance can be attached to them.

As is explained in more detail in Chapter 7, the process of democratization of municipal government in Canada, in terms of extension of the vote and easing of qualifications which candidates for office are required to meet, is still under way, but had begun to accelerate after the turn of the century. What the process of democratization does is to weaken the domination over city politics by those wealthier people who are owners of property in the city. The property qualifications attached to the franchise and to candidature had ensured that city politics would not be dominated by property-less masses who would (it was thought) conduct city affairs in a spendthrift manner. Bearing in mind that the bulk of municipal revenue has always been derived from taxation of property in the municipality, it is not beyond reason to expect that those who were substantial owners of property would be concerned about their financial interests as the process of democratization permitted greater participation in municipal affairs by those who were not owners of property. In this sense, therefore, the emergence of associations of ratepayers (that is, those who pay municipal taxes directly on property that they own) can be interpreted as a defensive reaction to protect and further the members' vested interests.

The municipal reform movement in the United States, especially in the 1890s, is the second development. The movement was a reaction to municipal corruption, "bossism", political machines, and mismanagement in the United States, and the movement spilled over into Canada even though few Canadian municipalities were then or even later experiencing the evils of a magnitude at all like that of American cities. The origins of the city manager structure of decision making in Canada have already been attributed in part to that imported reform movement. Ratepayer associations can also be linked to that movement which postulated "good government", the application of business-like principles (presumably including financial caution, if not austerity) to municipal affairs, and the notion that progress is best measured by growth. Thus ratepayer associations can be considered to have been an integral part of that reform movement.

Ratepayer associations were and continue to be primarily protective/reactive groups, but they do sometimes function as advocacy groups that initiate proposals and actions, particularly schemes to promote growth of the city. As Kaplan wrote, ratepayer associations ". . . were designed to protect the homeowner from skyrocketing municipal taxes, to defend the neighborhood from re-zoning and unwelcome intrusions, and to secure more services and improvement projects for the neighborhood."[16]

Kaplan, among others, tends to deal with ratepayer associations as a type of neighbourhood group. While in general he is probably correct in positing that they now tend to have a neighbourhood areal focus, many of them are organized on a larger geographical basis, and in earlier times they were usually organized on a city-wide basis. Their basic unifying interest was with regard to property taxation and financial management, but this interest cannot easily be narrowed down to geographical sections because it applies to *all* sections of the city. Hence, the organizational basis of ratepayer groups is one criterion that can be used to distinguish them from the newer style of citizen associations.

With regard to political resources, ratepayer associations have traditionally been in an advantageous position. Being propertied, the membership tended to be able to make political use of their economic power.

Those who were elected to council were themselves property owners because of required qualifications for office, and thus there was a sort of communion of interest between the associations and councillors. Hence the need to use such tactics as demonstrations, petitions, deputations, publicity, and so on (what can be called pressure tactics) was minimal, especially in light of a comparative absence of competing groups. Personal contact with one's business colleagues on council, or neighbours on council, or friends on council, or relatives on council, probably sufficed in most cases. The associations could also count on support, if needed, from the corporate interests with which they had connections. Also, the fact that ratepayer associations minimized an advocative or initiating role meant that the political resources they possessed could be expended sparingly. On the whole it is safe to say that they have been effective and successful as group actors in city affairs. But their success may be more historical than current, in part because the process of democratization has made them something of an anachronism and has presented them with competition. A number of ratepayer associations have recently dropped their home-*owner* orientation, thus transforming themselves into the newer type of citizen group.

THE NEW STYLE

The ratepayer associations were (and in many cases remain) rather exclusive. However, as the municipal franchise became more universal, the extent to which ratepayers could dominate non-electoral municipal participation was reduced, for significant and growing numbers of people were left out of their associations. New group actors began to emerge— what used to be referred to as "neighbourhood" groups, now more commonly referred to as "community associations". As these terms suggest, this kind of citizen group tends to be organized on a smaller geographical basis in cities. They are often referred to as the Ward x Community Association, or the Lower Town Residents Association, which reflects their areal focus. In a sense such groups are as exclusive as ratepayer associations were traditionally, but exclusive on the basis of geographical sector rather than property ownership. Membership and participation in these new group actors is customarily open to anyone who lives in the particular area, whether those people are property owners or tenants.

Community associations are largely a product of the 1960s, although there were instances of neighbourhood groups occasionally active earlier on. Some possible explanations of the flowering of this newer type of group actor have been suggested above and therefore need only be briefly restated as pressures and consequences of urbanization, structural changes of cities (municipal reorganization, and change from decision making to policy making), and societal changes (the popularization of the value-laden term "participatory democracy"). There is the related fact that people's expectations of government generally and of city government specifically have been heightened and that their demands for governmental intervention and action have correspondingly increased in scope and number. The community associations can be seen as a new medium by which these demands are channelled to those elected and appointed people who formally make decisions for the city.

The use of the word "demands" here is particularly apt, for it suggests that community associations tend to take a more pronounced advocative or initiating role than ratepayer associations have customarily taken. Also, the scope of their demands tends to be broader. This approach is reflected in the tactics used by these groups in attempting to exercise political influence. Their actions are generally more visible to the public through the media because the tactics are often those of confrontation politics—holding open meetings, circulating petitions, and conducting demonstrations, among other means. It would, however, be a mistake to assume that community associations use only such tactics because the quieter and less visible techniques used by ratepayer associations are employed too. Resorting more frequently to more activist kinds of tactics is attributable not only to the nature of the demands, but perhaps also to the relative youthfulness and inexperience of community associations.

Of considerable importance also is the fact that community associations frequently go beyond just seeking particular outcomes of the formal decision-making processes, such as stopping an expressway, having recreation facilities provided, and so on. They are frequently concerned with changing the *processes* of decision making—opening the process to public scrutiny, requiring consultation with people who might be affected by policy outcomes, and changing the traditional trustee-type roles of city councillors. In contrast, ratepayer associations have tended to accept the decision-making processes as given. The tactics employed to exercise influence, the constant readiness to be critical, and the less clear property basis of the membership all combine to give community associations less legitimacy than ratepayer associations in the eyes of elected and appointed city officials. The problem of legitimacy is even more severe for community associations than it is for Winnipeg's RAGS, for at least the latter have formal statutory recognition. If a group lacks legitimacy or has comparatively less than competing organized interests, then the group is less likely to be successful in its attempts to exercise political influence.

Citizen associations of both the older and the newer types have several common deficiencies in terms of political resources. One of these is the difficulty of sustaining their membership and their organization as such. The history of city politics in Canada is strewn with masses of citizen associations that have been formed and then become defunct or inactive. Citizen associations, especially of the newer type, tend to be based on and dependent on issues, forming in response to an existing issue such as the building of a roadway, a request for spot rezoning, or a lack of recreational facilities. The perennial problem that such groups encounter is that if or when the original issue is somehow resolved, their *raison d'être* is gone, and the group either falls apart or becomes inactive until another issue comes along. In either case its momentum and continuity are gone or sharply reduced, and so is its ability to mobilize citizens. Connected to this is the problem citizen groups of both sorts encounter in attracting and holding members. One of the most valuable political resources that an organized interest can have when it is trying to impress elected public officials is numbers of people, for the numbers indicate something about the representativeness and electoral power of the group. The representativeness of citizen associations is open to question by those they are trying to influence. They are frequently vulnerable on this point, and can only fall back on the counter-question of the representativeness of the elected public officials. Given the low turn-out at municipal elections (usually between 20 and 40 per cent) and the fact that councillors are often elected with a mere plurality of those who actually vote, the retort has some force. But it does not answer the question of representativeness of citizen groups. The problem of sustaining the group's membership poses the danger of the group being effectively dominated by a select and interested few. Especially with regard to community associations, these few are often pejoratively labelled as activists, or even as agitators or radicals.

Perhaps the other most impressive political resource that an organized interest can have is a substantial information base to back up its demands and objectives. But the formation of such a base requires time and technical expertise, which resources in turn require money, or at least access to the city's own information base. Given the tradition of governmental secrecy ("in camera" meetings, and confidentiality of city documents), citizen associations cannot count on this access and must therefore attempt to build up an adequate base of their own. Since participation in citizen associations is always voluntary and the group is dependent on small membership fees and donations, the amount of income they have is not enough to enable them to hire professional/technical staff. Therefore their ability to compile information of their own is severely restricted. To overcome this deficiency, they occasionally seek grants of money from government. There is a danger, though, of citizen groups compromising themselves by accepting such money. Their financial autonomy is jeopardized. The long-run effectiveness of citizen associations is likely to be greater if the group relies on its own membership for its finance (provided of course that the group is able to sustain itself between issue crises) although their short-run effectiveness may be reduced by self-reliance.

The problem of legitimacy was referred to above in connection with community associations, but to some extent the ratepayer associations are deficient in this regard too. The Bureau of Municipal Research in Toronto found in a study of the City of Toronto that there were fundamental disagreements between civic politicians and neighbourhood associations, particularly over the role that such groups ought to play in city politics.[17] The politicians tended to deny that the groups were representative of the areas they purported to represent and insisted that the groups should not attempt to pressure politicians into any particular course of action on an issue. For their part the groups felt that politicians were unjustly trying to monopolize power and should rely less on their own interpretation of the best interests of the constituents and rely more on the groups' expressions of those interests. Replicating the study five years later, the Bureau of Municipal Research found that groups seemed to have acquired more legitimacy in the eyes of the civic politicians. Positing the four levels or concepts of participation to which reference was made in the previous chapter (an information role being the lowest level, then consultation, then partnership, with "citizen control" being the highest level of participation), it was found that only two out of twenty-two elected officials felt that groups should participate only in the minimal information role. But only one of the elected officials was prepared to accept citizen control participation.[18] Half of the elected officials felt that citizens should have a partnership role wherein citizens would be allowed to share planning and decision-making power through such devices as joint planning committees, and more than half the elected officials felt that at least the consultation role was appropriate. With the exception of rather favourable responses from city planners to having citizens and groups participate at a high level, appointed officials generally minimized the participatory role that should be permitted. Therefore it appears that at least in Toronto citizen associations are acquiring greater legitimacy as far as elected officials and city planners are concerned, but have yet to win the battle for legitimacy in the minds of other appointed city officials. It should be recalled that appointed civic officials in Winnipeg were similarly unimpressed with the Resident Advisory Groups.[19]

Because community associations (and ratepayer associations too, though to a lesser extent) are usually organized on a sectional basis rather than on a city-wide basis, each city has many such groups among which there is typically little co-ordination of activities, sharing of resources, or even exchanging of information. Their concerns are thus largely focused on one particular sector of the city, which sometimes creates conflicts between groups. Attempts are made from time to time to create umbrella organizations of citizen associations but such coalitions have not been notably successful in maintaining their momentum. For instance, the Metro Toronto Residents and Ratepayers Association (METRRA), formed in 1970 as a coalition of citizen groups in Metro Toronto, rather quickly became dormant, at least temporarily. CORRA (the City-wide Confederation of Resident and Ratepayer Associations) has had more durability in Toronto. Formed in 1969, it had thirty-six affiliated group members by 1972.

The differences between the older and newer styles of citizen associations are increasingly being blurred. The older type have begun to

transform themselves by adopting new tactics and by relaxing their qualifications for membership. Indeed the word "ratepayer" in the official
names of some groups is no longer of much significance in itself, and tells
little about the makeup of the membership, the tactics used, or the likelihood of their being effective group actors in urban politics. In other words
a researcher cannot necessarily assume things about a group just from its
name. But any researcher is likely to find that the customary fragmentation of citizen associations puts them at something of a disadvantage
relative to other interests which are not organized on a sectional basis.

Non-Corporate Specific-Interest Groups

This category of group actors in city politics differs from the previous
ones in having a more or less specific policy interest such as transportation
or environmental pollution. Also this type of group tends not to have a
specific areal focus other than that of the city as a whole. But like the
groups dealt with above they are generally comprised of citizen members
rather than corporate members. The organization known variously as
Pollution Probe and Ecology Action is an example of a non-corporate
specific-interest group, its concern being primarily environmental pollution and ecology. The most widely known example is the Stop Spadina
movement which achieved spectacular (though in the end only temporary) success in getting the Spadina Expressway in Toronto stopped,
even after construction of the expressway was already well advanced.[20]
The temporarily abandoned and unpaved roadbed stood as a most
unusual and highly visible monument to the possibilities of concerted
action by citizens.

Although the Spadina Expressway (its official name was the William
R. Allen Expressway, named after the man who became Chairman of
Metro Toronto in 1961 after the retirement of Frederick Gardiner, who
also had an expressway named after him) was officially stopped (actually
just postponed) in 1971, it had been a reality since March of 1962 when
the Metropolitan Toronto Council approved about $74 million for its
construction. In fact the idea of the expressway dates back even before
1954 when Metro Toronto was formed, but it was only when the
area-wide decision-making structure of Metro Toronto was created with
responsibility for a Metro roads system that the expressway could really

be built because it would pass through several municipalities. The issue came before the Ontario Municipal Board several times, such as in 1963 when objections to the project were filed by two municipalities and six individual ratepayers or ratepayers' associations. A few proponents of the expressway were active as well, orchestrating a remarkable campaign to demand an immediate start on its construction.[21] The OMB gave its approval in 1963, but by 1969, the issue of the expressway had assumed a new dimension, with the Stop Spadina Save Our City Co-ordinating Committee (sssoccc) becoming an active group focused on this one specific interest. This committee, formed under the leadership of Alan Powell (a sociologist at the University of Toronto), was the key to co-ordinating the activities of other groups and individuals, making the Spadina issue a salient one by keeping it in the limelight, and mobilizing opposition to the scheme. The committee helped to co-ordinate the 220 briefs that were submitted to Metro Toronto Council's Transportation Committee in 1970.

Coupled with the sssoccc was the Spadina Review Corporation which was formed to fight the expressway at the Ontario Municipal Board's hearings in 1971 by raising money and hiring legal advisors. The movement had an initial success in getting Metro Council, at least temporarily, to halt construction of the expressway (after almost $70 million had already been spent on construction) in order to conduct a review of the project. A combination of such tactics as inserting commercials in the media, holding demonstrations and parades, selling buttons, presenting briefs, and hiring legal advisors thus produced initial success. That success appeared to be short-lived, however, for Metro Council applied to the Ontario Municipal Board for authorization to borrow more money to complete an extended Spadina Expressway. The OMB did authorize completion of the expressway but one of the three board members who heard the case did not concur with the decision. That and the added fact that the member who did not concur was Mr. J. A. Kennedy, then Chairman of the OMB, was some encouragement to the Stop Spadina movement, which then decided to exercise its right to appeal the board's decision to the Ontario Cabinet. In a stunning move not long before the 1971 provincial election, Premier Davis announced to the Ontario Legislature that the Ontario Municipal Board's decision was in effect being over-turned—that the provincial government would not proceed in support of the plan for the Spadina Expressway.[22]

While opponents of Spadina celebrated, the proponents were working to revive it. The provincial government refused in 1972 to rescind the earlier OMB and Metro Toronto Council decisions which approved the expressway. In early 1975 the Soberman Report was released, recommending either a southerly extension of the unfinished Spadina expressway or a southerly extension of Highway 400 right into the city centre.[23] It should be noted, though, that the Soberman Report's recommendations on this matter were intended to be taken in a context of other recommendations in the report. In fact, the report as a whole tends not to support major roadways for private cars. Nevertheless, in August of 1975 Premier Davis announced that the provincial government would permit and subsidize the paving of the Spadina ditch as a four-lane arterial road. As a "bonus", Highway 400 would also be extended as a four-lane arterial road. The on-again, off-again Spadina expressway was on again, and so was the Highway 400 extension. Metro Toronto Council hastened to call tenders for construction, opposition groups were galvanized into action, and the City of Toronto obtained a Supreme Court injunction that temporarily prevented Metro Toronto from paving the mile-long Spadina extension. In April of 1976 the Court denied the City's application for a permanent injunction, and in May a contract for the paving was awarded.

Out of all this it is apparent that the only lasting effects of all the opposition to Spadina were to delay its construction and to have it scaled down somewhat. But even these effects can be called an achievement, though a disappointing one.

The case of the Spadina Expressway does not stand alone as an instance of the kind of success (sometimes limited) that non-corporate specific-interest groups occasionally enjoy. From Vancouver, with the issues of the third crossing over Burrard Inlet and the East End Expressway, to Halifax, with the regional garbage dump and the Quinpool Road development, this kind of group action has become a common phenomenon since the 1960s, though not all attempts by such groups to influence urban decision making have been so highly publicized as the Spadina Expressway issue. The few examples cited here happen to be of an essentially protective/reactive nature, but there are instances where this kind of group does engage in advocative/initiator activity, such as the rehabilitation of Vancouver's Gastown area. Such groups remain less common than the other kinds of citizen associations, for an issue must be highly salient for the movements to be effective, and the kinds and quantities of politically valuable resources of the sort employed in the Stop Spadina movement are not often readily available.

Corporate Groups

The apparent political power of corporate interests in city affairs has received considerable attention.[24] The gist of this literature is that individual companies, particularly those whose business is real estate, construction, or development, have long wielded formidable influence in city halls, and that when these companies are confronted by citizen groups, they are almost always victorious. The concern here though is with groups rather than individual companies.[25]

Every city has its chamber of commerce, board of trade, or an equivalent organization of business interests, and these organizations have a long tradition of involvement in city government and politics. They have a continuity over time that most other organized groups do not have, and ready access to the kind of detailed information that is most likely to impress elected and appointed city officials. Given the background and experience of large proportions of elected officials, there is an obvious affinity between them and this kind of corporate group actor, an affinity that provides the latter with comparatively easy access to public officials.

In addition to chambers of commerce, which are organized on a city-wide basis and which are therefore not fragmented in the way that citizen associations are, there are also a number of corporate groups in Canada. They do not have an exclusively municipal focus but are at least occasionally active participants in urban government and politics. The two principal examples are the Urban Development Institute and the Housing and Urban Development Association of Canada.

The Urban Development Institute (UDI) is a national organization with branches in at least five provinces (Alberta, British Columbia, Manitoba, Nova Scotia, and Ontario). First established in Ontario in 1957, the membership is composed of companies and individuals that are engaged generally in the real estate and development industry, including mortgage companies, land and property developers, owners and managers of all sorts of property (commercial, industrial, and residential), engineers, architects, lawyers, planning consultants, and even the City of Halifax's Development Department. The UDI styles itself the "national voice of the development industry". Although the number of members is small (about thirty-five in the Nova Scotia branch, and in Canada about 550 overall), their financial power is impressive. For example, the UDI claims that its members' construction projects account for about 70 to 75 per cent of all apartment units built each year in Metro Toronto.

The UDI generates its revenue from membership fees ($250 a year for each active member and $125 a year for associate members) and is able to hire professional staff, engage lawyers to act on the institute's behalf, and to mount substantial public relations campaigns. For example, in 1975 it decided to engage a political consulting firm in Ottawa at $26,000 a year, and $8,000 was budgeted in 1975 to underwrite a course at the University of Waterloo to train land developers for private industry. The annual budget of the Ontario branch is several hundred thousand dollars. The institute has been active in campaigning against rent controls in British Columbia and also in Ontario, where shortly before that province's 1975 election the UDI paid for a series of half-page advertisements in major daily newspapers. Also, the UDI engaged lawyers to represent it at the Ontario Municipal Board's hearings concerning the City of Toronto "45-foot" by-law in 1974.[26] Among its other actions over city by-laws was the active campaign against a 1976 Toronto by-law which put restrictions on "adults only" apartment buildings, and the institute's appeal before Nova Scotia's Planning Appeal Board concerning the City of Halifax's attempt to protect views from Citadel Hill (the UDI eventually dropped its appeal in this case).

The Housing and Urban Development Association of Canada (HUDAC) is also a national organization with provincial branches, and its members are mainly but not exclusively residential builders. The association claims that its 4800 members produced 85 per cent of all housing starts in Canada in 1974, but is attempting to expand its membership to 5200 in order to give HUDAC wider industry representation, additional financial resources, and more "clout" when presenting briefs to various governments.[27] These tasks are facilitated by a research director. Among HUDAC's concerns have been increasing the supply of mortgage money for residential construction and generally improving the image of builders in Canada. When it became apparent that the federal and provincial governments might establish a compulsory national warranty program for newly built housing, the association attempted to stave off that move by setting up a warranty scheme that would give the builders themselves control over the warranty council. Such a builder-controlled warranty scheme was set up in Alberta in 1975, and after the government-sponsored national scheme fell through, HUDAC set up plans similar to Alberta's in Ontario, Manitoba, and the Atlantic provinces in 1976. Members of HUDAC were also represented by lawyers at the Ontario Municipal Board's hearings concerning the "45-foot" by-law of the City of Toronto.

What these two organizations lack in numbers (as a proportion of the population) they make up for in other ways. With their overlapping memberships and overlapping boards of directors, they are able to form coalitions with each other as well as with other associated organizations. It is of interest to note that in the case of the City of Toronto's building-height by-law those who registered objections before the OMB included not only the UDI and members of HUDAC but also such connected industry organizations as the Canadian Institute of Public Real Estate Companies, the Toronto chapter of the Ontario Association of Architects (which later reversed its opposition to the by-law), the Toronto RAC Committee (successor to the Redevelopment Advisory Council, representing big businesses in downtown Toronto but not developers), the Toronto Building Trades Council, and the Toronto Construction Association. Also, when the Borough of Scarborough's 1975 urban design by-law was at issue, the UDI protested in concert with the Toronto Home Builders Association. These groups eventually won the right to sit on a committee created by the borough council to revise the by-law. In addition to being able to mobilize other organizations, such groups are able to arrange legal representation to an extent that citizen groups are rarely able to do because of lack of financial resources. The battery of lawyers at the OMB hearings representing appellants to the "45-foot" by-law was what has been described as a "galaxy" of the Toronto legal profession, including some of the best known (and presumably most expensive) names in that profession.[28] The pool of legal expertise available to the appellants puts citizen associations (who generally supported the by-law) at a considerable disadvantage. For example, one developer's solicitors successfully argued that the OMB could not allow unincorporated ratepayer groups to appear before the Board on the grounds that such groups could not be considered as "persons" under Ontario's Statutory Powers and Procedures Act. The OMB's decision to refuse to allow such groups to appear before it was subsequently upheld in August of 1974 by the Ontario Cabinet.

Coupled with their financial resources, groups such as the UDI and HUDAC have the experience and research capability to assemble technical information which is useful not only for buttressing their case when presented to elected and appointed public officials at any level of government, but which is often sought by those officials. Thus the relationships between such organizations and public officials tend to be more reciprocal than is the case with citizen groups, and it more or less follows that corporate associations have traditionally had a higher level of legitimacy in the minds of public officials than do their disadvantaged counterparts. This is no doubt supported by exchanges of personnel such as the appointment in 1973 of Mr. William Teron (who had been a major Ottawa developer) as president of the Central Mortgage and Housing Corporation and in late 1975 as deputy minister of Urban Affairs in Ottawa, and of a recent Atlantic regional director of CMHC moving to manage a development company in Alberta. Because of their organizational bases and resources, corporate groups are far less confined than are citizen groups to exerting influence at just the municipal level of government—corporate group actors can easily shift the focus of their activities to provincial and federal officials too.

Their traditional legitimacy and connections make it unnecessary for corporate groups to utilize such tactics as presenting petitions or holding demonstrations. Because so many of their activities are based on frequent contact with public officials directly and privately, it is impossible to judge their success as interest groups with as much assuredness as it is to judge the success of citizen associations. In a sense one would be judging different things, in that corporate groups have long had success in having some voice in public decision making, whereas citizen groups, especially of the newer type, are still faced with the task of merely acquiring a legitimately recognized voice. This is a goal which must first be obtained before they can have success in achieving more specific ends. If one is to judge the success of corporate groups on the basis of such cases as the

"45-foot" by-law and the available literature, corporate groups have indeed enjoyed a substantial measure of success.

The Media of Mass Communication

Although the media of mass communication are not group actors in urban politics in the same sense as the kinds of groups with which this chapter has been concerned, the media deserve some attention. The most obvious role that the media play is the dissemination of information to the general public. The importance of this lies in the fact that the *kind* of information disseminated by the media and the *way* in which they disseminate that information affect people's interest in urban government and politics, and reinforce or change their views on particular issues. The other important aspect about the media's role is that this is the main way in which issues can become widely salient and by which the level of that salience is maintained, diminished, or heightened. If something like the issue of replacement of the farmers' market in Kitchener, Ontario is reported briefly and buried in the back pages of newspapers, then the issue is unlikely to become important except to those people who are directly affected. On the other hand, if such an issue receives continual front-page coverage, then it will become more highly salient even for people who are not directly affected.

The information role of the media of mass communication is more complex than the simple communication (or non-communication) of information to the general public. The same information is also communicated to elected and appointed public officials and to group actors of the sort dealt with above. But these more specialized audiences are far less reliant on the media for their information than is the general public, for public officials in particular and some group actors as well have their own information bases to which the general public does not have easy access. The media function to some extent as communicators of information from the general public and assorted groups to city officials in the form of open-line radio programs and letters to newspaper editors. It is impossible to guess what proportion of public officials tune themselves in to such expressions of opinion, or what their reactions are, but presumably some do pay attention and are somehow affected.

Editorial policy of the media takes basically two forms. The less obvious form includes selecting what news to disseminate, and the way in which it will be communicated—how much time or space will be devoted to a topic, what prominence will be given to that topic (front page or back page, top of the news or incidental, pictures or no pictures), and whether all sides (presuming that the issue is controversial) will be stated with equal prominence or whether the information will be slanted to one position. The more obvious form of editorializing is seen on the editorial page of newspapers and editorial comment on public affairs programs. In these ways the media openly favour or oppose courses of action on particular issues, or endorse particular candidates in city elections.

With regard especially to the printed media of mass communication it is useful to distinguish two main types on the basis of their tendency to editorialize and the kind of editorial comments they make.

THE "ESTABLISHMENT" MEDIA

The big daily newspapers generally profess to restrict all editorializing to the editorial page and to page seven (opposite the editorial page), but in terms of the first, more covert form of editorializing, they are not so restrictive. Announcements of major new development projects are frequently accompanied by idealized artist's sketches. The reporting generally appears to be entirely factual, yet the impression such press announcements tend to convey is that the development will be a good and desirable one. Later news items about opposition from citizen groups or non-corporate specific-interest groups tend to receive less prominent coverage. It is also sometimes the case that major advertising clients of the dailies (clients who are or might be involved in political issues or projects) receive unusually careful treatment by the media.[29]

Sources of advertising revenue and the fact that the media themselves have major stakes in cities by virtue of their own property holdings go some way to explaining the dominant impressions conveyed. A more important cause of this orientation is to be found in the ownership and control of the major media of mass communication. As the Senate's committee on the mass media found, almost three-quarters of Canada's newspapers were owned by chains, as was a large proportion of radio and television stations.[30] In other words, the media are to a large and increasing extent a part of the large corporate establishment, a fact which in itself would lead one to expect a commonality of interests and perspectives between the owners of the media and other corporate interests. Further, it has been found that there are more direct connections between media and corporate interests, such as the Irving family's ownership of all English-language daily newspapers in New Brunswick, one radio station and two television stations, besides such other businesses as petroleum, shipping, and lumber. The diversified Power Corporation of Montreal is another example, owning a number of French-language daily and weekly newspapers in Quebec. Even if the owners of conglomerates do not dictate the editorial policies of the media they own, the connections are sufficient to ensure that the management of the establishment media and their owners will share general philosophical and political perspectives.

In his study of politics in Metro Toronto, Kaplan found that there was little group involvement except for the three daily newspapers. They were regular participants in Metro issues, taking stands on over 90 per cent of the fifty-five issues that Kaplan examined.[31] He also found that the daily newspapers had the indirect but pervasive effect of helping set the ideological climate of Metro politics particularly with respect to the bloc of City of Toronto members on Metro Council.

THE "ALTERNATE" MEDIA

In contrast to the above kinds of media are what can be called the "alternate" media. This category includes independently owned weekly newspapers, neighbourhood newspapers, and several periodicals. They differ from the other media most importantly by being rather more explicitly editorial, and by being rather more critical of city politics, city officials, and corporate interests. The "underground" newspapers that flourished in the 1960s (such as the *Georgia Straight* in Vancouver, Toronto's *Citizen*, the *Prairie Dog* in Winnipeg, and the *4th Estate* in Halifax) left no doubt that their sympathies did not lie with developers but with citizen groups. Because of their smaller and more specialized audiences, this kind of newspaper probably has had less direct effect on public officials, but by acting as a catalyst for citizen group activity their impact has not been insignificant.

Among the journals and periodicals generally aimed at even more specialized audiences, and about which it is difficult even to guess at the impact they have on city politics is *City Hall*. This was published fortnightly beginning in 1970 by four "reform" aldermen elected in the 1969 Toronto election.[32] It began as a news-sheet devoted to detailed reports on aldermen's votes in committee and council, and on debates on important issues. From time to time it also presented detailed descriptive accounts of the machinery of Toronto's government, but primarily it was designed to give an openly subjective interpretation of what happens within Toronto's political system. Another example is *City Magazine* which was the outcome in 1974 of an unsuccessful attempt by several disaffected members of the Town Planning Institute of Canada to persuade members of the institute to examine themselves and the institute. They were particularly concerned with the relations of members of the institute with the development industry and with groups of citizens. The magazine is concerned most with issues involving planning and citizen participation in city planning. Like other examples of the alternate media *City Magazine* prints articles that are in-depth case studies of issues, analyses which make no pretences of being value-neutral.

Urban politics in Canada is characterized by a much larger number and somewhat wider variety of group actors than had been the case at the time Metropolitan Toronto was created. As a consequence urban politics has become both more complex and more interesting. While these group actors participate in urban politics in a multitude of ways, they commonly refrain from participating in the sense of directly seeking election to public office. It is with elections and the one kind of group actor which is directly involved in elections that the following chapter is concerned.

NOTES

1. Harold Kaplan, *Urban Political Systems: A Functional Analysis of Metro Toronto* (New York: Columbia University Press, 1967), pp. 209–11.
2. Mildred A. Schwartz, *Politics and Territory: The Sociology of Regional Persistence in Canada* (Montreal: McGill-Queen's University Press,

1974), Table 9-3, p. 222.
3. John Woods, "The City in (Conceptual) Space," workshop paper presented to the Annual Meeting of the Canadian Political Science Association (Toronto, June, 1974), Figure 1, p. 3.
4. Many other examples related to such areas of policy as housing are

recounted by Boyce Richardson, *The Future of Canadian Cities* (Toronto: New Press, 1972).

5. George M. Betts, "Citizen Participation and Local Government in Canada: A Background Paper," presented to the October, 1971 International Union of Local Authorities Conference in Zagreb, Yugoslavia, p. 4. This paper is available from the Institute of Local Government at Queen's University, Kingston, Ontario.

6. Bureau of Municipal Research, *Citizen Participation in Metro Toronto: Climate for Cooperation?* (Toronto: Bureau of Municipal Research, 1975).

7. Kaplan, *Urban Political Systems*, p. 167.

8. For an account of this case see *City Magazine*, September, 1974, and October, 1974. The city eventually bought the land in dispute.

9. Dr. P. H. Wichern, Jr., "Patterns of Public Participation in Canadian Urban Policy Making: The Case of Winnipeg's Resident Advisory Groups," presented at the first annual meeting of the Atlantic Provinces Political Studies Association (Antigonish, Nova Scotia, October, 1975), p. 1. Note for example the list of special-purpose bodies in the City of Calgary in this regard in Chapter 3.

10. There are several accounts of Winnipeg's Resident Advisory Groups, two useful accounts being Wichern, "Patterns of Public Participation in Canadian Urban Policy Making"; and Lloyd Axworthy and Jim Cassidy, *Unicity: The Transition*, Future City Series No. 4 (Winnipeg: Institute of Urban Studies of the University of Winnipeg, undated but likely 1974), especially pp. 89–135 and 213–15.

11. See, for example, Lloyd Axworthy, "Winnipeg: An Experiment in Innovation," *Canadian Forum* (May–June, 1972); reprinted in L. Axworthy and James M. Gillies, eds., *The City: Canada's Prospects,*

Canada's Problems (Toronto: Butterworths, 1973), pp. 276–83.

12. In this connection see David C. Walker, "Resident Advisory Groups in Winnipeg: A Short Commentary," presented at the first annual meeting of the Atlantic Provinces Political Studies Association (Antigonish, Nova Scotia, October, 1975).

13. Axworthy and Cassidy, *Unicity: The Transition*, p. 120.

14. Wichern, "Patterns of Public Participation in Canadian Urban Policy Making," p. 5.

15. For several case studies see David Ley, ed., *Community Participation and the Spatial Order of the City* (Vancouver: Tantalus, 1973); and James A. Draper, ed., *Citizen Participation: Canada, A Book of Readings* (Toronto: New Press, 1971). Other useful books include Donald Gutstein, *Vancouver Ltd.* (Toronto: James Lorimer, 1975); John Sewell *et al.*, *Inside City Hall* (Toronto: Hakkert, 1971); James Lorimer, *The Real World of City Politics* (Toronto: James Lewis and Samuel, 1970); and James Lorimer, *A Citizen's Guide to City Politics* (Toronto: James Lewis and Samuel, 1972), especially Chapter 13.

16. Kaplan, *Urban Political Systems*, p. 168.

17. Bureau of Municipal Research, *Neighbourhood Participation in Local Government: A Study of the City of Toronto* (Toronto, January, 1970).

18. Bureau of Municipal Research, *Citizen Participation in Metro Toronto*, p. 46.

19. Wichern, "Patterns of Public Participation in Canadian Urban Policy Making," p. 10.

20. For a chronicle of the Spadina Expressway up to the point when construction was halted see David and Nadine Nowlan, *The Bad Trip: The Untold Story of the Spadina Expressway* (Toronto: New Press/ House of Anansi, 1970). In different contexts see Graham Fraser, *Fighting Back: Urban Renewal in Trefann*

Court (Toronto: Hakkert, 1972); and Jack Pasternak, *The Kitchener Market Fight* (Toronto: Hakkert, 1975).

21. See two columns written by Ron Haggart in the *Toronto Daily Star* (February 26, 1962, and March 1, 1962). These are reprinted in Nowlan, *The Bad Trip*, as appendices.

22. For the Ontario Municipal Board's decision and Premier Davis' statement see Lionel D. Feldman and Michael D. Goldrick (ed.), *Politics and Government of Urban Canada: Selected Readings*, 2nd ed. (Toronto: Methuen, 1972), pp. 198–211.

23. Metropolitan Toronto Transportation Plan Review, *Choices for the Future: Summary Report*, report no. 64 (Toronto, January, 1975).

24. See, for example, Lorimer, *A Citizen's Guide to City Politics*; David Lewis Stein, *Toronto for Sale: The Destruction of a City* (Toronto: New Press, 1972); J. L. Granatstein, *Marlborough Marathon: One Street Against a Developer* (Toronto: Hakkert, 1971); and Gutstein, *Vancouver Ltd.*

25. In this connection see the important and extremely well documented study by Peter Spurr, *Land and Urban Development: A Preliminary Study* (Toronto: James Lorimer, 1976). The report is basically a data book, and as such does not purport to analyze the political power of the land development industry in Canada. But the implications are obvious.

26. The OMB supported the institute's position by rejecting the city's by-law designed to limit the height of new construction in part of the city to 45 feet unless certain conditions were met by the developer.

27. Report of an interview with Mr. Bernard Denault, President of HUDAC for 1976, in *The Globe and Mail* (Toronto), February 7, 1975, p. B11.

28. *The Globe and Mail* (Toronto), October 28, 1974, p. 5.

29. See, for example, Wallace Clement, *The Canadian Corporate Elite: An Analysis of Economic Power* (Toronto: McClelland and Stewart, 1975), p. 294. Chapters 6 and 7 of his book are particularly interesting regarding the media. See also Lorimer, *A Citizen's Guide to City Politics*, Chapter 10.

30. Canada, *Report of the Special Senate Committee on Mass Media*, 3 volumes (Ottawa: Queen's Printer, 1970). This report is known as the Davey Report.

31. Kaplan, *Urban Political Systems*, p. 167.

32. A selection of stories from the first year's issues of *City Hall* was republished by John Sewell, *et al*, *Inside City Hall*.

Parties and Elections

The distinction between organized groups of the sorts examined in the previous chapter and political parties is not always clear-cut, except in terms of whether the organization does or does not openly and directly contest civic elections. The distinction is clouded by the fact that non-party groups sometimes privately sponsor or openly endorse one or more candidates for elective office. That connection is occasionally carried over after the election to the extent that successful candidates are sometimes seen as spokesmen on council for particular group interests. It also happens from time to time that non-party groups become transformed into a sort of party because they begin to contest city elections with a full or partial slate of candidates. Finally, there is considerable overlap in the functions performed by non-party organized groups and by parties.

The political function normally associated with organized interest groups is interest articulation, which is to say that the group becomes a focal point of particular interests and communicates information about those interests to the elected and appointed city officials who are in formal positions to translate that input into outputs. In contrast, political parties are most associated with performing an interest-aggregation function, which means that parties sift and sort among a diversity of interests and demands, rejecting some, accepting some, working out compromises, correlating those accepted, and ordering them into priorities. However, these two functions are not completely separate. While each organized interest group has a relatively narrow range of interests and concerns, such groups must also perform the interest-aggregation function. Especially when the membership of the group is fairly large, there may well be competing demands and interests within the group itself, necessitating much the same sifting and sorting, compromising, and ordering of priorities that parties do. Also, parties must go beyond interest aggregation—they have to publicize (i.e. articulate) the interests which they have aggregated, and communicate to some audience (the general public and/or appointed and elected public officials) the party's program or platform. And both parties and interest groups function as mechanisms linking the public to city government.

For the present purposes the distinction between organized interest groups and parties hinges on whether or not an active and open role is taken in city elections. So the word "party" is used to apply to any organized group of people who nominate or openly endorse several candidates (not necessarily a full slate, but more than one candidate) for a city election, provide those candidates with organizational and/or financial support in the election, and perhaps provide direction to and exercise influence over its candidates if they are elected to council.

City politics in Canada is now characterized by two basic kinds of parties—what can be called "civic" parties, and units or branches of the major national/provincial political parties that contest city elections.

Civic Parties[1]

Civic parties are specifically *local* parties, their activities and concerns being oriented to single municipalities. Hence one does not find the same civic party active in two or more cities, and in fact not all cities have them. It is also the case that civic parties are local in the sense of being oriented only to a municipality and not to the provincial and federal governments except in the most incidental ways. For reasons that are made clear below, it is useful to distinguish a newer style of civic party from an older style. As in the case of citizen associations, the older and newer versions tend to differ in the time period of their blossoming, but the older style can still be found in many major cities, and some of the newer ones have been transformed into the style of their more aged counterparts. Clear examples of the older version that are still active in 1976 include the Civic Party formed in Montreal in 1960, the Civic Non-Partisan Association formed in Vancouver in 1936, and in Winnipeg the Independent Citizens Election Committee whose predecessors date back to 1919. Civic parties that are clearly of the newer style include Vancouver's Committee of Progressive Electors that was formed in 1968 and the Montreal Citizens Movement formed in 1974. It can be argued that the Electors Action Movement in Vancouver (TEAM, formed in 1968) is an example of a party that began in the new mode and subsequently changed to the old.

Civic parties originally were a phenomenon transplanted into Canada from the United States, having been in that country an integral part of the reform movement of the 1890s. As noted in Chapter 3, the city manager form of decision-making structure developed during the reform movement in the United States as an attempt to apply business principles of efficiency and economy to municipal government. Civic parties, at least those of that time, were a second manifestation of the reform movement. Their purpose was to eliminate "politics" from municipal government so that civic affairs would be managed according to those same principles. Like the transplanting into Canada of the city manager structure, civic parties developed in the early part of the twentieth century. One of the earliest was the Westmount Municipal Association in Quebec in 1909, formed four years before Westmount became the first municipality in Canada to adopt the city manager structure of decision making.

The earliest civic parties in Canada were adamant in their insistence that they were not parties. They professed to be non-partisan and this reflected an anti-political, pro-business approach to city politics. It is this aspect that most importantly unites the older-style civic parties across Canada. They share a definite ideologically related perspective that stands in quite sharp contrast to the newer-style examples. The more recent manifestations of the phenomenon have been less bothered about calling themselves (or being called) parties.

Whether old or recent, all civic parties at least initially view themselves as parties seeking reform. But there is a qualitative difference in the kind of reform sought. The older type has sought to reform civic affairs by de-politicizing them and managing them as a board of directors would manage a business corporation's affairs. As a consequence, such election platforms as they have had emphasize "good government" and financial frugality, sentiments that reflect an ideology of conservatism. The newer form, on the other hand, tends to have broader and more specific platforms that are indicative of competitive if not confrontation politics. The Saskatoon Citizens' Committee formed in 1973 is one of these that present this kind of ideologically based comprehensive program that could be described as liberalism, but other examples of newer-style civic parties take a more socialist perspective. In a sense the newer version argues for reform in terms of removing the older form's domination over city affairs. In fact the reform sought by both types amounts to little more than the removal of the other from control over the decision-making structure of the city.

The newer and older forms of civic parties differ also in terms of their sources of membership and support. The older form, as one would expect, have been organizations dominated especially by people in business (usually small-scale business) and some professionals—in other words, middle-class people who are generally middle-aged, or older. The membership of those groups is generally small, rarely exceeding a hundred or so people. In so far as they have small memberships, the older-style civic parties are not mass movements. Nevertheless in some cities they have been particularly powerful in terms of controlling nominations for elective public office and controlling council once the election is over. But as Joyce and Hossé point out, these parties tend to have little ability to maintain their organizational continuity; most of them rather quickly become either defunct or dormant.[2] They seem to be particularly subject to breaking up when they encounter some sort of crisis—crises of leadership, of policy, the absence of a more or less left-wing opposition, or whatever. In view of their comparatively small memberships, this susceptibility to crises seems somewhat surprising, for the small membership should lead to rather strong internal cohesion. However the apparent paradox may be resolved by considering the fact that such civic parties frequently revolve around either an individual leader (or a very small group of leading members) or the existence of a left-leaning opposition. If the opposition is removed or neutralized, then part of the party's *raison d'être* is removed too. Alternatively, if the leadership of the party splits or abdicates, it may be left like a ship without a rudder in a storm—floundering. Two additional factors that may account for the relative instability of the older type of civic parties are the facts that they tend to be largely an election phenomenon, lapsing into inactivity between elections, and that they do not have a sufficiently explicit and unifying ideology or philosophy. A call for "good, efficient, economical civic management" is not a stirring rallying cry which can be depended upon when there is internal disagreement over tactics or leadership. So there is little on which older civic parties can fall back in times of crisis.

The newer style of civic parties tends to be somewhat broader based in its membership, both in the kinds of people who are members (they are not so identifiably of any particular age group or occupational category), and in the number of members. For example, within a few months of its formation, Vancouver's TEAM had about one thousand paid-up members.[3] Until the October crisis of 1970 (with implementation of the War Measures Act) virtually destroyed Montreal's FRAP, it too had about one thousand card-carrying members. Although these examples are from two of Canada's three largest cities, memberships anywhere nearly as large as these are almost unheard of with respect to the older form of civic parties. Hence the newer versions more closely resemble mass political movements. Moreover these civic parties tend to have an explicit and coherent organizing ideology which serves as a basis for election campaigns, enables the party to maintain a degree of continuity between elections, and may also serve as a means of retaining a committed membership. Although some of these ideologies do tend to be "left", some of them are more moderately liberal. As noted earlier some that seem to be more or less left-wing initially become transformed over time—the ideology is eventually discarded for pragmatic purposes of gaining office because the electorate in Canada's major cities is generally unprepared to vote a clearly radical party into office at city hall.

It is impossible to state how many civic parties there are or have ever been in Canada, but it is safe to say that there have been several hundred of them. Almost all cities have (or have had) at least one.[4] But records are incomplete, many civic parties have dissolved, and many others are dormant. Space does not allow a full examination of examples of such parties, but for purposes of illustration it is useful to look briefly at two cities where they are active.

MONTREAL

Jean Drapeau first became mayor of the city of Montreal in 1954. He ran as the candidate of the Civic Action League (which opposed him in 1962) and ran on a reform platform, pledging to bring efficiency to the city's administration and to root out corruption in city hall. He entered the campaign fresh from a dazzling performance as chief prosecutor for the Caron inquiry into the city's police force. Mr. Drapeau was defeated in 1957 after one term of office and formed the Civic Party shortly before the 1960 election, which he won. The Civic Party was and is in effect the Drapeau Party, having been formed by Mr. Drapeau and being quite completely controlled by him. His party is a unique one in Canadian city politics, characterized as it is by a strength of discipline that is unknown in any other civic parties.[5] Hence the Civic Party is much more than simply an election phenomenon, unlike a good many others among its counterparts. The relationship between Drapeau and the party is not unlike that between a strongly individual prime minister and the governing party in the House of Commons, except that Drapeau's control over his party's members of council is, if anything, more complete than that of a prime minister. Party candidates are screened by Mr. Drapeau, and are not normally selected by public nomination meetings. The Civic Party does not hold conventions nor policy conferences but its councillors do meet in caucus periodically. What meetings it does hold are usually shrouded in secrecy by Mr. Drapeau.

Although the Civic Party is not old, it is of the older style. It is composed largely of business interests (small and large) plus some professionals, but not organized labour. Further, it initially styled itself as a party of reform, but in 1974, for example, it contested the election mainly on its past accomplishments rather than on change for the future. It, like Drapeau (it is virtually impossible to separate the two analytically) is associated less with policy than with such decisions or attractions as Expo '67, the Olympics, the Métro, and Place des Arts. In terms of election of members to Montreal City Council, Drapeau's Civic Party has been extraordinarily successful, and has had a clear majority in every election it has contested: 1960 (forty-five of the sixty-six council seats); 1962 (forty-one of the forty-five seats), 1966 (forty-five of forty-eight seats, including thirty-three by acclamation), 1970 (all fifty-two seats), and 1974. So complete was the party's control, and so complete was Drapeau's control over the party that the locus of decision making was clearly the mayor's office, and the six-member Executive Committee (which is in the mayor's firm control). Council is called into session infrequently (normally five or six times a year) and traditionally rubber-stamped decisions already taken by Mr. Drapeau.

The first serious attempt to create a new party to dislodge Drapeau's was in May of 1970. The Front d'Action Politique (FRAP) was formed as a sort of coalition of existing citizens' associations with support from the Confederation of National Trade Unions (CNTU), the Parti Quebecois, and the provincial wing of the NDP.[6] FRAP was very much a newer-style civic party. It had a fairly large membership, had a broad and specific policy platform, tended to be dominated by younger people, and had a rather distinct left-wing ideology. Its ideology and its support from the separatist Parti Quebecois enabled Mr. Drapeau to link it with the Front de Liberation du Quebec (FLQ) just before the 1970 city election which was held at the height of the October Crisis. This denunciation was reinforced when Mr. Jean Marchand, a powerful member of the federal cabinet, publicly labelled FRAP as a "front" for the FLQ. Although the charges were never substantiated, FRAP was effectively destroyed (though it received about 20 per cent of the vote) with Mr. Drapeau's Civic Party defeating every FRAP candidate for council and winning all fifty-two council seats.

By 1974, FRAP was replaced by the Montreal Citizens Movement (MCM) as the major opposition to the Civic Party. A second but much smaller opposition party, called Democracy Montreal, was formed to join the fray. It was led by one of several disillusioned former Drapeau councillors. The MCM, like FRAP, was formed only six months before contesting its first city election, and like FRAP it was a sort of coalition of citizens' associations with support from the Parti Quebecois, the NDP, politically active trade unionists, and some academics.[7] Its platform was broad and specific, and included decentralization of city government, citizen participation, new roles for councillors and neighbourhood groups, and financial reform. Position papers were also prepared on specific subjects such as public transit. The MCM fielded candidates for all seats on council and ran Jacques Couture, a Jesuit priest and community worker, as its mayoralty candidate opposing Mr. Drapeau. The MCM, lacking the kind of financial resources that enabled Drapeau's Civic Party to buy hour-long slots of radio time to broadcast speeches by Mr. Drapeau, relied on a small army of volunteer workers that conducted extensive door-to-door campaigning. Although neither the MCM nor Democracy Montreal won a majority of the seats on Council in the November election of 1974, the Civic Party for the first time since 1960 was confronted with substantial and more or less unified opposition in Montreal City Council. With regard to candidates for council seats, the Civic Party received 50.7 per cent of the vote (getting thirty-six seats, or 65 per cent of them, after recounts), while the MCM's candidates for council got 45.3 per cent of the vote and eighteen seats (33 per cent of the seats). The fifty-fifth seat was won by a candidate of the Democracy Montreal party. Of course Mr. Drapeau retained his mayoralty with 55 per cent of the vote, while his MCM opponent received 40 per cent of the votes cast. The Civic Party was left with one seat short of a two-thirds majority. Since some decisions of Montreal City Council require that majority to pass, politics in Montreal became considerably more lively and exciting than they had been for many years. But the MCM is not unified on the prominence that its ideology should be given. The party is split between those who insist that the party should retain its ideological purity, and those who believe that a more flexible election-oriented program should be adopted so as to broaden the party's bases of electoral support. Unless the MCM can resolve this division, Mr. Drapeau's Civic Party is not likely to meet an early demise.

VANCOUVER

Vancouver was one of the first Canadian cities to have its council clearly and consistently dominated by civic parties. In 1936 the Civic Non-Partisan Association (NPA) was formed, and this older-style party controlled city council for thirty-five continuous years after its first election in 1937. The NPA was formed basically to keep the CCF (Co-operative Commonwealth Federation) out of power in Vancouver. It was composed of anti-CCF, anti-socialist, anti-labour people associated with the Liberal and Progressive Conservative parties, later being joined by Social Credit Party supporters. In this sense the Non-Partisan Association's name was a misnomer, for rather than being non-partisan, it was more accurately a multi-partisan coalition united by opposition to the CCF. The NPA enjoyed very considerable success in getting its candidates elected to council, although a CCF candidate (Dr. J. Lyle Telford) was elected mayor in 1939. In large part its long reign may be attributed to the abolition of a ward basis of representation on council after a plebiscite held in December of 1935 voted to abandon wards (only 20 per cent of the eligible voters voted in that plebiscite). As a consequence, all candidates for council had to run at large, an electoral system which almost always requires much greater financial resources to wage a successful election campaign than does a ward system, because candidates in such elections must cover the entire electorate of the city. Because of the nature of its membership, it was only the NPA that was able to acquire the substantial finances that could enable its candidates to mount effective campaigns. The much less wealthy CCF was left virtually out in the cold. A second consequence of the abolition of wards was the fact that members of Vancouver City Council were almost invariably residents of the more prestigious west side of the city rather than of the generally more working-class east side.

After more than thirty years of continuous control of council, the NPA experienced serious opposition. The Electors Action Movement (TEAM) was created in 1968 and began as one of the newer style of civic parties— younger people, more concerned with citizen participation, critical of unrestrained development, and proposing decentralization of the planning process. It was much less a party led by owners, managers, and officials in business than was the NPA,[8] and within a few months of its creation TEAM had a paid-up membership of about one thousand people. It is usually seen as being connected with the Liberal Party. The NPA had additional opposition in the form of the Committee of Progressive Electors (COPE) which was also formed in 1968. This party was of the newer style too, but more left-wing than TEAM. COPE is usually perceived as being connected with the left-wing of the NDP, and its leadership is drawn mainly from such occupational categories as union officials, skilled and unskilled labourers, and school teachers. Of the three civic parties, it had the most explicit ideology.

In the election for council held in December of 1968, the NPA retained control but two TEAM candidates won, as did one COPE candidate. In 1970 the New Democratic Party entered the civic election with a slate of five aldermanic candidates, all of whom lost the election. By 1972, the NPA had run into trouble, and its mayoralty candidate withdrew from the election campaign because of an allegation of conflict of interest. Both the NDP and COPE ran full slates of candidates, thus splitting the remaining reform votes that had not gone to TEAM. The latter swept into power with its mayoralty candidate and with eight out of ten aldermanic seats. COPE retained its one council seat, and the NPA was reduced to one alderman. By November of 1974 the NPA (renamed the New Non-Partisans) had somewhat recovered from its 1972 electoral disaster, with four of its aldermanic candidates being elected. The one incumbent from

COPE was re-elected, but TEAM retained control of council with its candidate for mayor and five of its aldermanic candidates being successful.

Between 1972 and 1974, TEAM appears to have changed a great deal and to have become much less reformist than it was at first. For example, the party had originally been in favour of reforming Vancouver's elections by reintroducing a ward basis of representation to council. But when a plebiscite was held on this question in October of 1973, it was split on the issue and no longer solidly and publicly favoured a return to a full ward system. TEAM now officially favoured a partial ward system, which meant that only part of council would be elected by ward, the rest being elected at large. The result of the confusing plebiscite in 1973 was that about 60 per cent of those who voted (the voter turnout was only 21 per cent) favoured retention of the at-large system. TEAM changed in other ways too. Gutstein argues persuasively that by 1974 it had become in effect the NPA under a new name, even though the NPA still existed as a civic party with one seat on council. Gutstein examined not only the voting record of members of Vancouver City Council but business ties as well, and concluded that TEAM ceased being a civic party of the newer reform style and that it represented "exactly the same" interests as the NPA.[9] Still, the NPA was more dominated by businessmen while TEAM was more dominated by professionals, and more closely associated with the Liberal Party. Whether this transformation is real or not, it does represent a continuation of Vancouver's long tradition of domination by civic parties, a domination so complete that in the 1970 civic election there, independent candidates received less than 5 per cent of the votes cast. There have been no independent councillors on Vancouver City Council for some years.

National/Provincial Parties

Until the late 1960s the major national/provincial political parties rarely took an active part in city politics in terms of directly contesting civic elections. What few examples there were of earlier civic election activity of non-civic parties are found mainly in Western Canada, such as the CCF's running candidates in Vancouver in the 1930s and 1940s, Social Credit slates of candidates in Calgary in the later 1930s, and Communist

Party candidates in such cities as Winnipeg.[10] As this suggests, it was largely the protest parties that were involved earliest, mainly during the Great Depression when cities, especially those of the prairie provinces, were experiencing formidable financial problems. The parties' success in getting candidates elected to city councils was limited and sporadic. As the depression faded into the economic boom of the Second World War, non-civic party involvement in city politics faded too. Only in Winnipeg did overt activity by this kind of party really persist. There, the CCF and the Communist Party continued to run their own candidates with some measure of success. In fact, Winnipeg was perhaps the earliest Canadian city to be characterized by non-civic politics, one of the ancestors of the CCF-NDP first running candidates in the election of 1920, after the political upheaval culminating in the famous Winnipeg General Strike of 1919.

A number of reasons can be advanced for the historical absence of the major national or provincial political parties in city politics.[11] Bearing in mind that Canada's form of municipal government was to a considerable extent a transplant of the English model in the latter part of the nineteenth century, this absence can similarly be viewed as a transplant of the English experience, for the system of municipal government in England was not at that time characterized by overt partisanship. Further, in most provinces of Canada, the systems of municipal government either evolved after the reform movement in the United States, or were significantly affected by that movement with its emphasis on non-partisan local government. It can also be argued that the major parties were aware that city electorates did not want them. The several brief and unsuccessful forays made by some parties earlier demonstrated that electorates did not view the major parties as legitimate contenders for civic office.

An important reason for lack of involvement in city politics by the major parties in Canada was quite simply a lack of interest on their part. When the cities were engaged so largely in non-controversial house-keeping decisions there was comparatively little need for an interest-aggregation function to be performed in the cities and hence little need for parties. And the stakes involved in city government were not substantial enough. About the only possible payoff for major parties to become active by contesting city elections was that such involvement could facilitate the recruitment of candidates for provincial and federal elections. In other words, municipal government could be considered a sort of training ground whereby the major political parties could assess the performance and the basis of popularity of councillors, with the thought in mind that some of those councillors could be recruited to contest elections that were, in the eyes of the parties, more important. But as Chapter 8 explains, the training ground theory is not solidly supported by facts, and in any case the parties could recruit councillors without overtly and directly taking part in municipal politics. It has by no means been uncommon for the major political parties to be involved in municipal elections behind the scenes, in terms of contributing organizational support to selected candidates for municipal office, but overt and direct participation by national/provincial parties in civic politics was generally confined to the protest parties. Only the CCF had long been interested in contesting city elections, but it usually lacked sufficient resources to make much of a showing.

However, with the pressures of urbanization, reorganization of city government, expanded scope of governmental activity generally (including that of city government), and the shift in city government from short-term, non-controversial decision making to more politicized policy making, the major national/provincial political parties became increasingly interested and involved in city politics in the later 1960s. The stakes involved had become worthwhile, and the major parties sensed a growing need for the kind of interest-aggregating expertise that they possessed. Clarkson attributes much importance to a need felt by the major parties for city reform in a period of urban crises during which city governments seemed weak and ineffectual.[12]

Aside from very minor parties such as Marxist-Leninists, and perhaps with the exception of the NDP, the major political parties did not exactly leap into the breach in involving themselves in city elections. The decisions to enter city politics directly have not come from the national offices of the parties, nor from the provincial headquarters. Rather, it has been a case of smaller organizational units of the major parties taking the decision (often contrary to the wishes of the provincial organization) to contest elections, and in almost all cases those decisions have been in cities, not in non-urban areas. In Manitoba, the NDP provincial government designed Unicity Winnipeg in such a way as to entice (one might almost say to force) the introduction of party politics in the Unicity Council. The large number of council members (now fifty-one) plus the original intention to have the mayor selected by the elected members of council from their own ranks almost required that some kind of party organization be overlaid if some order is to evolve out of an otherwise chaotically large council. To have the mayor selected by and from among the elected councillors would be equivalent to having the largest grouping of councillors select a sort of prime minister, an action that would certainly be facilitated by having each grouping formed on party lines. But the Manitoba government reversed its earlier intention, and provided for the mayor to be directly elected.

It comes as no surprise to find that the New Democratic Party fielded a large slate of candidates for Winnipeg City Council in the civic election held in October of 1971, as well as in the election for Brandon City Council the same month. However, it appears that while the NDP may have been ready for city politics, the civic electorates were not ready for party politics, at least not for the New Democrats. Of the thirty-one candidates run by the party in Winnipeg, only seven were elected. The older-style civic party called the Independent Citizens Election Committee captured thirty-seven seats, and only five out of sixty-seven independents were successful. Hence the first election in Unicity Winnipeg was a disaster for the NDP, only slightly improved by a gain of two seats in 1974. But the Winnipeg disaster in 1971 was not so great as that in Manitoba's second largest city. In Brandon, all of the party's seven candidates for the ten council seats were defeated, and the NDP's mayoralty candidate came in a very distant third.

In the City of Toronto, the election of 1969 was a particularly interesting one, for two major parties were directly involved, the Liberal Party and the NDP.[13] Local associations of the NDP first contested Toronto elections in 1966, but did not run a full slate of candidates and were inhibited from running a mayoralty candidate because of the Toronto Labour Council's support for Mr. William Dennison, who was the incumbent mayor. The NDP was divided on the wisdom of seeking municipal office in Toronto, and the efforts of the local associations of the party lacked the wholehearted support of its organization. In 1967, Metro Toronto's municipal structure was reorganized, and citizens' associations had become an important element in civic affairs in Toronto in the earlier 1960s. Therefore the political climate of Toronto was changing. City Council after the 1966 election was a rather mixed group of traditional and reformist councillors, and Council became a confusing battlefield characterized by minimal co-ordination of councillors within each type. After the NDP's tentative foot in the water in the 1966 Toronto election, the party made gains in the provincial election of 1967. This strengthened its interest in seriously and directly contesting elections for Toronto City Council, and in 1968 the party's provincial convention endorsed moves by its local branches to contest the Toronto election of the following year.

Meanwhile, the Liberal Party emerged triumphant from the 1968 federal election campaign, and greatly invigorated by Pierre Trudeau's leadership. But at the same time, the Liberal Party faced a long-entrenched Progressive Conservative government in Ontario. If the party was to ever eliminate the massive majority that the PC's held in the Ontario legislature, it was apparent that it had to create a stronger base in Toronto. The question of its involvement in Toronto city politics was first raised in the latter part of 1967, primarily by younger elements in the party. The question was taken up at the Toronto and District Liberal Executive's annual meeting in 1968. After considerable debate and some hesitation, the executive passed a motion which favoured direct participation by the party in the next city election. This decision was approved by the party's general meeting for Toronto and District in January of 1969, but only after more hot debate. Dissidents brought the matter up again at the annual meeting of the Ontario Liberal Party held in March, and that meeting eventually endorsed the right of local associations of the party to contest municipal elections directly. It was clear that the Liberal Party was internally split over the propriety of entering municipal politics, and this resulted in a less than wholehearted effort in the Toronto election of November 1969.

The election itself did not go well for either major party. The Liberal Party's mayoralty candidate (Stephen Clarkson) came in third with about 21 per cent of the votes cast, being defeated by the incumbent mayor, William Dennison, who was associated with the NDP but who refused to run as an NDP candidate. Dennison received 43 per cent of the votes cast. Each of the two major parties nominated only sixteen aldermanic candidates out of a possible twenty-two, so neither ran a full slate. Only three candidates of the New Democratic Party and two of the Liberal Party's candidates for alderman were elected, and only five more NDP and two more Liberal candidates were serious challengers for office in terms of getting at least half as many votes as the junior alderman received in a given ward.[14] Therefore the results of the 1969 election in the City of Toronto were no more a triumph for either party than were the results in Winnipeg in 1971 a triumph for the NDP.

The voters in both cities seem to have been singularly unimpressed by this new feature in city elections. Involvement of the parties seems to have had little effect on voter turnout, so the introduction of major party politics does not appear to have been especially exciting for the electorate. The two parties in Toronto were very much humbled by their 1969 experience, and reverted to indirect involvement in subsequent elections.

What factors account for this lack of success by the major political parties? Clearly, part of the problem in Toronto especially was that the involvement of the parties was somewhat less than wholehearted, the Liberals being especially fraught with internal dissension over the propriety of openly entering city politics. In fact several candidates for council refused to run as party candidates despite their known connections with major parties. Additionally, Clarkson maintains that there were substantial institutional, legal, and cultural barriers to the entry of parties in Toronto.[15] For example, the franchise differed in the City of Toronto compared to that for federal and provincial elections. Therefore lists of the parties' faithful for provincial and federal elections were not particularly useful for the municipal election. Also, the local associations of the parties lacked the financial resources necessary to utilize the kind of advertising techniques they were accustomed to using for higher-level elections. Attempts to formulate and publicize campaign platforms were inconsistent with the usual expectations of the civic electorate. In short, the major national/provincial parties had difficulty in adapting themselves to the context of city politics.

Non-Partisan City Politics?

Without doubt one significant factor mitigating against the entry of non-civic parties in city politics is the popular view that the conduct of city affairs should be non-partisan. As mentioned before, this view is buttressed by such structural features as comparatively small councils that approximate corporate boards of directors, the city manager structure in smaller cities, and the Ryerson tradition of isolating some kinds of functions (public education, for example) from any taint of politics at the municipal level. Furthermore, party politics in cities are commonly viewed as unsavoury, "dirty" politics, a view that is in part a spill-over from American bossism, party machines, and patronage, but from time to time reinforced by scandals in Canadian city halls. Just why "dirty" party politics should somehow be more tolerable in the provincial and federal contexts than in the city context is inexplicable. What is also inexplicable is that city electorates are commonly aware of the party affiliation of members of council who profess an ability to discard such connections. Thus partisan individuals on council are perceived (and profess) to be apolitical when it comes to performing their roles as councillors. In other words, while the individuals are partisan, city politics is non-partisan. Or so the myth has it.

In fact, there may be considerable validity to that ironic statement. Except in cases where a city council is composed almost entirely of people from the same party, voting coalitions on council frequently cross party affiliations. As a consequence, the fact that most councillors do have an affiliation to one major party or another is not necessarily of significance in terms of their behaviour (voting or otherwise) in council. Major party affiliation is not always a useful indicator for predicting how a particular councillor will vote on any specific issues. The Liberal and Progressive Conservative parties are not coherently ideological parties at the federal or provincial levels, and there is even less reason to expect that they would (or could) offer explicit ideology in city politics. The New Democratic Party is the one major political party that one might expect to be the exception on issues in the city arena because of its more obvious ideological stances in federal and provincial politics. Therefore one would expect that city councillors who are connected to the NDP, either by having run for council as an NDP candidate, or by privately being a member of the party, would be those councillors most likely to be partisan and to co-ordinate their activities and views in council. But the NDP has neither dominated nor constituted a significant bloc of members except briefly in a few city councils. Therefore one cannot say that councillors who are known to be associated with major parties, even though publicly non-partisan in city elections, are especially partisan in terms of their behaviour as members of council.

Nor in the case of municipal election campaigns can any considerable evidence of partisanship be detected, except in those few and isolated cases where the major parties have run slates of candidates. Co-ordination of election campaigns by candidates who privately share a major party affiliation is very rare. It is somewhat more common with civic parties, but even in the case of these parties (especially of the older style) most candidates run independently, not as co-ordinated slates with a common policy platform, co-ordinated campaign organization, and so on.

Even though party affiliation (civic or non-civic) is not always meaningful or significant, it is still interesting to look at the composition of councils of a few Canadian cities for which data are available. After the 1968 election in Edmonton, council consisted of six Liberals, three Conservatives, one NDP member, and three aldermen whose major party affiliation (if any) was unknown. After the 1971 election there, council was composed of five Liberals, two Conservatives, two NDP members, and three whose affiliation, again, was unknown.[16] While the major parties were not directly involved in those elections, one older-style civic party was. In the 1968 election, the United Civic Action Party (UCAP, previously called the Better Civic Government Committee, and before that known as the Civic Government Association) had five members on council, and there were seven councillors who had run as independents. In his 1968–69 study of Fort William (since 1970 part of the City of Thunder Bay), Alexander interviewed seven of the twelve members of council. The previous civic election was entirely non-partisan, with no civic or non-civic parties having been involved. Five of those seven were formal members of the Progressive Conservative Party, and the other two were formal members of the Liberal Party.[17] Voters in Halifax's 1974 election, also an entirely non-partisan contest, elected six Liberals as aldermen, two Progressive Conservatives, a mayor who had been a PC Member of Parliament, and two aldermen whose major party affiliations (if any) were not known.

Whether city politics should be partisan or not is a matter of hot debate. It would seem from the disastrous attempts by the NDP in Winnipeg and by the Liberal Party and NDP in Toronto that the electorate is not convinced that the major non-civic parties ought to be directly involved. But the electorate is clearly much more favourably disposed to direct involvement by civic parties. It is questionable, though, whether the civic parties are really "parties" in terms of being more than just a label attached to candidates for election to council. As was pointed out earlier, the newer type of civic party, with more or less specific and broad policy platforms, and with caucusing (though without strong discipline in council) more closely represent partisan city politics than do their older counterparts. The latter tend to be basically just election phenomena.

The usual arguments offered in opposition to openly partisan city politics include the belief that such politics are connected with bribery and corruption, that political parties represent vested special interests as opposed to the general interest, that party caucusing would result in public decisions being shrouded in privacy and secrecy, that a city council controlled by a party different from that controlling the city's provincial government would be in trouble, and that well qualified potential candidates for civic office would be deterred from running for office if they had to publicly acknowledge or adopt a party label.[18] On the other hand, there are those who argue that the process of urbanization has changed the nature of the cities and that the structures and processes must reflect that change, that the best way to reduce the chaos of non-partisan city councils would be to have political parties to organize and clarify competing viewpoints, that parties would be a mechanism whereby councils and councillors could better be held accountable and responsible to the electorate, that parties would be a mechanism whereby the citizens could be better informed, and that parties would be an additional avenue of participation in city politics for citizens who do not wish to run for elective office themselves. It is not the intention here to attempt to assess each of these propositions favouring or opposing partisan politics in the city context. But it should be understood that few councils in Canada's major cities have demonstrated much will or ability to grasp and cope with the stresses and consequences of urbanization. Analysts such as Jane Jacobs have argued convincingly that the cities face an urban crisis.[19] Having significant and direct party involvement in city councils is in itself unlikely to be the cure-all for the ills of cities that some proponents seem to hope. Nevertheless, parties, whether purely local ones or branches of major existing ones, can be important in the sense of clarifying, sorting out, and instilling some orderliness and intelligibility in city politics. If parties are to be effective in this regard, then clearly some structural changes in the decision-making processes are required. It is difficult if not impossible to conceive of the parliamentary model of governing and opposition parties working in a context of councils that are as small as those of so many cities in Canada; in a context where the mayor is elected at large rather than by and from among elected councillors; or in a context where a kind of cabinet (i.e. board of control) is also elected at large. Perhaps the most important qualifier of party success in city politics is that the cities' electorates have yet to be convinced that parties and the parliamentary model ought to be applied in city politics. Thus, before disciplined political parties win council seats at the polls, they have to win legitimacy in the minds of their electorate.

City Elections

As the Liberal Party found to its dismay in Toronto in 1969, city elections are not like provincial and federal elections. They rarely generate levels of excitement characteristic of federal and provincial general elections, media coverage of them tends to be less extensive and less prominent, and there are inevitable and predictable sighs about voter apathy in city elections. There are other differences too. Part of the interest in provincial and federal general elections may be due to an element of mystery surrounding their timing, which is not fixed (there is only a five-year maximum between elections), so rumours, speculation, and denials are rife before such an election is called. In contrast, city elections are regular and predictable in their timing—everyone knows (or can know) with absolute confidence when the next city election will be. The charter or municipal act tells us exactly. Also, when one goes to the polling station, the voter in local elections is presented with a different and generally more complex task than he faces when voting in federal and provincial elections. In the latter cases, the voter marks one simple "X" on one piece of paper. In city elections, one is confronted with choices not just for one office but a number of offices: typically one or two "X"s for aldermen, another for mayor, perhaps four for board of control, sometimes a dozen or so for school board, and in some cities, some "X"s for hydro-electric commissioners. To complicate matters, city voters must sometimes also vote on plebiscites to approve a city bond issue or water fluoridation, for example. The result is what is known as a "bed sheet" ballot, denoting the size of the ballot paper needed to accommodate the number of elective offices and the number of choices available.

To take one example, in Ottawa's 1972 civic election a voter was faced with choosing twelve people out of forty-six candidates for the Board of Education (if the voter was not a Catholic school supporter), choosing four out of ten candidates for Board of Control, choosing one out of four candidates for mayor, and (if the voter was in Britannia Ward) choosing one out of ten candidates for alderman. In total, therefore, the voter was expected to vote for as many as eighteen out of seventy candidates. Taking all wards and all Board of Education seats into account, there were in that one city election 132 names of candidates on the ballots. Understandably, some concern was expressed about the ability of the electorate to cope with such a selection in a reasoned and informed way. In situations such as this those candidates who are incumbents have a definite advantage, and so do candidates whose names begin with the letters A, B, and C, because names are usually printed in alphabetical order on the ballots. Voters who are not familiar with all or many of the candidates tend to select the names at the top of the ballot.

The other aspects of city elections that need consideration are electorates, candidature, and campaigns.

THE ELECTORATE

Who are the people that are confronted with tasks like that in the 1972 election in Ottawa? The legal qualifications for electors in municipal elections are generally specified in city charters, general municipal acts of the provincial legislatures, or municipal elections acts of the provincial legislatures. As a result there is a high level of uniformity in elector qualifications within each province, though there are some variations from province to province.

When K. G. Crawford wrote his book in 1952, it was common for electors to have to meet a property qualification, either as an owner or as a tenant of property assessed at some specified minimum value.[20] Spouses of those owners or tenants were usually considered to have met that qualification too. The two subsequent decades have witnessed a considerable democratization of the municipal franchise, with electors in Canada's larger cities (population of 100,000 or more) no longer having to meet such a condition in order to vote. In Montreal, for example, it is only since 1970 that the municipal franchise has been virtually universal, and the process of election reform began in Montreal only in 1962. Before that, most tenants were disenfranchised, in a city where some 80 per cent of the people are tenants. Residence within the city for a specified minimum period of time (typically no more than one year prior to the election) usually suffices, if the person also is at least 18 (in some places 19) years old, and is either a Canadian citizen or a British subject. Therefore the usual qualifications for municipal electorates are citizenship, age, and residence. However, in many of the larger cities there is still a property qualification of sorts, in that people who own property in a city are included on the electoral roll even if they do not reside in that particular municipality or in the particular ward. For example, people who own a business in a city can often vote even if they do not live there. In Ontario's cities it is the case that some property owners have multiple votes, being able to vote in any and all municipalities and/or wards within which they own land, as well as having a vote in the municipality and ward in which they reside. There is an added quirk in Montreal, where *companies* that own property are also entitled to a vote, that vote being cast by a designated representative of the firm.

The fact that the municipal franchise is not completely uniform, and that it is not identical to the franchise for federal and provincial elections, does not pose a particularly serious problem in comparing voter turnout among cities, and between local elections and federal or provincial elections. Voter turnout in federal general elections from 1900 to 1974 ranged from a low of 66.4 per cent (in 1925) to a high of 79.4 per cent (in 1958). Turnout in provincial general elections tends to range both higher and lower, sometimes being well over 80 per cent, and sometimes dipping below 60 per cent, but the usual turnout is two-thirds to three-quarters of the electorate. These figures constitute a somewhat startling comparison relative to voter turnout in Canada's larger cities. Figures for the most recent municipal election up to August of 1975 are shown in Table 7:1.

Only the cities of Laval and Thunder Bay had voter participation that equals or exceeds the general minimum in provincial elections. The average of these municipal voter turnouts is about 35 per cent, or about half the average in federal or provincial general elections.

Nor are the above figures atypical of the historical norm. With regard to Winnipeg, for example, the average turnout in all twenty municipal

Table 7:1   Voter Turnout by City (%)

city	turnout	city	turnout
Montreal	38	London	33
Toronto	30	Windsor	38
Winnipeg	35	Quebec	*
North York	27	Mississauga	37
Edmonton	48	York	30
Vancouver	32	Regina	41
Calgary	45	Saskatoon	20
Scarborough	25	Halifax	42
Hamilton	35	Kitchener	35
Ottawa	35	St. Catharines	25
Etobicoke	28	Thunder Bay	58
Laval	61	East York	28

*no figure is given because in the 1973 election, candidates were acclaimed in all except two wards.

elections from 1945 to 1964 was about 39 per cent, ranging from a low of about 23 per cent (in 1963) to a high of about 57 per cent (in 1956).[21] Also, the above figures are comparable to those reported in a study published in 1967 of municipal voter turnout in the fourteen Canadian cities that then had populations of at least 100,000.[22]

Although Table 7:1 does not clearly show a connection between population size of municipalities and the percentage of voter turnout, the Canadian Federation of Mayors and Municipalities found in both that 1967 study and a 1957 study of 122 municipalities that there was a tendency for turnout to be inversely connected to population size—that is, the more populous the municipality, the lower the percentage turnout of voters.[23] This aspect of scale also suggests that voter turnout is likely to increase the smaller the population of wards. There are factors other than just the population size of cities, though. There is clear evidence that voter participation is directly related to such factors as occupational status and level of education, the assessed value of a home-owner's house, and the assessed value of a tenant's residence.[24] Also, it has been fairly common in Canadian cities to have staggered elections, whereby only part of council is elected at any one civic election, the rest being elected at a subsequent one. Therefore some city elections do not always involve the election of a mayor. However, when a mayoralty contest is included, the turnout of electors is higher than in other elections.

Some explanations for low voter turnout in city elections compared to federal and provincial general elections have already been offered in the two preceding chapters, so need not be repeated here. It was noted in Chapter 6 that the timing of civic elections (usually late autumn or early winter) may reduce voter turnout because of the likelihood of inclement weather. It does seem rather unlikely that this factor has high explanatory value; such other factors as level of interest in local politics seem more probable because an excited voter will tend to vote regardless of the weather. Simply changing the timing of city elections would not result in any dramatic increase of citizen participation.

CANDITATURE

It has become standard practice that the qualifications of candidates for city council are the same as the qualifications of the electorate. In other words, it is almost always the case that anyone on the electoral roll can run for council. Such has not always been true, for it was once common that the qualifications for candidature were more restrictive than those for the electorate, especially in terms of property ownership and/or length of residence in the city. The City of Mississauga, for example, still requires that candidates for council have assessable property in the ward they are contesting.

Aside from voting and being a member of interest groups which concern themselves with city affairs, being a candidate in city elections is one of the main avenues of participation available in city politics because of the number of directly elective seats, as shown in Table 7:2. Whether or not one also takes into account such other municipal elective offices as seats on school boards, the point remains that there are far more opportunities to participate in local politics by running for office than there are at either the federal or provincial levels. While a higher proportion of the electorate runs for municipal office than in federal or provincial elections, it is not always the case that city elections are more hotly contested, in terms of the number of candidates for each available office. In the federal general election of 1974, there were 1207 candidates for 264 seats in the

Table 7:2 Number of Directly Elective Council Seats, by Type, by City (1975)

city	aldermen	other	total	city	aldermen	other	total
Montreal	55 (19 wards)	mayor	56	London	14 (7 wards)	mayor, 4 controllers	19
Toronto	22 (11 wards)	mayor	23	Windsor	8 (at large)	mayor	9
Winnipeg	50 (50 wards)	mayor	51	Quebec	16 (7 wards)	mayor	17
North York	14 (14 wards)	mayor, 4 controllers	19	Mississauga	9 (9 wards)	mayor	10
Edmonton	12 (4 wards)	mayor	13	York	8 (8 wards)	mayor, 2 controllers	11
Vancouver	10 (at large)	mayor	11	Regina	10 (10 wards)	mayor	11
Calgary	12 (6 wards)	mayor	13	Saskatoon	10 (10 wards)	mayor	11
Scarborough	12 (12 wards)	mayor, 4 controllers	17	Halifax	10 (10 wards)	mayor	11
Hamilton	16 (8 wards)	mayor, 4 controllers	21	Kitchener*	10 (at large)	mayor	11
Ottawa	11 (11 wards)	mayor, 4 controllers	16	St. Catharines	12 (6 wards)	mayor	13
Etobicoke	10 (5 wards)	mayor, 4 controllers	15	Thunder Bay	12 (at large)	mayor	13
Laval	21 (8 wards)	mayor	22	East York	8 (4 wards)	mayor	9

*in a plebiscite conducted during the 1974 election, voters in the city approved the adoption of a ward system.

House of Commons, or an average of 4.6 candidates per available seat. This compares with the City of Ottawa election in 1972 where there was an average of 4.0 candidates for the sixteen council seats, and an average of only 2.6 candidates for each of seventeen seats on the Ottawa School Board. In Halifax's city election in 1974, the average number of candidates per council seat was only 3.3. In contrast, a by-election for one aldermanic seat in Hamilton in 1976 produced an incredible seventeen candidates. It is not uncommon in city elections for council seats to be uncontested, but acclamation almost never occurs in federal or provincial elections. In the 1974 Halifax example, one seat was filled by acclamation, as was one of the seats in the 1972 Ottawa city election. In the 1956 election for Halifax city council, six out of fourteen seats were filled by acclamation. The mayor's chair in Winnipeg was filled by acclamation in both 1958 and 1960. In 1974, two of Scarborough's aldermanic seats were also filled by acclamation, as were thirty school board seats in Metro Toronto. And in Quebec City in 1973 all council seats from five of the seven wards were filled by acclamation. Although it rarely happens in major city contexts, it is worth noting that sometimes no candidates at all offer for municipal elective office.

Although there are times and places (such as the Hamilton by-election) where elections to major city councils are highly contested, the overall impression is that they tend to be somewhat less competitive than the federal or provincial equivalents. Of the many factors that help explain this, probably the most important one is the general absence of major party structures in city elections. In the context of the federal and provincial governments, it is normally the case that each of the Liberal, Progressive Conservative, and New Democratic parties runs a candidate for each seat, as well as the Social Credit Party in some areas. Therefore one expects three or four party candidates for each seat, plus the occasional independent candidate, although the number of independents tends to be small because of the long-term monopoly held by the major parties. But in municipal elections, political parties of the national/provincial variety have no such monopoly, and in most cases the newer-style civic parties are too new to have acquired any sort of monopoly. Local parties of the older style have a history of dominance in many cities, which minimizes the likelihood of slates of opposition candidates from contesting city elections. This means that there is generally a relatively low level of competitiveness in city elections, but it also means a low degree of predictability concerning the number of candidates that are likely to contest an aldermanic seat on council. When a long dominant civic party appears to be on the brink of decline, one is likely to see a rush of independent candidates come forward. Otherwise, few will contest the election, and acclamations may result.

Also, the rate of turnover on city councils tends to be extremely low. It is not unusual for as many as 80 per cent of incumbent councillors who stand for re-election to be re-elected. Whether or not such councillors are associated with a civic party, they obviously tend to monopolize the votes in their ward or in the city as a whole. This very strong advantage of incumbency therefore tends to dissuade other possible candidates from entering the fray and helps make city elections relatively uncompetitive.

In addition to these and such previously mentioned factors as generally low interest of the electorate in city affairs, the relative uncompetitiveness of city elections may be related to the deposits that candidates must put up in many cities. In Montreal, for example, candidates for mayor and for aldermen must post a $200 deposit which is refunded only if the candidate wins the seat or receives at least 50 per cent of the winner's total vote. This deposit is the same as that which candidates in federal elections must post. In Vancouver, candidates for mayor must post a $300 deposit which is refunded if the candidate receives at least 5 per cent of the votes cast. Some cities (such as Toronto) do not require that deposits be posted by candidates—they need only be nominated by ten qualified voters. The idea of deposits is basically to dissuade "nuisance" candidates, to ensure that only the serious will run. However, the ability to post a deposit is not the best possible indicator of a candidate's "seriousness". Requiring a substantial cash deposit may not only dissuade some worthwhile candidates from seeking election, it can also be viewed as undemocratic in the sense of limiting candidature to particular kinds of people—those who either can personally afford it, or those who have friends, family, or business associates that can afford it. A better test is the candidate's ability to get a reasonable number of qualified electors to sign the nomination form.

Finally, some mention of wards is necessary. As the previous table shows, most of Canada's larger cities have some form of ward basis for purposes of civic elections, but a few cities (Thunder Bay, Windsor, Vancouver, and, until recently, Kitchener) require that all candidates run "at large", there being no electoral wards at all. Several consequences arise from having either no wards at all or having a very small number of very large wards (such as Edmonton), some of which have multiple members on council. One consequence is that aldermen can quite safely ignore some sectors of the city or large ward, in the knowledge that at the next civic election they will not likely be voted out of office by the ignored people. It is lower-income people that are most likely to be ignored because of the greater tendency for the middle classes to vote. There is, therefore, the fundamental question about the capacity (and perhaps willingness) of aldermen to represent all sectors, to respond to inputs from all sectors, and to be really accountable to all sectors. Second, having to contest an election either at large or in very large wards requires a widely recognized name, or financial and/or organizational resources that are simply not available to the bulk of the electors who could run as candidates. This is likely to depress the competitiveness of elections. There are two basic kinds of wards—block wards and strip wards, the terms referring to the shape of the area.[25] If carefully drawn, and if sufficiently numerous, it is possible for block-ward boundaries to coincide fairly closely with perceived communities. Strip wards of the sort proposed for the City of Toronto in 1969 do not respect perceived communities; rather, each tends to include bits of a number of widely disparate sectors. Thus strip wards tend to divide communities, and are subject to the kinds of difficulties associated with large-ward or no-ward electoral systems. The Unicity Winnipeg example goes a considerable distance toward ensuring that sectors of the population do not go essentially unrepresented, and that candidature is not greatly discouraged.

CAMPAIGNS

There are several fundamental differences between campaigns for a city election and campaigns for federal or provincial elections. The fact that the date of a city's next election is always precisely known makes it possible for the incumbents and for potential candidates to have their strategies mapped out and put into operation well before nomination day. In contrast, the timing of federal and provincial elections is never known to candidates until the premier or prime minister announces the date. A second fundamental difference lies in the fact that even when candidates for city elective office are running under the name of a civic party, they run essentially as independents. Hence it is the individual candidates themselves (plus any advisors that they may have) that plan and run an entire and separate campaign, instead of fitting in to a party's plans. Raising funds, arranging publicity, formulating a platform, deciding strategy, recruiting workers, and so on, are done for each candidate separately. If the candidate is sponsored by an organized interest or by a party, some assistance may be given to him or her, especially if the party is either of the newer type of civic party or a branch of a major national/provincial political party. This isolation is one factor that accounts for the scarcity of detailed and comprehensive campaign platforms in so many city elections. Typically, a candidate for council states only that he or she will endeavour, if elected, to promote good government, more consultation with citizens, and other such generalities. The absence of comprehensive policy platforms is largely a matter of recognizing realities; the candidates are running as independents (more or less) and will be elected as independents. As such, they have no assurance of stable support from other members of council. To promise other than vague generalities exposes the candidate to the likelihood of being accused at the subsequent election of not having fulfilled the pledges made in the preceding election. It is somehow viewed as more reprehensible for incumbent candidates to be open to this accusation than to make no promises at all, or promises of only a highly general nature. Traditionally, the most common and probably the most popularly accepted promise made in city election campaigns has been to keep the tax rate down. However, city electorates are no longer dominated by property owners, to whom such promises are mainly directed. Therefore vows of financial frugality are somewhat less universal than has long been the case, though they are prevalent still.

The most essential objective of candidates in city elections is to get their names known, if they are not already widely recognized. This is because the still rather minimal direct involvement by the major national/provincial political parties make it less possible for candidates to rely on a party name than can be done in provincial and federal elections. Therefore city election campaigns are organized in such a way as to maximize exposure of the candidate and his or her name, using such tested and traditional tactics as door-to-door canvassing and blitz-type distribution of printed material throughout the ward. Typically the blanket distribution of campaign literature is done more than once during the campaign, and the literature itself emphasizes, again, the candidate's name rather than statements of policy.[26]

For candidates who are not incumbents running for re-election, this publicity exercise can be an expensive one. Incumbents have a definite head start, for their names are likely to be already widely recognized. Reliable information about campaign finance, both with respect to amounts raised and to amounts spent, is extremely scarce because of lack of controls over it and because of an absence of disclosure requirements.[27] There is presumably a connection between the population size of a constituency (whether a ward, or an entire city in the case of at-large elections) and the amount of resources necessary to conduct more than a token campaign. Some support for this is found in a study in Metropolitan Toronto.[28] Of *successful* aldermanic candidates in 1974, the average campaign costs were $1,566 in the Borough of York, which had the smallest average-size wards (17,550 people). In contrast, the average costs of aldermen in the City of Toronto, which had the largest average number of people per ward (62,023) of any of the six municipalities in Metro, were $8,075. However, the study excluded unsuccessful candidates, 79.3 per cent of the respondents were not newcomers to office, and there was not a uniform connection between average campaign costs and average size of wards. The same study found that the election expenses of successful aldermen (elected by ward) tended to be much less than those of the mayors and controllers, who are elected at large. None of the aldermen interviewed reported spending more than $15,000, but eight of the twenty people elected at large reported spending more than $15,000 on their campaigns.[29] Candidates for mayor in the City of Toronto's 1969 election reported that they expected their campaigns to cost between $12,500 and $25,000, figures that appear to be somewhat understated.[30] Candidates for mayor in Halifax in 1974 expected their campaigns to cost as little as $8,000 and as much as $30,000. One would expect that incumbents seeking re-election to council need not raise and spend as much money as non-incumbents, for their names are already known, and they can sometimes recycle signs and so on from previous campaigns. The expenditures are highest when campaign workers are paid rather than voluntary. It is generally the case that campaigns for aldermanic seats in wards rely largely on volunteered help—unpaid personnel to man the headquarters, to formulate strategy, to distribute literature and post signs, and to drive voters to the polls. It is in these areas that the major political parties have been covertly active. Additionally, candidates often receive donated goods and services, such as the use of office space, so even if reliable figures were available for campaign revenue and expenditure, those figures would not represent a particularly accurate value of all the actual costs involved in running for city council.

The problem of campaign finance is one which has become increasingly important in more than just the sense of the amounts of money needed dissuading interested people from participating in urban politics by contesting elective office. Of growing concern are the ramifications of donations (whether of cash, goods, or services) in terms of possible influence on those who are elected. The problem of conflict of interest is raised further in the next chapter, but clearly one highly important aspect of this matter concerns the sources of campaign funds and any strings that may be attached implicitly or explicitly to donations. For federal elections as well as for most provincial elections, there now exist laws requiring some degree of public disclosure of the sources of campaign finance, and sometimes setting limits on the amounts that can be spent. As imperfect as much of that legislation is, it does present a sharp contrast with municipal elections, which are financial free-for-alls.

Especially in the more expensive city election campaigns, candidates are seldom self-sufficient for election finance. Incumbent candidates are likely to find it easier than newcomers to get contributions from others, but newcomers are likely to have greater need for outside contributions if there is an incumbent councillor running as competition. In the study of successful candidates in Metro Toronto's 1974 elections only nineteen of the eighty-five councillors reported that they received no financial contributions.[31] While some refused to accept any contributions, seventeen of the eighty-five councillors received donations that paid for between 76 and 100 per cent of their campaign expenses.

The property industry has long been reputed to be the largest contributor to city election campaigns. As usual, there are virtually no reliable figures on either the size or the recipients of donations from building contractors, land developers, large property owners, and so on, but rumours abound in virtually every city from time to time. For example, it was alleged that the Meridian Building Group "bankrolled" twenty-three individual campaigns in Toronto's 1969 election, including at least eight of the successful candidates, and several people claimed that they had been offered at least $11,000 each by Meridian to run as aldermanic candidates for council. While the company's president partially denied the rumours, he was quoted as saying that he would support ". . . anyone who is not a Maoist. I would be too happy to support anyone who runs who is not a burn-baby-burn type".[32] Whether the rumours are correct or not, city councillors tend to be extremely sensitive about the issue of public disclosure and in recent years have attempted to head off demands for it by announcing that they, as individual candidates, will voluntarily put a ceiling on the size of donations coming from any one source, the limits ranging as high as $1000. This does not of course resolve either the issue of the expectations or strings attached to a donation, or the issue of the amount of money required to wage a competitive election campaign. Elections in major cities are not poor men's games, especially for first-time serious candidates. If broader participation in city politics, in the sense of contesting elective office, is to be facilitated, and the chances of success arc to bc made less dependent on personal wealth or on connections with wealth, then reform of the financial aspect of city elections is very much needed. An equally important reform necessary to facilitate such participation is enlarging the size of most city councils, increasing the number of wards, and decreasing the size of wards. Of course at-large elections for any council offices would need to be eliminated. Not only would such reforms lead to a significant reduction in the need for substantial campaign resources but they would generally democratize city politics by enabling wider participation and ensuring that there are not significant sectors of cities' populations that go underrepresented or entirely unrepresented.

NOTES

1. The most exhaustive study of civic parties in Canada is found in J. G. Joyce and H. A. Hossé, *Civic Parties in Canada* (Ottawa: Canadian Federation of Mayors and Municipalities, 1970). Their definition of civic parties is wider than the one used here in that their definition includes branches of the federal/provincial parties.

2. Ibid., Appendix A.

3. Robert Easton and Paul Tennant, "Vancouver Civic Party Leadership: Backgrounds, Attitudes and Non-Civic Party Affiliations," in Jack K. Masson and James D. Anderson, eds., *Emerging Party Politics in Urban Canada* (Toronto: McClelland and Stewart, 1972), p. 110.

4. Joyce and Hossé, *Civic Parties in Canada.* Appendix c of their book indicates that twenty-four of twenty-eight cities examined in 1969 had at least one active civic party (generally of the older style) as the term is defined in this present book.

5. For an interesting but now dated analysis of the Civic Party see Peter Michaelson, "Montreal's Civic Party: the king, the duke and the vassals," *Civic Administration*, April, 1968, pp. 38–9 and 56. See also the articles by Jeff Simpson in *The Globe and Mail* (Toronto), February 4, 1976, p. 33; and February 5, 1976, p. 10.

6. See Margaret Daly, "Montreal Poor Challenge Mayor Drapeau's Regime," reprinted in Masson and Anderson, *Emerging Party Politics in Urban Canada*, pp. 76–82.

7. See *City Magazine*, vol. 1, no. 4 (May-June, 1975), pp. 4–5; and Henry Milner, "City Politics: Some Possibilities," *Our Generation*, vol. 10, no. 4 (Winter, 1975), pp. 47–60.

8. Robert Easton and Paul Tennant, "Vancouver Civic Party Leadership: Backgrounds, Attitudes and Non-Civic Party Affiliations," in Masson and Anderson, *Emerging Party Politics in Urban Canada*, p. 113.

9. Donald Gutstein, "The Developers' TEAM: Vancouver's 'Reform' Party in Power," *City Magazine*, vol. 1, no. 2 (December, 1974–January, 1975), pp. 13–28. See also Donald Gutstein, *Vancouver Ltd.* (Toronto: James Lorimer, 1975), especially chapters 26 and 28.

10. Joyce and Hossé, *Civic Parties in Canada*, pp. 35–6.

11. For example, see James Lightbody, "The Rise of Party Politics in Canadian Local Elections," *Journal of Canadian Studies*, February, 1971; and Stephen Clarkson, "Barriers to Entry of Parties into Toronto's Civic Politics: Towards a Theory of Party Penetration," *Canadian Journal of Political Science*, vol. IV, no. 2 (June, 1971), pp. 206–23. Both articles are reprinted in L. Axworthy and James M. Gillies, eds., *The City: Canada's Prospects, Canada's Problems* (Toronto: Butterworths, 1973).

12. Axworthy and Gillies, ibid., p. 209.

13. For an interesting chronical and analysis of that election see Stephen Clarkson, *City Lib: Parties and Reform* (Toronto: Hakkert, 1972); Bureau of Municipal Research, *Parties to Change: The Introduction of Political Parties in the 1969 Toronto Municipal Election* (Toronto, 1971); and E. P. Fowler and M. D. Goldrick, "The Toronto Election of 1969: Patterns of Partisan and Non-Partisan Balloting," a paper presented at the annual meeting of the Canadian Political Science Association, Winnipeg, 1970.

14. P. Silcox, "Postscript: The City Council Results," in Bureau of Municipal Research, *Parties to Change*, pp. 54–6. The term "junior alderman" refers to the alderman in each ward who gets the second largest number of votes. Each ward has two seats on Council.

15. Clarkson, "Barriers to Entry of Parties into Toronto's Civic Politics."

16. J. D. Anderson, "Non-Partisan Urban Politics in Canadian Cities", in Masson and Anderson, *Emerging Party Politics in Urban Canada*, p. 7.

17. Alan Alexander, "The Institutional and Role Perceptions of Local Aldermen," a paper presented to the annual meeting of the Canadian Political Science Association, Winnipeg, 1970, p. 22 (reprinted both in Masson and Anderson, *Emerging Party Politics in Urban Canada*, pp. 124–40; and Lionel D. Feldman and

Michael D. Goldrick (ed.), *Politics and Government of Urban Canada: Selected Readings*, 2nd ed. (Toronto: Methuen, 1972), pp. 139–52.

18. See, for example, the selections by Wickett, Gaetz, and Lighthall reprinted in Masson and Anderson, *Emerging Party Politics in Urban Canada*, pp. 22–32.

19. Jane Jacobs, *The Death and Life of Great American Cities* (New York: Random House, 1961). See also N. H. Lithwick, *Urban Canada: Problems and Prospects* (Ottawa: Central Mortgage and Housing Corporation, 1970).

20. K. Grant Crawford, *Canadian Municipal Government* (Toronto: University of Toronto Press, 1954), Appendix A, pp. 159–60.

21. M. S. Donnelly, "Ethnic Participation in Municipal Government: Winnipeg, St. Boniface and the Metropolitan Corporation of Greater Winnipeg," in Feldman and Goldrick, *Politics and Government of Urban Canada*, p. 56.

22. Canadian Federation of Mayors and Municipalities, *Survey of Municipal Voting in Fourteen Canadian Urban Centres of 100,000 or More Population* (May, 1967), Table 1.

23. Ibid., p. 1.

24. See, for example, Jerry F. Hough, "Voters' Turnout and the Responsiveness of Local Government: The Case of Toronto, 1969," in Paul W. Fox, ed., *Politics: Canada*, 3rd ed. (Toronto: McGraw-Hill, 1970), pp. 284–96; and Robert Vaison and

Peter Aucoin,"Class and Voting in Recent Halifax Mayoralty Elections," in Feldman and Goldrick, *Politics and Government of Urban Canada*, pp. 153–72.

25. In this connection see James Lorimer, *A Citizen's Guide to City Politics* (Toronto: James Lewis and Samuel, 1972), pp. 110–12. See also his book *The Real World of City Politics* (Toronto: James Lewis and Samuel, 1970), Chapter 2.

26. For interesting accounts of two successful campaigns, see Irene Harris, "How to Run and Win," *City Magazine*, vol. 1, no. 3 (February-March, 1975), pp. 14–23 and 26–7; and John Sewell, *Up Against City Hall* (Toronto: James Lewis and Samuel, 1972), Chapter 3.

27. The best study to date is of eighty-seven successful candidates in metropolitan Toronto, including mayors, controllers, and aldermen in the city and the boroughs (unsuccessful candidates were not included): The Royal Commission on Metropolitan Toronto, *Political Life in Metropolitan Toronto: A Survey of Municipal Councillors*, staff study (Toronto, April, 1976).

28. Ibid., p. 56, Table 5.3.

29. Ibid., p. 58, Table 5.4.

30. Clarkson, *City Lib: Parties and Reform*, p. 201.

31. Royal Commission on Metropolitan Toronto, *Political Life in Metropolitan Toronto*, pp. 59–62.

32. Reported in *The Globe and Mail* (Toronto), October 17, 1972, p. 35.

What kinds of people emerge victorious out of city elections, and how do they behave once elected? It is to such questions that this chapter is directed.

Who is Elected?

After the civic elections in Metro Toronto in 1962, the Bureau of Municipal Research constructed a profile of the candidates for councils and school boards.[1] Mr. Metro Politician was a male, about fifty years old, married with a family, owner of his own home, active in his church (Anglican), active in business organizations and in citizen and charity organizations, well-educated, earning a middle-to-upper level of income, a businessman or professional, a member of a major political party (most likely the Progressive Conservative Party), born in Ontario of parents who were born in England or Canada, and resident in his present municipality for fifteen years or more. He entered city politics out of a sense of duty, and felt that the most important issues were rising debt charges, rising tax rates, and citizen apathy, and he believed that the key to good local government was the application of good business methods and managerial experience.

As is the case with all stereotypes, this one disguises what differences there were among the candidates in that election, both for council office and for school board office. While there were indeed variations from that stereotype, the most striking feature of the candidates was the similarity of their social and economic positions—they constituted ". . . a middle-class group representative of the old Metro Toronto rather than the new."[2] There were large segments of the electorate in Metro Toronto that were unrepresented by candidates for municipal elective office, notably minority ethnic groups of all types and people of lower socio-economic status. It is also interesting that those candidates who did not very closely fit the mold of the Metro politician were effectively sifted out in the election process, so that those who were elected constituted an even more homogeneous group than the candidates as a whole.

The occupational distribution of the successful candidates, especially for council seats, was particularly interesting. Almost a third (31 per cent) were professionals, half of whom were lawyers. Thirty-four per cent of the successful candidates were managers, officials or proprietors, of whom close to three-quarters were small businessmen. This category was defined as including self-employed managers or proprietors with fewer than twenty employees. These kinds of occupations provide councillors with more freedom to devote time to political activities without a great loss of income than do occupations which require the individual to put in a regular nine-to-five day, or to work steady shifts. Adding the 13 per cent of successful candidates who were either retired or who were housewives gives a total of over three-quarters of the elected councillors included in the survey that were the kinds of people who could devote time to city affairs because they were somewhat independent of regular occupational obligations. The importance of this point will be drawn out shortly.

That profile constructed by the Bureau of Municipal Research applied specifically to candidates only in Metro Toronto, and only for 1962. In the 1969 election to Toronto City Council, the largest single occupational category of successful candidates was lawyers (six out of twenty-three councillors), followed by five businessmen. There were seven other professionals.[3] The sifting-out process in that election resulted in more than half of the eleven lawyer candidates and five of the twelve businessman candidates being elected, but none of the ten clerical/sales candidates nor any of the five skilled worker candidates were successful. Nevertheless, the complexion of council changed in 1969 with a group of newer-style councillors elected. The election of 1972 saw a further shift in the complexion of Toronto City Council,[4] and this was continued into the 1974 election. These elections saw the emergence of such untraditional reform-bloc councillors as M. D. Goldrick, John Sewell, Janet Howard, and Dorothy Thomas. The stereotype of "Mr. Metro Politician" was weakening in Toronto.

City councils elsewhere shared Toronto's pre-1972 councillor stereotype, with women, people of lower socio-economic status, and minority ethnic groups being under-represented on council. For example, Vancouver's eleven-member council in 1971–72 had only one woman, no people with other than Anglo-Saxon surnames, and seven people that Lorimer identified as having occupations connected to the property industry.[5] Even alderman Harry Rankin of the leftist Committee of Progressive Electors was a lawyer, for trade unions. In Winnipeg, the fifty-one-member council of 1972–74 had substantial ethnic representation, but there were only four women, and only seven members that Lorimer classified as having occupations other than those connected with the professions, the property industry, or other business interests.[6] Using other occupational categories, another study described that council as having seventeen businessmen, sixteen professionals, four salesmen, four retired people, three housewives, three technical/tradesmen, and one full-time politician.[7]

As the Toronto election of 1972 showed, stereotypes are subject to change over time. The Bureau of Municipal Research's profile continues to fit a large proportion of candidates for and members of councils in Canada's major cities, but it has ceased to be as widely applicable in the middle 1970s as it was in the early 1960s. The wide-scale emergence of the newer type of civic party and the political activism of citizen associations have thrust larger numbers of people who deviate from that stereotype onto the electoral stage, and sometimes into council. Most major city councils now have a complement of members who are not seen as part of the "group" of old-time civic politicians. But these new-style politicians only constitute minority groups on city councils, although they tend to be vocal and visible. As so many people who have been long-time observers of individual city councils have commented, councils used to have very much the atmosphere of a club. City councillors themselves may prefer to see their councils as a family rather than as a club, but whichever term is used the newer type of councillor does not fit in, at least not when first elected. In fact it can often be said that such people run for office at least partly to change the clubby atmosphere of city councils, an environment that is not conducive to public clarification of controversial issues. John Sewell, elected to Toronto City Council in 1969 as a new-style councillor, relates his astonishment at then-Mayor Dennison's welcoming him onto the "team" the day after the election.[8] Sewell's involvement as a community organizer in the Trefann Court case among others, the issue-basis of his campaign for election to council, and his objectives as a councillor made it quite clear that he certainly did not see himself fitting easily into the role as a member of a cohesive team or family.

What, then, distinguishes the newer type of councillor from the older-style city politician? There are generally some background differences between the two. The newer example is not likely a businessman, either as a corporate manager or as a proprietor. They may be professionals, but generally of a type different from or with a clientele different from those older-style city politicians with a professional occupational background. For example, newer-style city politicians who are or have been lawyers do not usually have property developers or other kinds of corporations as clients so much as community associations and individuals that are involved in litigation against property developers. University teachers (especially those in the social sciences) constitute another professional occupation category from which a number of such councillors emerge. One could also say that the few union members who become city councillors tend to be of the more modern style (at least initially), but people with this kind of occupational background generally do not have the flexibility of working hours that has become almost a prerequisite of active membership on city councils. Thus in terms of occupational backgrounds, newer-style city politicians are not greatly different from their older-style colleagues. One would probably be correct in supposing that the newer type is younger and has a lower-income background than the other. One would also expect that involvement in groups prior to election differs between the two. The older type is more likely to have been involved in such associations as church groups, business groups, and perhaps ratepayers groups, whereas the newer one tends to have been much more involved in the recent phenomenon of community associations. In fact one could go so far as to say that involvement in such groups is not only a prerequisite for the newer type of city politician (the group forming the politician's election base and stimulus to run for council) but constitutes one of the main features that distinguish the two styles. This point is pursued later under the heading of roles.

The newer style of urban politician is fundamentally different from his or her more traditional counterpart in that he views council as a necessarily *political* forum rather than as an overseer of city administration and management. Therefore he tends to see council as a focus for the public clarification and resolution of often highly contentious issues, as a means of informing, mobilizing, and representing the public on all sides of the issues. This orientation has required that he try to remove the shrouds of secrecy that have so often characterized so many city councils —"in camera" meetings, confidentiality of city documents and information, and informal private meetings with companies and groups seeking particular action by council. In short, this politician is committed to opening things up and to stimulating informed public debate well before council commits itself to any particular course of action. One can call this an attempt to democratize (some might say anarchize) the decision-making process in city hall.

Typically, the concerns of the newer-style urban politician have a specific focus, namely, the property development industry. Indeed it is almost a truism to say that the chief stimulus in such a politician's decision to run for election to council in the first place is first-hand involvement in a confrontation between a developer and a group of citizens. In such confrontations, city council is perceived as a handmaiden of the developer, and it is this perceived relationship that demands of some people a try for elective office so as to change that relationship. As a consequence, this kind of councillor tends to be stereotyped as anti-development. This stereotyping is almost always overstated, though, and it is more accurate to say that, in general, newer-style city politicians are simply more selective and more demanding about the nature and scale of development. They are anxious to ensure that city council not be (and not be seen to be) in collusion with property developers to the detriment of the public interest.

In much the same sense that the two kinds of civic parties tend to differ in their ideological orientations, so do councillors. The Montreal Citizens Movement and many of its members on council are characterized by a strongly anti-capitalist viewpoint. While they tend to be more vocal and explicit about their political stance than similar councillors in other cities, they nevertheless highlight the kind of ideological differences that distinguish the two types of councillors. As in the case with most generalizations, however, there are exceptions to this one. Such people as Winnipeg's Joe Zukin and Vancouver's Harry Rankin are in many respects of the older style, but are far from having conservative ideological perspectives.

Because they are only a minority in city halls, the newer style of city politician inevitably encounters frustration and discouragement. It is a trying and often lonely task to take upon one's self and to maintain the role of a continual minority, a persistent "radical" on council. These people run the danger of slipping into the easier model of the majority on councils, in a sense being transformed from the newer type to the older type of city politician. The other easy way out of the likely frustration and disappointment is to not seek re-election.

Terms and Conditions of Office

Except for mayors and a small handful of other members of council (such as controllers in Ontario), being a member of a city council is not intended to be a full-time position. It is also a position that offers little security even though incumbents usually do get re-elected. In most of Canada's major cities, the term of council office is two (in places three or four) years, compared to a norm of about four years for members of provincial legislatures and for the House of Commons. The apparent advantage of having a comparatively short term of office at the municipal level is that members of council can be held accountable to their electorate more frequently. This, in theory, exemplifies the status of municipal government as grass-roots democratic government.

In an absence of other mechanisms by which city councillors can be held accountable and responsible, there may be some force of logic to this notion, but it runs into considerable difficulty in operation. As stated earlier, it has been traditional in Canada for candidates to run for council as independents, and it is not unreasonable for councillors seeking re-election to say that they tried but failed, for lack of a majority in council, to get earlier campaign promises adopted by council. It is also the case that so many decisions are taken by city councils outside the glare of publicity and full public debate that the electorate really has little information on which to judge the performance of its representatives. Further, most city councils do not even record all votes taken in council. Nor can the electorate rely on party affiliation or on past party policy as an indicator of how its members of council have voted on specific issues. While the media occasionally report individual votes in council, they very seldom report council proceedings in full. It is the rare elector indeed who can keep track of all votes. Therefore the relative frequency of city elections does not in itself provide a particularly useful means of holding members of council accountable for their actions.

Longer terms of office may of course exacerbate this problem of accountability, but one clear advantage is that it would tend to facilitate the making of long-term policy by council rather than emphasizing short-term decision making. The phenomenon of urbanization requires a greater emphasis on the creation of policies for the future, but city councils with terms of office of as few as two years are much constrained in their ability to do this, for councillors' eyes are continually focused on the next election. The optimum solution would be to have longer terms of office (at least three years) to facilitate policy making, coupled with additional mechanisms to facilitate accountability; these might include making all city documents public except in very few and special circumstances, recording and publishing all council votes, virtually eliminating "in camera" meetings, regularizing frequent contact between members of council and the public, and providing ward offices for aldermen.

Perhaps most important of all is the necessity of revising the conditions of council office so that all members of council (not just the mayor) can function on a full-time basis as councillors and therefore as representatives. Presently, the level of compensation granted to aldermen is modest, with some notable exceptions. Therefore, unless aldermen can afford to give up their jobs or unless they have occupations that permit them to take time off, they are not often able to devote their full attention to city affairs, either in terms of working in city hall or in terms of maintaining close contact with their constituents. Table 8:1 shows the amounts of compensation paid to members of council in Canada's larger cities.

These figures understate the actual remuneration received by many councillors. In almost all cities one third of the salary is counted as tax-free expense money. In addition, members of some councils receive additional compensation. For example, those councillors who sit on the Metropolitan Toronto Council receive an extra $6,000 a year; members of Quebec City Council's executive committee receive an extra $10,500; Hamilton-Wentworth Regional councillors receive an additional $8,500; all members of Montreal City Council also sit on the Montreal Urban Community Council, for which they receive an additional $2,500 a year; and Mississauga's members on the Peel Regional Council receive an

Table 8:1   Annual Compensation Paid to Councillors
(most recent figures available as of August, 1975)*

city	aldermen	mayor	controllers
Montreal	$ 5,000	$28,500	—
Toronto	18,000	31,000	—
Winnipeg	6,555	35,000	—
North York	12,600	27,000	$23,000
Edmonton	12,000	35,000	—
Vancouver	13,200	30,000	—
Calgary	9,000	30,000	—
Scarborough	13,000	28,500	20,100
Hamilton	7,500	24,000	15,500
Ottawa	10,374	25,874	16,874
Etobicoke	9,820	25,680	18,890
Laval	6,795	30,200	—
London	7,000	24,500	13,000
Windsor	10,500	26,000	—
Quebec	7,000	30,000	—
Mississauga	10,000	20,000	—
York	10,122	27,072	17,655
Regina	6,000	21,000	—
Saskatoon	5,400	23,000	—
Halifax	10,000	27,000	—
Kitchener	7,489	18,500	—
St. Catharines	3,600	16,000	—
Thunder Bay	6,000	21,000	—
East York	8,250	16,500	—

*In almost all cases the figures given were supplied by the respective city. Not included in these figures are additional payments made to members of council who have additional functions.

extra $10,000. In general, then, people who are members of both upper-tier and lower-tier municipal councils receive extra remuneration, as do councillors who are members of some special-purpose bodies such as police commissions in Ontario or executive committees. Therefore the actual compensation received by some councillors is substantially higher than that indicated in the above table. In the case of the City of Toronto, the eleven senior aldermen received a total of at least $24,000 (some of it tax-free) a year in 1975, an amount that should have enabled these people to be full-time professional aldermen. In a survey conducted in January of 1975, it was found that seventeen of the City of Toronto's twenty-two aldermen did operate in this manner, but two of the five aldermen who continued to work at least part-time in their private occupations were senior aldermen who received the extra compensation as members of Metro Council.[9] In the five boroughs in Metro Toronto, all the mayors were full-time public officials, as were five of Scarborough's twelve aldermen, four of the eight East York aldermen, four of the fourteen aldermen in North York, only one of York's eight aldermen, and three of Etobicoke's ten aldermen. All borough controllers, with one exception, functioned on a full-time basis. Particularly in the less populous major cities the incidence of full-time city politicians, excluding mayors, is low.

Increasing their levels of compensation is one of the most thorny issues with which members of city councils are faced, particularly because the councillors themselves must make the decision. When councils propose raising their salaries, there is almost inevitably a public outcry, usually accompanied by protesting editorials in the newspapers. Controversy is especially heated when such proposals are made shortly after a city election. In an attempt to defuse and deflect the invariable unpopularity of being seen to increase their own salaries, it has become fairly common practice for city councils to emulate the practice of federal and provincial legislatures by entrusting the responsibility for proposing increases to independent commissions. But the responsibility for legislating increases remains with the councillors themselves, so the only real utility in using this method is presumably to make public the workload and amount of time put in by councillors, without an analysis of their effectiveness or the quality of the work done.

When one takes into account the amount of money spent by candidates in their campaigns for election to council (assuming that many pay the bulk of their campaign expenses themselves), the compensation paid to councillors in many of Canada's major cities is clearly not designed to enable them to be professional elected officials. While remuneration has generally gone up, not only in absolute dollar terms but also relative to the consumer price index, being a member of a city council in many cases still borders on "charity" work of a sort that only a small proportion of the electorate can reasonably afford. This tends to limit council seats to people with particular kinds of occupations or with personal wealth. No doubt some councillors do not earn the amount of money they receive, but it seems reasonable to expect that the overall calibre and the representativeness of candidates for city council office will increase as the compensation is made more attractive.

It remains exceptional for councillors to be given access to facilities of a sort that would assist them in being more professional and effective in their legislative and representative roles. Research assistance is provided for councillors only in a handful of the major cities (Toronto, Scarborough, Laval, London, Windsor, Quebec, and Thunder Bay) but even in these cases it tends to be mainly a matter of city departments passing information on to councillors by request. Most cities claim to provide their members of council with some sort of secretarial service, exceptions being Windsor, Saskatoon, and St. Catharines. Even office space is not provided at all for aldermen in some cities (such as Montreal, Laval, Windsor, Saskatoon, St. Catharines, and Thunder Bay), and in some other cities only very limited office space is made available. For example, in Winnipeg only committee chairmen have office space; London's fourteen aldermen share two offices; and Regina's aldermen share a lounge. In summary, there persists a general reluctance to provide all members of council with all the tools necessary for them to function as effectively as they might.

Being a member of a city council can be a very time-consuming occupation, but the workload of councillors is greatly variable. Mayors of major cities are expected to work full-time, as are controllers and executive committee members, for these people have executive responsibilities and therefore have more or less specific jobs to perform. For aldermen, though, there is no specified job, and their workload is determined basically by how they individually perceive their roles and by what demands they allow to be made on their time. Therefore it is difficult to generalize about the nature of the workload of all aldermen, or even of those in particular cities. In addition to the time taken for meetings of council, of committees of council, and sometimes of special-purpose bodies such as planning boards, aldermen generally spend time preparing for those meetings by reading reports and briefs and possibly by conducting research. All these tasks relate to their legislative role. The third area in which aldermen find they must spend time is dealing with constituency matters—meeting with groups in the constituency, acting as an inter-mediary between city staff and constituents, and generally trying to solve constituents' problems. Simple day-to-day matters like getting the engineering department to unplug someone's blocked sewer, getting someone else's pothole in the road filled, rectifying complaints about garbage not being collected, or about streets not being plowed are not only time-consuming, but they can also seriously disrupt the councillor's private life.

A study of Halifax aldermen in 1975 found that they reported putting into their roles as many as seventy or more hours a week, but half of them put in an average total of forty to fifty hours a week.[10] The amount of time spent in an average week on meetings ranged from fewer than nine hours to between twenty and twenty-nine hours. Six hours a week were spent on average for research, study, and preparation. Although no figures were given for time spent on constituency matters, one can surmise that the average would be about ten hours per week. A study conducted in Toronto and the five Metro boroughs in 1975–76 found that a majority of the aldermen interviewed reported a total workload taking up an average of 43 hours a week.[11] Preparation for council meetings took an average of 2.5 hours per week, and 13.4 hours a week were spent on constituency matters. The average number of hours spent per week on council meetings ranged from 2.3 in East York to 6.6 in Toronto. Average time spent on standing committees ranged from 2.3 hours per week in York to eight in Toronto. Regarding local boards, aldermen's average hours per week ranged from 1.7 in East York to 2.2 in Toronto. In addition to these aspects, time would also have been spent on special committees, sub-committees, and ceremonial and social functions.

Representative Roles

It was suggested earlier that the one factor most useful in distinguishing the newer type of urban politician from the older type is the individual's perception of the kind of connection or interaction that is most desired between citizens (especially those organized in groups) and the formal decision-making structure. The less tradition-bound councillor aims at democratizing that structure by encouraging citizen participation in the governing process at times other than during the frenzy of an election. In short, he perceives himself to be an agent for his constituents. The older-style civic leader, in contrast, considers himself to have been elected to make decisions for others, and consultation with his constituents occurs, effectively, only at election time.

The most widely known representative role theory has been derived from Edmund Burke's "Speech to the Electors of Bristol", which has been analyzed and formalized into representative role theory, most notably by Heinz Eulau.[12] Two basic representative role *styles* are implicit in Burke's speech and are drawn out by Eulau. One of these is what is known as the *trustee* role style, by which is meant that the elected representative perceives his or her role as that of a free agent who has been elected primarily to make decisions for others on the basis of his or her own "unbiased opinion", "mature judgement", and "enlightened conscience" (to use Burke's words). It therefore follows that the representative ought not to sacrifice these to the opinion of the constituents. The trustee feels required neither to consult with them nor to seek out their opinions. In the event that constituents do inform their elected representative of their views, the trustee does not consider those views to be in any sense binding instructions on the position he or she takes on issues. In contrast to this role style is that of the *delegate*.[13] A representative who perceives his or her role in this way takes the position of a servant or agent relative to his or her constituent masters, and feels bound by instructions from them. Delegates are not only receptive to input from the constituents but actively seek it out by consulting with them frequently and perhaps going so far as attempting to organize them into groups (if they are not already organized) in order to maximize such input. Hence a delegate role is not necessarily a passive one, although it may be. A third category, called the *politico* style, is a sort of residual category necessary to take into account the kind of councillor who sometimes takes a trustee role but at other times a delegate role, depending on the particular issue at hand. For example, if taking a position on a particular issue would seem to require a great deal of highly technical information that is not available to the general citizenry, the politico councillor would probably take the trustee style. But on non-technical matters, the same councillor would opt for the delegate style.

There is a second aspect of representative role theory. In addition to role style is role *focus*, which refers to the geographical area that a councillor believes should be represented. The theory has normally been applied in the context of national legislatures or provincial/state legislatures more so than to cities.[14] In these contexts role focus hinges on the question of whether the representative perceives his or her focus as their particular geographic constituency or as the country/province as a whole —in other words, a *particular* or a *general* geographical area. In cities that do not have a ward basis for election of aldermen to council, and in the case of offices such as mayor that are normally contested on a city-wide basis, the distinction is virtually inapplicable because there is no apparent basis for sectional constituencies. However the distinction can be used in the case of aldermen who are elected to represent a specific ward. Such aldermen can perceive either the interests of their particular ward or the interests of the city as a whole as paramount. One must add a third type of role focus, similar to the residual one for role style, to take account of those councillors who feel that whether they should take a particular or a general focus depends on the nature of the particular issue at hand. This can be called a *mixed*-role focus.

Since the two residual categories (politico style and mixed focus) are really combinations of the two basic categories of style and of focus (combinations depending on specific circumstances), there are four main ways to categorize elected representatives on city councils. The possibilities are: 1) trustees who emphasize a particular geographical section of the city; 2) trustees who emphasize the geographical city in general; 3) delegates who emphasize a particular geographical section of the city; and 4) delegates who emphasize the geographical city in general.

Edmund Burke made his "Speech to the Electors of Bristol" in 1774,

Figure 8:1

	role style		
role focus	trustee	delegate	politico
particular	cell **a**	cell **b**	
general	cell **c**	cell **d**	
mixed			

at a time preceding the development of disciplined political parties in the British Parliament, and Eulau formalized the theory of representative roles in the American context, which is not characterized by highly disciplined political parties. Application of the theory in present-day parliamentary systems such as Canada's House of Commons has been attempted,[15] but runs into difficulty primarily because the tradition of strong party discipline greatly mitigates against the freedom of members of the House of Commons to rely either on their own judgment or on instructions from constituents. All members of all parties in the House of Commons are, in the ultimate sense, *party* delegates; that is, they are generally bound to abide by decisions reached in party caucus. Given the general absence of direct and successful involvement by these national parties in Canadian city council elections, this problem of the applicability of representative role theory really does not arise. Nor is its applicability to city councillors seriously affected by the presence of civic parties, since such parties are rarely characterized by strong party discipline.

As noted above, application of the theory to the urban context does present difficulties in those cities that have all or some council offices elected at large, for there is no *prima facie* basis for identifying a geographical focus. In the case of cities that have a ward basis of election for aldermen, the obvious geographical sectors are the wards themselves, so that aldermen who adopt the particular role focus will perceive the interests of their ward as superior in importance to the interests of other wards or of the city as a whole. Aldermen who adopt the general role focus will emphasize the interests of the whole city rather than of his or her ward. Aldermen who adopt the delegate role style are likely to adopt the particular geographical focus (cell B above), and trustees may be expected to adopt the general role focus (cell C). But the other two cells, and the residual categories of politico style and mixed focus, remain possibilities that fit some councillors.

In view of their connections with citizens groups and their objective of opening up the decision-making process generally, councillors of the newer style are likely to perceive their representative role style as that of a delegate. Their concern is at least as much with *how* decisions are taken as with *what* decisions are made. The position is concisely summed up by alderman John Sewell:

The way to survive, I have found, is to be responsible to definable groups of citizens who can tell me what to say on their behalf. As a spokesman for such groups I make no claims to be "objective", but am consciously trying to represent the interests of those community groups which have managed to get formed. That, to me, is what democracy is all about: as an alderman, I represent real people and do what they want after they have had a chance to discuss it among themselves. Democracy isn't about "the common good", or the developers' good, but rather about people having a voice in decisions so that politicians do what they want.[16]

With regard to the older style of urban politician, one would expect that their role style perceptions would tend to be of the trustee type. Yet the blossoming of citizen associations and the popularization of participatory democracy makes this a difficult style to sustain. As noted in Chapter 6, data from Winnipeg and Toronto suggest that there are now few city councillors who will admit an unwillingness to accord at least some minimum participatory role to the citizenry.[17] To admit such an unwillingness would likely lead to defeat at the next election. Therefore it is probably less accurate to typify the older-style urban politicians as being of the trustee role style than to describe them as perceiving a politico style for themselves.

What people say is not necessarily descriptive of what they do, however. Therefore it is necessary to make a distinction between representative role *perceptions* (or expectations) and their *enactment*—a distinction, then, between theory and practice. Newer-style urban politicians, initially seeing themselves in the delegate role, can, after spending some time on council, decide that some issues are too complex or too technical to warrant their obeying instructions from their constituents. Therefore these representatives would be enacting a politico role style. Similarly, some older-style urban politicians may perceive a politico role, yet in practice give so little weight to their constituents' views that they actually become trustees.

Legislative Behaviour

Whether or not the bulk of the members of a particular city council enact any one role, the absence of disciplined parties in the councils of Canada's major cities suggests that it is extremely difficult to predict accurately the behaviour of council on any controversial issues coming to a vote. One would expect, though, that "family" councils would be characterized by fairly high levels of consensus in votes taken in council, and indeed that there would be considerable efforts made to reach a consensus before votes were taken. As noted earlier, however, the club atmosphere of councils has in many cities diminished as newer-type councillors appeared. This suggests that there may be a kind of developmental process in urban legislatures, a process which is not so much the result of any structural changes in city councils as the result of the composition of those councils. Composition of councils in turn is a reflection of the extra-legislative environment—deeper and more widespread public concern about the present nature and future prospects of the city, and greater activity by citizens' associations and political parties of both main types.

If there is a developmental process tending to transform city councils from cohesiveness in a club atmosphere to divisiveness based on existing societal cleavages and competing interests and demands, the process could be viewed as taking a particular form. In the first stage, council is composed mainly or entirely of members elected as independents of the older style (trustee role style) who share the common concern and objective of administering the city on business principles of economy and efficiency. This commonality tends to produce consensus in council, with considerable efforts being made to ensure it if at all possible. Therefore votes cast in council are usually unanimous votes, exceptions being rare and any minority votes being limited to only one or two councillors. In stage two, one civic party of the older type has become involved directly and successfully in elections for council because of the emergence of an important issue or scandal, and the party's councillors may be joined on council by a number of independents. In both cases the councillors are of the older style, assume a trustee role, and are more or less united in trying to ensure that the city is run, again, on business principles. Therefore there are still efforts made to search for consensus before votes are taken in council and the incidence of unanimous votes continues to be quite high, split votes low, but results that are only near-unanimous (one or two councillors in the minority) increase in frequency. In stage three the civic party that emerged for stage two encounters organized opposition from one or more other civic parties also of the older type. The search for consensus on council continues, but not with so much conviction or success. Thus votes taken in council demonstrate greater factionalism, and the proportion of unanimous votes declines. In stage four, the existing older-style civic parties have encountered opposition from one of the newer type or perhaps from a branch of a major national/provincial party for the kinds of reasons given in Chapter 7, and the new party has succeeded in getting several members elected. One of the older-style parties may have been eliminated in the election. The council is now a mixture of both types of politicians, and a mixture of delegates, trustees, and politicos. The search for consensus falters badly and is abandoned. Unanimous votes become proportionately fewer and occur mainly on matters viewed by all as unimportant, and the proportion of split votes increases. The fifth and last stage is the consequence of a fading out of the older type of civic party, the members of council now being aligned into two or three parties that are more or less disciplined. The trustee role style is infrequently seen and the councillors tend to be party delegates or, occasionally, politicos. The dominance of disciplined parties drives constituency delegates out of council. Unanimous votes by council are infrequent; debate in council is often heated; and decisions taken by council are marked by split votes corresponding to the size of the parties. Council has now taken on most of the aspects of a parliamentary legislature. This process is illustrated in Table 8:2.

Because of a lack of sufficient data, no proof can be offered for this notion of a developmental process with a focus on the voting behaviour of councillors (the last column of the table), or the processes involved in producing the outcomes (the second last column of the table). Voting behaviour in Canadian city councils has only quite recently begun to receive attention and systematic analysis, and frequently encounters a problem in that in only a few major cities (notably Edmonton, Ottawa, Toronto, Winnipeg, and Vancouver) are the votes cast by each member of council recorded as a matter of course so that one can tell who voted how. In most major cities, this record is kept only at the request of a member of council, typically on divisive motions, and council minutes normally record simply the aggregate number of votes for and against each motion. While such figures can be useful for determining the frequency of unanimous, near-unanimous, and split votes (and for detecting changes in the frequencies of those votes over a period of time), they are

Table 8:2 Developmental Process of City Councils

stage	type of party, if any	type of politician	type of role	level of cohesion	frequency of votes by type
1	none (all independents)	older style	trustee	high, result of seeking consensus before votes	unanimous—high near-unanimous—low split—low
2	one civic party (older type) plus independents	older style	trustee	quite high, result of seeking consensus before votes	unanimous—quite high near-unanimous—moderate split—low
3	two or more civic parties (older type), perhaps some independents	older style plus perhaps a few newer-style ones	mixture of all three types	moderate, some seeking of consensus before votes	unanimous—moderate near-unanimous—quite high split—moderate
4	one or more older-style civic parties plus one or more newer-style	mixture	mixture, but more politicos	quite low, little consensus-seeking	unanimous—low near-unanimous—quite low split—quite high
5	two or more disciplined parties	newer style (?)	party delegates, plus perhaps a few politicos	low, consensus only with each caucus	unanimous—low near-unanimous—low split—high

useless for the purposes of measuring the level and stability of cohesion within parties or within non-party blocs on council. Also, any proof of this developmental process would require analysis of more than just that handful of cities for which adequate data are available and analyses possible.[18]

In none of Canada's major city councils has stage five yet been reached. One might speculate that Montreal City Council is (since the 1974 city election there) near, but because the council members of the Montreal Citizens Movement, as the major opposition party, do not constitute a highly disciplined party, the council is probably closer to stage four. Roll-call data on council votes are not sufficiently available yet to verify this.

Studies conducted in the City of Toronto and the City of Vancouver suggest that both cities' councils have recently moved along the stages of the developmental process. In Toronto, Kay found a clear effect on the votes of some members of council resulting from the influx of a group of new-style "reformer" councillors in the city's election of 1969. What Kay did was to examine the change in cohesiveness (in terms of voting the same way) of the twelve people who were members of council both before and after that election. In the period 1967 to 1969 these twelve had an average of 52.4 per cent agreement in those votes that Kay analyzed. In the period 1970 to 1972, however, these same twelve councillors had an average of 73.3 per cent agreement in the council votes analyzed. In other words the twelve older-style Toronto politicians were being transformed into a more cohesive voting bloc as a consequence of the entry into council of the reformers. From 1970 to 1972, the average agreement of the eight reformers was 77.3 per cent. Kay's findings ". . . therefore tended to be consistent with the notion, that both 'reformers' and 'non-reformers' were more likely to gain backing among members within their own groupings in the construction of motion-supporting coalitions."[19] In terms of their legislative behaviour, Toronto's councillors were forming themselves into two distinct voting coalitions— two quasi-parties. By 1972, then, Toronto's City Council would seem to have moved from stage two to stage three and toward stage four, although Kay eliminated all unanimous and near-unanimous vote outcomes from his analysis.

In Vancouver, council roll-call votes have been recorded as a matter of course only since February of 1973, after the Electors Action Movement won a majority (nine of eleven seats). The election in 1974 saw some recovery of the Civic Non-Partisan Association which increased its number of seats in council from one in 1972 to four, and a reduction to six seats for TEAM. Tennant's analysis of council votes after that election manifests some change in the legislative behaviour of councillors. In the first four months of 1974 only 18.6 per cent of the council vote outcomes were not unanimous, while the percentage for 1975 was 31.9 per cent. However, TEAM has not been a highly disciplined party on council either before or after the 1974 election. Excluding all unanimous votes, the average extent of agreement of the nine TEAM councillors in 1973 was 68.4 per cent (the overall average for council being 64.9 per cent) and among the six TEAM councillors in 1975 was 69.1 per cent (the overall average being 62.0 per cent). For the four NPA members of council, the average agreement in non-unanimous vote outcomes for the same four months in 1975 was 62.8 per cent.[20] Given the change in unanimity of votes and the change in the structure of council from dominance by one party to a fairly close balance of two parties, it would seem that Vancouver's City Council shifted from stage two to stage three of the developmental process.

In his study of voting behaviour in the Edmonton City Council from 1966 to 1972, Masson found that ". . . the voting behaviour of Edmonton city councilmen revealed no relationship between members having campaigned together as an electoral party/slate and uniformity of voting in council. . . ."[21] Given the composition of council over that time period (one civic party plus a number of independents), Edmonton would seem to be at stage two of the developmental process, although no figures are available on the frequency of unanimous or split votes. In contrast to Edmonton, Winnipeg's City Council of 1972–73 seems to have been at stage four, with two parties in council (thirty-seven members of the older-style civic party called the Independent Citizens Election Committee, six members of the NDP, plus seven independents, one of whom was elected under the label of the Labour Election Committee). The NDP was a relatively disciplined (or, perhaps more accurately, cohesive) party. Majorities of ICEC and NDP councillors were opposed to each other on thirty out of forty-one roll call votes examined, but the ICEC did not vote as consistently as a bloc as the NDP did. In votes examined for 1972, the NDP members were completely united on all motions examined, but in 1974 the cohesion dropped so that its members were at least 90 per cent cohesive on only 68 per cent of the motions examined.[22] Sixty-four per cent of all voting outcomes from 1972 to 1974 can be counted as split votes because at least one-quarter of voting councillors voted in a minority on them.

Although it does not meet the minimum criterion of major city status used here (population of 100,000 or more), the City of Dartmouth in Nova Scotia is fairly populous (about 65,000 people) and is part of the Halifax metropolitan area. With fifteen members of council, each elected as an independent, and with no parties of any kind directly involved in the elections, the composition of council suggests that it is still at a very early stage of legislative development. Voting outcomes support this positioning, since 71.1 per cent of the 1442 motions between November of 1973 and April of 1975 were passed unanimously. Another 8.4 per cent of those motions were passed with only one dissenter, and an additional 7.6 per cent were passed with only two dissenters. Hence only a tiny proportion of all motions met even a most minimal criterion of split votes. Consensus-seeking and bargaining was often prevalent before votes were taken, and those efforts had a high degree of success. Dartmouth's council is, therefore, only at stage one.

If the positioning of these few cities at the various stages of legislative development is appropriate, there are two other points about the process that become evident: progression through the stages seems to be contingent on the size of council, larger councils being closest to stage five. Therefore as a city's council is increased in size, the probability of split voting increases, consensus-seeking falters and is displaced by caucusing within parties or blocs, and council becomes polarized. It also seems that the progression through the stages of legislative development is associated with the population size of the city, since the most populous cities are nearest stage five while the less populous ones are at earlier stages of legislative development.

It was noted that the newer-style urban politician described earlier is likely to encounter difficulty if or when the city's council reaches stage five. Being a *constituency delegate* is a hallmark of this kind of politician, but the fifth stage of legislative development is characterized by *party delegates*, so the possibilities for representatives to feel bound by instructions from constituents in determining their actions in council are sharply curtailed. It is for this reason that a question mark was put beside "newer style" in the developmental process table for stage five. What seems likely, therefore, is that constituency-delegate politicians will leave urban councils and will be active (if at all) outside of council.

Exits for Urban Politicians: Onward and Ever Upward (or Out)

Having considered how urban councillors get involved in electoral and council politics, it is appropriate to consider briefly how and why they eventually leave that realm. Possible reasons are electoral defeat, retirement from politics entirely, moving on to provincial or federal politics, and forced removal or voluntary resignation.

Once people are elected to a city council, the chances are much greater than one out of two (more often about four out of five) that they will be re-elected in subsequent elections if they choose to run for office again. For example, in Ottawa's 1972 election, the mayor was returned to office, all four members of the Board of Control were returned, as were aldermen in seven of the eleven wards. Only three incumbent councillors were defeated. In some wards, councillors were seeking a fourth or fifth term on council. In the 1975–76 study of councillors in Metro Toronto's six municipalities, it was found that York's councillors had held elective office for an average of 9.8 years, and that the overall average for the six municipalities was 7.3 years.[23] This kind of situation is characteristic of Canada's major cities. Therefore it is not usually a case of councillors leaving city politics by decision of the electorate. No doubt some councillors retire in the expectation that they would be defeated in the next election, but retirement can simply indicate that they feel they have done their duty, that it is time for new blood in council, that the rewards of office are insufficient, or that city politics is too time-consuming and/or too frustrating.

The two most interesting exits that some city politicians make are forced removal or resignation from office under clouded circumstances, and moving "onward and upward" in politics. It is sufficiently infrequent in Canada for councillors to be removed from office or to resign in the face of scandal that those instances receive considerable publicity. Unfortunately, they have received rather little scholarly examination.[24] "Conflict of interest" is a term that has very broad and usually vague legal meaning. As one analyst has noted, "The fundamental difficulty with a general statement of the principles involved in conflict of interest is that it does not lead to unambiguous conclusions about specific cases."[25] It therefore becomes necessary to define "conflict of interest" in terms of situations. Mayo identifies three basic types of such situations: 1) the primary situation, where a councillor accepts some sort of remuneration from private interests for government-related services; 2) a situation in which the councillor's personal financial interests are affected by contracts with government or by business activities that are subject to regulation by government; and 3) a situation involving the disclosure of confidential information, or the use of it, for personal gain.[26]

Legal provisions applying to conflict-of-interest situations that might affect municipal councillors are contained in provincial governments' statutes, usually in the provinces' general municipal acts. Most provinces have taken two basic approaches: prohibiting people who would be most likely placed in conflict of interest situations (such people as municipal employees, judges, and people in debt to the municipality) from running for election in the first place; and secondly, removing from office and/or applying some other sort of penalty to councillors who are convicted of conflict of interest. A sort of third approach is a requirement for councillors who have a private interest in a matter being considered by council to disclose their interest and to refrain from taking any part in council's deliberations on that matter. Provincial legislation is far from uniform across Canada, and much of the legislation has assorted deficiencies.[27] It tends to be particularly weak on penalties imposed on councillors who have been found to have conflicts of interest.

"Conflict of interest" includes both fairly innocuous and highly unsavoury behaviour. In January of 1973, Mr. Dennis Flynn was disqualified as the mayor of Etobicoke on the grounds that he had been an employee of the City of Toronto on the day that he was elected mayor of Etobicoke, although municipal employees were prohibited from running for office in any municipality in Ontario. No moral reprehension there. In Ontario's provincial election of 1971, at least eight elected members of the legislature were at the same time members of municipal councils, and resignations from their council seats followed election to the provincial legislature. No moral reprehension there either.

Similarly, rather innocuous conflict of interest was involved in the court-ordered unseating of four of Thunder Bay's aldermen in 1972. The four were removed from office because it was found that companies in which they were involved were entering into contracts with the city while the four were councillors. As the judge noted, their actions contravened the Ontario Municipal Act, but the judge opined that the four had acted openly, in good faith, and (he believed) honestly. The judge also referred to the Act as "stupid" legislation.

Having a financial interest in matters considered by council has led to the downfall of some urban politicians. A semantic distinction is usually made between direct and indirect financial interest, but both kinds are generally supposed to require that the councillor concerned declare that he or she has a conflict of interest and that he or she is to refrain from moving, seconding, debating, and voting on the particular motion before council. The case of Mr. Benjamin Grys, an alderman on Toronto City Council in 1971, is only one of many possible examples concerning conflicts of interest that involve at least ostensibly indirect financial interest.[28] The amazing case of Mr. William Hawrelak involved more direct financial interest when he was mayor of Edmonton. Mr. Hawrelak was first elected mayor in 1951 and was repeatedly re-elected until he was forced to resign in 1959 when the Porter Royal Commission found him guilty of "gross misconduct" over land transactions. He ran for mayor again in 1963, and the electorate returned him to office with a majority of some eight thousand votes over his one opponent. Three years later, he was removed from office when the Supreme Court of Alberta declared the mayor's chair vacant after it was found that Mayor Hawrelak had violated the City Act in a land deal between the city and a company in which he was a principal. The court also ordered Mr. Hawrelak to pay the city some $72,000. He was defeated when he ran for mayor again in 1966, but in 1974 the electorate returned him yet again to the mayor's chair. Mr. Hawrelak died in office in 1975. One surmises that the electorate, at least in Edmonton, is tolerant of behaviour clearly involving conflict of interest.

Many major conflict-of-interest cases involve the property development industry in one way or another. The problem is a serious one, given the kinds of occupational backgrounds of a sizeable proportion of urban politicians—lawyers who have had clients engaged in the property industry, real estate agents who have acted on behalf of that industry, engineers who have done work for that industry, contractors (roofing firms, plumbing firms, etc.) who have done work for that industry, and so on. Although his classifications may be questioned, Lorimer presents a convincing analysis and calculated that seven of Vancouver's eleven City Council members in 1971–72 had property industry occupations, as did twenty-four of Winnipeg's fifty-one members of council in 1972–74, twelve of the City of Toronto's twenty-three council members in 1970–72, six of the thirteen members of Thunder Bay Council in 1971, five of the Borough of York's eleven councillors in 1971, and nine of the seventeen councillors of the Borough of North York in 1971.[29] Of any group, the property development industry is probably most often most directly affected by decisions of city councils and would certainly be expected to have a high level of interest in city affairs. It should therefore not be surprising that companies and individuals engaged in this industry cultivate a particular interest in elected city politicians as well as with appointed personnel in the city administration. Nor should it be surprising that such companies and individuals would provide financial assistance to selected candidates in their campaigns for election or re-election to council. The only way to avoid the exercise of undue influence on councillors and to avoid potential conflicts of interest is to combine much more stringent legislation (whether municipal or provincial) governing conflicts of interest with stringent regulation of campaign finance. Aside from the immediate consequences of cases involving conflict of interest, they have a serious long-term effect in producing a general cynicism among the electorate about the moral, ethical, and legal tone of city politics and city politicians.[30]

City politics is often thought to be a "stepping stone" to higher-level politics, and there is evidence to suggest that election to council is sometimes either intended or merely happens to become such an aid. The theory is that politically ambitious people first seek election as an alderman, then attempt to advance their political career by becoming a mayor (in Ontario, the board of control is often a step between alderman and mayor), and then onward and upward to either the provincial legislature or the federal parliament. Ward found that in each federal general election between 1900 and 1945, between 24 per cent (in 1940) and 45 per cent (in 1900) of the elected members of parliament did have backgrounds in municipal politics.[31] These figures are understated, for they refer to those MPs who had backgrounds only in municipal politics; that is, the figures exclude any MPs who had backgrounds in *both* provincial and municipal politics. While he does not give figures for those who had backgrounds in both, he does state that ". . . if members who have had local experience only were categorized with those who have had *both* local and legislative experience, it could probably be shown that more than half the federal members have started out in local politics, particularly in Central Canada."[32] Ward did detect a falling off in the tendency for members of the House of Commons to enter the House with prior experience in political elective office, and the 1975 edition of the *Parliamentary Guide* suggests that he was correct; although the data are incomplete, only 26 per cent of the members of the House of Commons in 1975 are shown to have had any prior municipal electoral experience, and in the case of eighteen of the sixty-nine MPs concerned, that experience was on boards of education rather than a municipal council.[33] With the notable exception of Ontario, only small proportions of provincial legislators in 1975 had prior experience on municipal councils, although again the data are incomplete and presumably understated: Alberta, 25 per cent; British Columbia, 18 per cent; Manitoba, 23 per cent; New Brunswick, 22 per cent; Newfoundland, 24 per cent; Nova Scotia, 17 per cent; Ontario, 46 per cent; Prince Edward Island, 13 per cent; Quebec, 13 per cent; and Saskatchewan, 15 per cent. It seems rather clear, then, that success in municipal elections is not a requisite for success in federal or provincial elections. Therefore, the stepping-stone theory is overplayed even though there are some people for whom it does apply.

The weakening of that theory perhaps indicates that city elective politics is increasingly being viewed by urban politicians as an appropriate context for the satisfaction of their political ambitions. The improving conditions of office, especially in terms of pay, perhaps account in part for this. But it may also reflect an awakening to the importance of urban problems, the possibilities for the resolution or mitigation of those problems, and the general significance of cities in Canada.

NOTES

1. Bureau of Municipal Research, *The Metro Politician: A Profile* (Toronto, June, 1963).
2. Ibid., p. 4. It was also noted that very few candidates, whether elected to council or not (3 per cent in both cases) had an annual income in 1962 exceeding $25,000.
3. P. Silcox, "Postscript: City Council Results," in Bureau of Municipal Research, *Parties to Change: The Introduction of Political Parties in the 1969 Toronto Municipal Election* (Toronto, 1971), p. 57.
4. In this connection see Jon Caulfield, *The Tiny Perfect Mayor* (Toronto: James Lorimer, 1974).
5. James Lorimer, *A Citizen's Guide to City Politics* (Toronto: James Lewis and Samuel, 1972), p. 97.
6. Ibid.
7. Lloyd Axworthy and Jim Cassidy, *Unicity: The Transition* (Winnipeg: Institute of Urban Studies of the University of Winnipeg, 1974), p. 43.
8. John Sewell, *Up Against City Hall* (Toronto: James Lewis and Samuel, 1972), p. 61.
9. Reported in *The Globe and Mail* (Toronto), January 20, 1975, p. 5.
10. *1975 Report of Stipends Committee of The City of Halifax* (Halifax, November 21, 1975), p. 20. Four aldermen averaged fewer than thirty-nine hours a week, while one reported spending an average of fifty or more hours per week.
11. Royal Commission on Metropolitan Toronto, *Political Life in Metropolitan Toronto: A Survey of Municipal Councillors*, staff study (Toronto, April, 1976), p. 29. The following data are derived from pp. 14–29.
12. Heinz Eulau, "The Legislator as Representative: Representative Roles," in John Wahlke *et al*, eds., *The Legislative System* (New York: John Wiley and Sons, 1962).
13. For a somewhat different application of the delegate type of representative role and for a different interpretation of role theory generally from that used here, see Harold Kaplan, *Urban Political Systems: A Functional Analysis of Metro Toronto* (New York: Columbia University Press, 1967), especially Chapter 8.
14. See for example Robert J. Jackson and Michael M. Atkinson, *The Canadian Legislative System* (Toronto: Macmillan of Canada, 1974), Chapter 7.
15. See for example Allan Kornberg, *Canadian Legislative Behaviour: A Study of the 25th Parliament* (New York: Holt, Rinehart and Winston, 1967), Chapter 6.
16. Sewell, *Up Against City Hall*, p. 168.
17. In this regard see the account of an all-candidates meeting, in James Lorimer, *The Real World of City Politics* (Toronto: James Lewis and Samuel, 1970), pp. 147–52.
18. See Barry J. Kay, "Voting Patterns in a Non-partisan Legislature: A Study of Toronto City Council", *Canadian Journal of Political Science*, vol. IV, no. 2 (June, 1971); Barry J. Kay, "A Model of Non-partisan Legislative Bargaining and the Impact of Toronto Council's Partisanization 1967–1972," (a paper presented to the annual meeting of the Canadian Political Science Association, 1974); Jack K. Masson, "Decision-making Patterns and Floating Coalitions in an Urban City Council (Edmonton)," (a paper presented to the annual meeting of the Canadian Political Science Association, 1973); Donald Higgins, "Mother Stubbs and her Fourteen Alderchildren: A Short Story of a Happy Family that Fell Apart," (a paper presented to the annual meeting of the Canadian Political Science Association, 1975); Paul Tennant, "Vancouver City Council Roll-Call Analysis," (comments for

the annual meeting of the Canadian Political Science Association, 1975); and P. H. Wichern, Jr., "Notes on the Analysis of Canadian City Council Roll Calls," (for the annual meeting of the Canadian Political Science Association, 1975). For an example of analysis of aggregate data on a council's votes see Kaplan, *Urban Political Systems*, especially tables 3.1 and 8.4.

19. Kay, "A Model of Non-partisan Legislative Bargaining and the Impact of Toronto's Partisanization 1967–1972," pp. 9–11.

20. These percentages are calculated from Tennant, "Vancouver City Council Roll-Call Analysis," tables 1 and 2.

21. Masson, "Decision-making Patterns and Floating Coalitions in an Urban City Council," p. 21.

22. P. H. Wichern, Jr., "Winnipeg's Unicity After Two Years: Evaluation of an Experiment in Urban Government," (a paper given at the annual meeting of the Canadian Political Science Association, 1974, p. 26).

23. Royal Commission on Metropolitan Toronto, *Political Life in Metropolitan Toronto*, p. 12.

24. Some useful material is contained in Kenneth M. Gibbons and Donald C. Rowat, eds., *Political Corruption in Canada: Cases, Causes and Cures* (Toronto: McClelland and Stewart, 1976).

25. Daniel H. Mayo, "Conflict of Interest in Canadian Municipalities" (unpublished Honours research essay, Carleton University, 1972), p. 11.

26. Ibid., pp. 12–14.

27. Ibid. Mayo's study is now slightly out of date, but is thorough and useful.

28. For accounts of this case, see Sewell, *Up Against City Hall*, Chapter 7; and John Sewell *et al, Inside City Hall: The Year of the Opposition* (Toronto: Hakkert, 1971)), pp. 93–106.

29. Lorimer, *A Citizen's Guide to City Politics*, pp. 97–9.

30. See Kenneth M. Gibbons, "The Political Culture of Corruption in Canada," in Kenneth M. Gibbons and Donald C. Rowat, eds., *Political Corruption in Canada: Cases, Causes and Cures* (Toronto: McClelland and Stewart, 1976), pp. 231–50. Although that article deals specifically with the federal and provincial contexts, it has some applicability to the city context as well.

31. Norman Ward, *The Canadian House of Commons: Representation*, 2nd ed. (Toronto: University of Toronto Press, 1963), p. 122.

32. Ibid., p. 124 (emphasis his).

33. Calculated from Pierre G. Normandin, ed., *The Canadian Parliamentary Guide, 1975* (Ottawa, 1975).

Conclusion

This book is intended to provide a reasonably comprehensive description and interpretation of the institutional and procedural framework within which the policy problems of urban Canada have been approached in the past and in the present. Such an intention has necessitated consideration of a very broad range of subject matter, so that a "tying-together" seems desirable here. At the same time, however, that very breadth makes such a tying-together rather difficult. In addition to the diversity of subject matter, there is a diversity in the kinds of urban governmental institutions and processes from province to province, and also some diversity within single provinces. With regard to this last arena, it is the case that the dynamics of political life within cities in a single province can vary substantially even when the municipal institutions do not happen to vary fundamentally within the province. For example, in institutional terms the cities of Calgary and Edmonton are similar, yet in their dynamics of urban politics they are not the same. So the range of subject matter is broad, and in application varies according to *place*.

In addition to these variations by place, this book has demonstrated that there have been substantial variations over *time*. Most cities in Canada have changed in their internal governmental institutions. Most of the major cities were affected during the 1960s by reorganization in terms of regional or metropolitan government, for example. All urban municipalities in Canada have also been significantly affected by external changes that have altered the nature of central-local relations. For example, it was maintained especially in Chapter 2 that the functional capacities or responsibilities of cities have quite steadily been whittled away by provincial governments, and their financial capacities have declined relative to the federal and provincial governments. While the pace of municipal reorganization that is initiated by provincial governments appears in 1976 to be slowing, it is safe to predict that there will be further changes in the future. Thus the making of generalized conclusions is not only somewhat difficult but also rather risky if those conclusions are to have much predictive capability. Imminent changes could conceivably nullify generalizations. One thinks of the Robarts Royal Commission on Metropolitan Toronto, the Whalen and Henley commissions' studies in Newfoundland, the Archer and Mayo review studies of regional government in Niagara and Ottawa-Carleton respectively, and continuing changes in the federal Ministry of State for Urban Affairs. An author of a book like this one is therefore conscious that the book may soon be overtaken by events.

As indicated in the Introduction, Canada is a predominantly urban country in much more than Statistics Canada's minimal definition of "urban". The majority of Canadians live in settlement areas that are large enough in population to justify the proposition that the residents in such areas experience a "city" way of life. The nature of economic and social interdependencies and the nature of the means of communication are such that in a sense *all* Canadians are urbanized, and thus are affected both by the opportunities and by the stresses that the process of urbanization produces.

While the process does not appear to be reversible (even if we wanted to reverse it), it can be modified by governmental action. Federal immigration policy can stem the influx of people into urban areas to some extent, both by controlling the number of people permitted to settle in Canada and possibly also by directing immigrants to take up residence in designated areas. Policies designed to foster the creation and growth of new urban areas and thereby reduce the population pressures on places that are already highly urbanized are in place now. It is significant, though, that the urban municipalities can have comparatively little effect on rates and locations of urbanization. It is the senior governments, federal and provincial, that have the primary capacity to control and direct the process of urbanization, and the municipalities are to a large extent left with the problem of reacting to the consequences of actions taken from up above.

Were it not for the fact that urbanization produces stresses, this largely reactive position of municipalities would not be of serious concern. But the process does produce stress. As the population of cities increases, so too do both the problems *in* cities and the problems *of* cities (to use Lithwick's terms). Historically, it has been the municipal level of government that was left to cope with what has been termed urban problems of policy—transportation, availability of housing, sprawl, pollution, poverty, land-use planning, noise, congestion, and so on. Of course the actual magnitude of many of these policy problems once was such that they were not highly visible. Even when they were recognized as problems, they were rarely recognized as problems that government (including municipal government) should be involved in mitigating or overcoming. The historical domination of municipal government by the propertied and wealthy few, the concern of such people with taxation of property, and the dominance of a *laissez-faire* perspective all helped to minimize the involvement of municipal government in urban problems of policy. Further, urban problems of process were accentuated only when municipal government became more democratized and when the population size of urban municipalities really began to swell. *How* policies were to be made was not of particular concern at the municipal level because the numbers of people who could directly participate in municipal government through voting, running for elective office, or holding elective office were relatively few. Those few had no particular problem of access to the municipal decision-making process. Municipal councils and their bureaucracies had few demands for action as well as few responsibilities that were viewed as legitimate areas for governmental activity. As noted earlier, though, the range of things that municipalities could do, by virtue of their special charters or by virtue of general municipal acts of the provincial legislatures, was very wide. What actions municipalities considered necessary or appropriate were therefore much less than what they were legally permitted to do.

Over time, several developments effectively reversed that statement, and thereby altered the role of urban municipalities. One of these was the process of urbanization itself. As the population of some municipalities increased in size, the importance of urban problems of policy grew and became more apparent, and continued urbanization creates new policy difficulties. There were in many municipalities increasing numbers of people who had to be educated and for whom new schools had to be built, more teachers hired, and so forth. Additionally, the advent of new technology (which is an inherent aspect of the economic dimension of urbanization) produced requirements for new kinds of municipal services as well as simply producing a greater need for existing kinds of services. The demands created by the automobile are the most obvious.

A second development was a shift in the dominant attitude toward government regulation, intervention, and involvement. To cite just a few of many possible examples, the relief of poverty ceased to be viewed as primarily a private charity or family responsibility. Private decisions over such things as the size and location of new commercial and residential development were seen to involve considerable public costs for the provision of even rudimentary levels of such services as water supply and sewage collection. As the population of cities increased, it became apparent that only governments could adequately deal with health problems that coincide with human congestion. Such changes in the dominant attitudes toward governmental intervention and control affected the municipal level of government in much the same way it affected the senior levels of government. The Great Depression of the 1930s and the popularization then of Keynesian economics were important factors that accelerated the shift in public attitudes. It was during the 1930s that the role (both actual and desired) of municipal government in Canada became particularly difficult. On the one hand, urban municipalities largely remained legally most responsible among the levels of government for providing an expanded range of needed social services, but the municipalities clearly lacked the financial capacity to undertake such services. As a consequence, many municipalities teetered on the brink of bankruptcy, and a number fell over. On the other hand, the provincial governments, which were not quite so strapped financially and which recognized a degree of responsibility for their creature municipalities, were understandably unprepared to rush to the financial aid of municipalities without having some means of controlling the kinds and levels of local services provided. Thus this period saw an increasing level of municipal dependence on financial support from the provincial governments, as well as a whittling down of municipalities' functional autonomy. It should also be recalled that most of the provinces that had not already established provincial bodies to oversee and supervise municipalities did so during the 1930s.

A third development that had an important effect on altering the role of municipal government and that created urban problems of process was the democratization of municipal government. As property qualifications for voters and for contestants for municipal elective office came down and were gradually abandoned, there was an increase in the numbers of people who, as individuals and as organized groups, made demands on municipal government. Of course the second development referred to above—dominant attitudes toward governmental involvement changing—also expanded the range of demands.

Institutions of government almost invariably trail behind changes in public attitudes. This has certainly been true of urban municipalities in Canada. Their institutions and processes of decision making had been designed for earlier circumstances, and were not readily adapted to the increasing pressures. City councils tended to remain small in size; the old and cumbersome council-committee structure of decision making was often retained. When it was abandoned, it tended to give way to the imported council-city manager structure which emphasized non-political, business-type administration, isolated from policy formulation. This was little better suited than the council-committee structure to the changing circumstances and expectations of urban municipal government. Another aspect of the inadequacy of urban municipal structures and processes was the failure of geographical boundaries of municipal jurisdiction to reflect changes in patterns of urban settlement, with the result being that most major cities were badly fragmented. There is probably no better example of the persistence of anachronistic municipal institutions and processes than this one of geographic boundaries. While there was a recognition that urban problems of policy such as crime, health, and pollution do not respect municipal boundaries, there remained a general reluctance of both municipal and provincial officials to alter the boundaries. Instead, the decision-making processes were made more complex and less comprehensible. The multitudinous special-purpose bodies, some of which were inter-municipal, were also not clearly responsible and accountable to the public.

The growing and increasingly apparent inadequacies of urban municipal government in both policy and process terms resulted in the reorganization of urban municipalities and their decision-making structures. In large part, the reorganizations were justified (and generally justifiable) by provincial governments on the grounds of planning. There were really two aspects of such a planning justification: first, the municipal fragmentation of major cities inhibited adequate development planning by urban municipalities. Planning is one traditional municipal function that in major cities requires a rather large geographic scale of jurisdiction.

Second, it can be argued that the fragmentation of major cities inhibited adequate planning by the provincial governments. In this sense the type of planning was not so much of strictly *urban* development as of overall development objectives, their associated financial expenditures, and the co-ordination of programs and policies of the provincial government. Both aspects of the planning problem were more apparent in the major cities, and it was there that the winds of change blew earliest and with the greatest velocity, beginning with the creation of two-tier metropolitan government in Toronto in 1954. Within a few years, the Toronto experience was emulated and adapted by Winnipeg, Montreal, Ottawa, Hamilton, Vancouver (in a much weakened form), Quebec, and others. All of these reorganizations were approached from a service perspective —a service requisite of scale. The common approach was therefore to create a second tier of municipal government, encompassing a number of smaller municipalities within a single urban area, and to endow that second tier with a range of service responsibilities that invariably included area-wide planning. The representation requisite of scale was presumed (if it was thought of at all) to be adequately met by the retention of lower-tier municipalities, although there has been a tendency to combine small lower-tier municipalities into fewer and larger ones. Unicity Winnipeg remains, in 1976, the single example of urban municipal reorganization that was a conscious attempt to develop new mechanisms designed to foster the representation requisite of scale in a geographic area that was big enough to satisfy the service requisite.

The representation requisite has therefore not been the dominant perspective from which urban municipal reorganization has been approached, but it is an important one when the social heterogeneity of all major cities is considered. As the territorial and population size of municipalities grows, the traditional notion that municipal government is grass-roots democracy runs into considerable difficulty. If the term "grass roots" is interpreted to mean that municipal government is direct, personal, intimate, informal, and face-to-face—in one word, "close"—then it is clear that the service perspective toward urban municipal reorganization tends to work against grass-roots municipal government. Also of relevance here is the fact that two-tier municipal government, with a division of governmental responsibilities, tends to be complex, and thus is neither adequately understood by residents in major cities nor adequately responsible and accountable to those residents. Largeness of scale runs counter to the perceptions that people have of "we-feeling", that is, of identification with others in some particular geographic area. The issue is not only the extent to which people in a major city identify with each other, but also the extent to which they can identify with their institutions, personalities, and processes of municipal government. If the level of identification is low in this second sense, then municipal government will be seen as remote rather than close. Further, a good case can be made for the proposition that public participation in government is partly a function of that level of identification, and therefore of the size of the governmental unit. Given the apparent connection between community size and participation, and the normative connection between democracy and participation, it can be concluded that large-scale municipal government is neither grass-roots government, nor as democratic as grass-roots government can be. In other words, units of municipal government should correspond in size and boundaries as closely as possible to identifiable areas of perceived community, and should change in size and boundaries as areas of perceived community change. Muncipal government in Canada's major cities does neither of these, with the possible exception of Unicity Winnipeg.

Since large-scale city government tends to minimize participation that is more than ritualistic, the possibility of city affairs being dominated by particular minorities is increased. The elected and appointed public officials are more likely to be familiar and sympathetic with the interests and demands of long-established and/or well-organized groups such as ratepayers' associations and organizations of business interests. Individual companies that are frequently affected in direct ways by actions of urban municipal government are similarly likely to be effective in exercising influence. These kinds of group actors have traditionally had rather high levels of legitimacy in the eyes of public officials, and indeed there is compelling evidence which indicates that many elected public officials often have very close connections with corporate interests. The legitimacy of such groups is derived partly from their obvious stake in decisions of city hall, partly from their persistence over time, and partly from their access to or possession of information of a kind that is most likely to impress public officials favourably. Such information is a politically valuable resource that other kinds of organized groups in urban politics lack. Yet in the middle and late 1960s, newer kinds of organized groups such as community associations, non-corporate specific-interest groups, and the alternate press emerged in considerable numbers. This is one of the outstanding features of Canadian urban politics in recent times, but there are signs that the significance and numbers of these organized interests is in a period of decline.

While such groups were, like the more traditional organized interests, concerned with problems of policy, the newer organized interests have at the same time been much concerned with problems of process, and they have also been less protective or reactive than some other kinds of interests. Hence newer kinds of organized groups have not only demanded or initiated action in such policy areas as public transportation and pollution control, they have also demanded that the processes of municipal decision making be made more open, more subject to public scrutiny, and involve greater consultation with the public. These groups therefore became important vehicles for public participation in city affairs. In some cities there have also been newer-style civic parties that have had close relations with community associations and with non-corporate specific-interest groups. In a number of cases, the newer civic parties have been an outgrowth of organized groups, and have espoused much the same kinds of demands, both in terms of policy problems and process problems. The kinds of reform that newer-style reform parties have sought have put them in conflict with the traditional civic parties which long dominated many city councils and which originally sought to de-politicize city affairs. Further complicating and further enlivening city elections has been the recent interest shown by major political parties, particularly the Liberals and the NDPs, although the protest parties (CCF, Social Credit, and Communists) had involved themselves openly in the 1930s and 1940s. Prior to the 1960s the major political parties had frequently been involved in municipal elections behind the scenes, but it was mainly in the late 1960s that they openly contested municipal elections as parties with slates of candidates and with more or less comprehensive policy platforms. It was argued in Chapter 7 that the stakes involved in city politics had become big enough by the late 1960s to interest the major parties, and that the expanding range and numbers of demands for city action created a clearer need for the kind of interest aggregation function that the major parties are used to performing. But this direct involvement in city elections by the major parties met with resistance from the electorate, and they appear now to have retreated to a role behind the scenes.

It is somewhat ironic that the excitement afforded by major parties' direct involvement and by the emergence of the newer style of civic parties in city elections appears to have had rather little impact in stimulating greater participation by city electorates. Voter turnouts remain considerably lower than is the norm in federal and provincial elections. However, the presence of newer-style civic parties often resulted in considerable changes in the composition of city councils. The stereotype of city councillors changed noticeably by the latter part of the 1960s and early 1970s. Councils have ceased to have so much of the atmosphere of a club or a board of directors. Instead, they have tended to become considerably more political forums characterized by less uniformity of ideology. Councils became seen as a focus for public clarification, debate, and resolution of often highly contentious issues, again both of policy and of process. New-style city politicians, at least when they are first elected to council, have been concerned with removing the shrouds of privacy and secrecy that had so often enveloped city councils in the past. Generally, these politicians have been more committed than their older-style counterparts to democratizing the process of decision making. This is seen in the removal of the last and anachronistic vestiges of property qualifications for voters and candidates. Additionally, the newer-style city councillors tend to be united in a concern about the nature, scale, and direction of urban development and more specifically about the property development industry; these councillors are not, however, necessarily anti-development. The role of such politicians is more difficult to sustain than that of older-style councillors, partly because of the demands the former allow to be made on their time, partly because they lack adequate tools (such as research assistance, office space, and, in many cities, salaries) to perform their jobs as well as they might. As a consequence, those councillors who emphasize the delegate role tend to suffer one or the other of two fates—they drop out of city council, or they revert into the less demanding trustee role that in most cities has traditionally characterized the bulk of councils' members. Nevertheless, the presence of even a small minority of newer-style delegate councillors has somewhat affected the role orientations of their older-style counterparts by making the latter more attentive to non-corporate organized groups.

The newer-style councillors can also be seen to have influenced the nature of cities' decision-making processes, particularly in terms of the way councils behave. Reflecting the contention that city councils have quite recently become more political forums than has been traditional are the clearer divisions within councils in terms of voting blocs. Councils tend to become more polarized, not just on single areas of policy but across a range of policy issues. However, the polarization is most evident on issues involving developers, particularly when developers' proposals are opposed by citizen groups, as is often the case. The cosy relationships of the past between councils and the property development industry have not been eliminated, but they are rather less cosy now, and the belief that high-rise, large-scale developments are necessarily good is increasingly being questioned. In part, this may be attributed to a sensitivity to possible conflicts of interest, but it may also be a factor of generally increasing and widening concern with the kind of city environment in which people wish to live. The scale of cities is a legitimate and important concern. Scale in terms of population size and density is, of course, one aspect of this, but the concern is a broader one that includes questions of the adequacy of opportunities for the public to participate in urban politics, the adequacy of existing institutions and processes of government to accommodate citizen involvement, and also the adequacy of the institutions and processes of urban government to produce the best possible kinds of policies and decisions. The point here is that complex and "big" government is not generally compatible with the valued notion of municipal government as grass-roots *local* government. Unless such a value is to be discarded as hopelessly anachronistic or Utopian, then the institutional structures and processes of decision making require more experimentation and innovation so that they will be more capable of fulfilling the wish for further democratization.

As this book has attempted to demonstrate, the nature of urban government and politics in Canada has been quite radically transformed over time, and especially within the past few years. Whether the momentum is to be maintained or not, or altered in direction, it is too early to predict. But continuing private and public concern with, and debate over, the kind of cities in which most Canadians now live, and in which an increasing proportion of Canadians will live in future, provides grounds for hope, if not optimism.

Suggested Readings

This list is arranged by chapter title and has been restricted to material that is fairly readily available to most readers. Thus it is by no means exhaustive. The main kinds of material excluded are most government documents and reports, early journal articles, and unpublished Learned Societies papers. Some of that material has been cited in footnotes, so the enterprising and interested reader may be able to track some of it down. A very useful bibliography is:

Canadian Council on Urban and Regional Research. *Urban and Regional References 1945–1969*. Ottawa, 1970. Updating volumes are published annually.

Introduction: Urbanization

ARTIBISE, ALAN F. J. *Winnipeg: A Social History of Urban Growth 1874–1914*. Montreal: McGill-Queen's University Press, 1975.

AXWORTHY, L. and GILLIES, JAMES M., eds. *The City: Canada's Prospects, Canada's Problems*. Toronto: Butterworths, 1973.

BOURNE, L. S. and MACKINNON, R. D., eds. *Urban Systems Development in Central Canada: Selected Papers*. Toronto: University of Toronto Press, 1972.

————; MACKINNON, ROSS D.; SIEGEL, J.; and SIMMONS, JAMES W., eds. *Urban Futures for Central Canada: Perspectives on Forecasting Urban Growth and Form*. Toronto: University of Toronto Press, 1974.

CLAIRMONT, DONALD H. and MAGILL, DENNIS WILLIAM. *Africville: The Life and Death of a Canadian Black Community*. Toronto: McClelland and Stewart, 1974.

CLARK, S. D. *The Suburban Society*. Toronto: University of Toronto Press, 1966.

DOSMAN, E. J. *Indians: The Urban Dilemma*. Toronto: McClelland and Stewart, 1972.

Economic Council of Canada. *Fourth Annual Review*. Ottawa, 1967.

FELDMAN, L. D. *A Survey of Alternative Urban Policies*. Urban Canada:

Problems and Prospects, Research Monograph 6. Ottawa: Central Mortgage and Housing Corporation, 1971.

———— and GOLDRICK, MICHAEL D., eds. *Politics and Government of Urban Canada: Selected Readings.* 2nd. ed. Toronto: Methuen, 1972.

GILLESPIE, W. I. *The Urban Public Economy.* Urban Canada: Problems and Prospects, Research Monograph 4. Ottawa: Central Mortgage and Housing Corporation, 1971.

GORACZ, A.; LITHWICK, I.; and STONE, L. O. *The Urban Future.* Urban Canada: Problems and Prospects, Research Monograph 5. Ottawa: Central Mortgage and Housing Corporation, 1971.

JACKSON, JOHN N. *The Canadian City: Space, Form, Quality.* Toronto: McGraw-Hill Ryerson, 1973.

KRUEGER, RALPH R. and BRYFOGLE, R. CHARLES, eds. *Urban Problems: A Canadian Reader.* Toronto: Holt, Rinehart and Winston, 1971.

LITHWICK, N. H. *Urban Canada: Problems and Prospects.* Ottawa: Central Mortgage and Housing Corporation, 1970.

————. *Urban Poverty.* Urban Canada: Problems and Prospects, Research Monograph 1. Ottawa: Central Mortgage and Housing Corporation, 1971.

———— and PAQUET, GILLES, eds. *Urban Studies: A Canadian Perspective.* Toronto: Methuen, 1968.

LORIMER, JAMES and PHILLIPS, MYFANWY. *Working People: Life in a Downtown City Neighbourhood.* Toronto: James Lewis and Samuel, 1971.

LUCAS, REX A. *Minetown, Milltown, Railtown.* Toronto: University of Toronto Press, 1971.

NADER, GEORGE A. *Cities of Canada, Volume One: Theoretical, Historical and Planning Perspectives.* Toronto: Macmillan, 1975.

————. *Cities of Canada, Volume Two: Profiles of Fifteen Metropolitan Centres.* Toronto: Macmillan, 1976.

POWELL, ALAN, ed. *The City: Attacking Modern Myths.* Toronto: McClelland and Stewart, 1972.

REYNOLDS, D. *The Urban Transport Problem in Canada, 1970–2000.* Urban Canada: Problems and Prospects, Research Monograph 3. Ottawa: Central Mortgage and Housing Corporation, 1971.

RICHARDSON, BOYCE. *The Future of Canadian Cities.* Toronto: New Press, 1972.

SEELEY, JOHN R.; SIM, R. ALEXANDER; and LOOSLEY, E. W. *Crestwood Heights: A Study of the Culture of Suburban Life*. Toronto: University of Toronto Press, 1956.

SIMMONS, JAMES and SIMMONS, ROBERT. *Urban Canada*. Toronto: Copp Clark, 1969.

SMITH, LAWRENCE B. *Housing in Canada: Market Structure and Policy Performance*. Urban Canada: Problems and Prospects, Research Monograph 2. Ottawa: Central Mortgage and Housing Corporation, 1971.

SPELT, JACOB. *Urban Development in South-Central Ontario*. Toronto: McClelland and Stewart, 1972.

SPREIREGEN, PAUL D., ed. *The Modern Metropolis: Its Origins, Growth, Characteristics, and Planning; Selected Essays by Hans Blumenfeld*. Montreal: Harvest House, 1971.

STONE, LEROY O. *Urban Development in Canada*. Ottawa: Dominion Bureau of Statistics, 1967.

YEATES, MAURICE. *Main Street: Windsor to Quebec City*. Toronto: Macmillan, 1975.

1: The Evolution of Municipal Government

ARTIBISE, ALAN F. J. *Winnipeg: A Social History of Urban Growth 1874–1914*. Montreal: McGill-Queen's University Press, 1975.

BECK, J. M. *The Government of Nova Scotia*. Toronto: University of Toronto Press, 1957.

———. *The Evolution of Municipal Government in Nova Scotia*. Halifax, 1973.

BOURASSA, GUY. "Les Élites politiques de Montréal: De l'aristocratie à la démocratie," *Canadian Journal of Economics and Political Science*, XXXI, 1 (February, 1965), 35–51.

BRITTAIN, HORACE L. *Local Government in Canada*. Toronto: Ryerson, 1951.

CRAWFORD, K. GRANT. *Canadian Municipal Government*. Toronto: University of Toronto Press, 1954.

CROSBIE, J. C. "Local Government in Newfoundland," *Canadian Journal of Economics and Political Science*, XXII, 3 (August, 1956), 332–46.

DAWSON, GEORGE F. *The Municipal System of Saskatchewan*, 3rd ed. Regina: Department of Municipal Affairs, 1955.

DONNELLY, M. S. *The Government of Manitoba.* Toronto: University of Toronto Press, 1963.

FERRIS, TERRY T. "Local Government Reform in Upper Canada," *Canadian Public Administration,* XII, 3 (1969), 387–410.

HANSON, ERIC. *Local Government in Alberta.* Toronto: McClelland and Stewart, 1956.

MACKINNON, FRANK. *The Government of Prince Edward Island.* Toronto: University of Toronto Press, 1951.

ROSS, ROMAINE K. *Local Government in Ontario.* 2nd ed. Toronto: Canada Law Book Company, 1962.

ROWAT, DONALD C. *Your Local Government.* 2nd ed. Toronto: Macmillan, 1975.

WHALEN, H. J. *The Development of Local Government in New Brunswick.* Fredericton, 1963.

WICKETT, S. MORLEY, ed. *Municipal Government in Canada.* Toronto: University of Toronto Library, 1907.

2: Central-Local Relations

ADAMSON, R. T. "Housing Policy and Urban Renewal," in N. H. Lithwick and Gilles Paquet, eds., *Urban Studies: A Canadian Perspective.* Toronto: Methuen, 1968.

ADLER, GERALD M. *Land Planning by Administrative Regulation: The Policies of the Ontario Municipal Board.* Toronto: University of Toronto Press, 1971.

ADRIAN, CHARLES R. *Governing Urban America.* 2nd ed. New York: McGraw-Hill, 1961.

AXWORTHY, LLOYD. "The Housing Task Force: A Case Study," in G. Bruce Doern and Peter Aucoin, eds., *The Structures of Policy-Making in Canada.* Toronto: Macmillan, 1971.

———— and GILLIES, JAMES M., eds. *The City: Canada's Prospects, Canada's Problems.* Toronto: Butterworths, 1973.

BETTISON, DAVID G. *The Politics of Canadian Urban Development.* Edmonton: University of Alberta Press, 1975.

————; KENWARD, J.; and TAYLOR, L. *Urban Affairs in Alberta.* Edmonton: University of Alberta Press, 1975.

BRITTAIN, HORACE L. *Local Government in Canada.* Toronto: Ryerson, 1951.

Bureau of Municipal Research. *Urban Development and the Ontario Municipal Board.* Toronto, 1971.

CAMERON, JOHN R. *Provincial-Municipal Relations in the Maritime Provinces.* Fredericton: Maritime Union Study, 1970.

CAMERON, DAVID M. "Urban Policy," in G. Bruce Doern and V. Seymour Wilson, eds., *Issues in Canadian Public Policy.* Toronto: Macmillan, 1974.

CARVER, HUMPHREY. *Compassionate Landscape.* Toronto: University of Toronto Press, 1975.

CHAPMAN, BRIAN. *Introduction to French Local Government.* London: George Allen and Unwin, 1953.

CRAWFORD, K. GRANT. *Canadian Municipal Government.* Toronto: University of Toronto Press, 1954.

DENNIS, MICHAEL and FISH, SUSAN. *Programs in Search of a Policy: Low Income Housing in Canada.* Toronto: Hakkert, 1972.

DUPRÉ, J. STEFAN. "Intergovernmental Relations and the Metropolitan Area," in Simon R. Miles, ed., *Metropolitan Problems: International Perspectives, A Search for Comprehensive Solutions.* Toronto: Methuen, 1970.

————. *Intergovernmental Finance in Ontario: A Provincial-Local Perspective.* Toronto: Queen's Printer, 1968.

FELDMAN, LIONEL D. "Legislative Control of Municipalities in Ontario," *Canadian Public Administration*, IV, 3 (September, 1961), 294–301.

———— and GOLDRICK, MICHAEL D., eds. *Politics and Government of Urban Canada: Selected Readings.* 2nd ed. Toronto: Methuen, 1972.

GOLDRICK, M. D. "Present Issues in the Growth of Cities," *Canadian Public Administration*, XIV, 3 (Fall, 1971), 452–9.

GRIFFITH, J. A. G. *Central Departments and Local Authorities.* London: George Allen and Unwin, 1966.

JOHNSON, J. A. "Provincial-Municipal Intergovernmental Fiscal Relations," *Canadian Public Administration*, XII, 2 (Summer, 1969), 166–80.

LITHWICK, N. H. *Urban Canada: Problems and Prospects.* Ottawa: Central Mortgage and Housing Corporation, 1970.

MCKAY, A. N. and SLATER, D. W. "The Scope of Urban Policy," in N. H.

Lithwick and Gilles Paquet, eds., *Urban Studies: A Canadian Perspective*. Toronto: Methuen, 1968.

MCKENNA, BRUCE. "The OMB: Citizens as Losers," *City Magazine*, 1, 7 (November, 1975), 40–6.

O'BRIEN, ALLEN. "Local Government Priorities for the Eighties," *Canadian Public Administration*, XIX, 1 (Spring, 1976).

Plan, Special Issue: National Urban Policy. 12, 1 (July, 1972).

RICHARDS, PETER G. *The Reformed Local Government System*. London: George Allen and Unwin, 1973.

RIDLEY, F. F. "Integrated Decentralization: Models of the Prefectoral System," *Political Studies*, XXI, 1 (March, 1973), 13–25.

——— and BLONDEL, J. *Public Administration in France*. 2nd ed. London: Routledge and Kegan Paul, 1969.

ROSS, ROMAINE K. *Local Government in Ontario*. 2nd ed. Toronto: Canada Law Book Company, 1962.

ROWAT, DONALD C. *The Canadian Municipal System: Essays on the Improvement of Local Government*. Toronto: McClelland and Stewart, 1969.

———. *Your Local Government*. 2nd ed. Toronto: Macmillan, 1975.

SMITH, LAWRENCE B. *Housing in Canada: Market Structure and Policy Performance*. Urban Canada: Problems and Prospects, Research Monograph 2. Ottawa: Central Mortgage and Housing Corporation, 1971.

WHALEN, HUGH. "Ideology, Democracy, and the Foundations of Local Self-Government," *Canadian Journal of Economics and Political Science*, XXVI, 3 (August, 1960), 377–95.

WICKWAR, W. HARDY. *The Political Theory of Local Government*. Columbia, South Carolina: University of South Carolina Press, 1970.

3: The Structures of Municipal Decision Making

BERNARD, ANDRÉ; LÉVEILLÉ, JACQUES; and LORD, GUY. *Profile: Calgary, The Political and Administrative Structures of the Metropolitan Region of Calgary*. Ottawa: Ministry of State for Urban Affairs, 1975.

———. *Profile: Edmonton, The Political and Administrative Structures of the Metropolitan Region of Edmonton*. Ottawa: Ministry of State for Urban Affairs, 1974.

————. *Profile: Halifax-Dartmouth, The Political and Administrative Structures of the Metropolitan Region of Halifax-Dartmouth.* Ottawa: Ministry of State for Urban Affairs, 1974.

————. *Profile: Hamilton-Wentworth, The Political and Administrative Structures of the Metropolitan Region of Hamilton-Wentworth.* Ottawa: Ministry of State for Urban Affairs, 1975.

————. *Profile: Montreal, The Political and Administrative Structures of the Metropolitan Region of Montreal.* Ottawa: Ministry of State for Urban Affairs, 1974.

————. *Profile: Ottawa-Hull, The Political and Administrative Structures of the Metropolitan Region of Ottawa-Hull.* Ottawa: Ministry of State for Urban Affairs, 1974.

————. *Profile: Quebec, The Political and Administrative Structures of the Metropolitan Region of Quebec.* Ottawa: Ministry of State for Urban Affairs, 1975.

————. *Profile: Toronto, The Political and Administrative Structures of the Metropolitan Region of Toronto.* Ottawa: Ministry of State for Urban Affairs, 1975.

————. *Profile: Vancouver, The Political and Administrative Structures of the Metropolitan Region of Vancouver.* Ottawa: Ministry of State for Urban Affairs, 1975.

————. *Profile: Winnipeg, The Political and Administrative Structures of the Metropolitan Region of Winnipeg.* Ottawa: Ministry of State for Urban Affairs, 1975.

Bureau of Municipal Research. *The 101 Governments of Metro Toronto.* Toronto, 1968.

CRAWFORD, K. GRANT. *Canadian Municipal Government.* Toronto: University of Toronto Press, 1954.

FELDMAN, LIONEL D. and GOLDRICK, MICHAEL D., eds. *Politics and Government of Urban Canada: Selected Readings.* 2nd ed. Toronto: Methuen, 1972.

PLUNKETT, THOMAS J. *Urban Canada and Its Government: A Study of Municipal Organization.* Toronto: Macmillan, 1968.

ROWAT, DONALD C. *The Canadian Municipal System: Essays on the Improvement of Local Government.* Toronto: McClelland and Stewart, 1969.

————. *Your Local Government.* 2nd ed. Toronto: Macmillan, 1975.

4: Municipal Reorganization

AXWORTHY, LLOYD. "Winnipeg: An Experiment in Innovation," in L. Axworthy and James M. Gillies, eds., *The City: Canada's Prospects, Canada's Problems*. Toronto: Butterworths, 1973.

BROWNSTONE, MEYER and FELDMAN, LIONEL D. "Innovation and City Government: Winnipeg 1972," *The Canadian Forum*, LII (May, 1972), 28–31.

Bureau of Municipal Research. *Regional Government—The Key to Genuine Local Autonomy*. Toronto, 1968.

————. *Reorganizing Local Government: A Brief Look at Four Provinces*. Toronto, 1972.

Canadian Public Policy, I, 3 (Summer, 1975), 342–92. This is a set of articles on Nova Scotia's Graham Royal Commission.

COOK, GAIL C. A. and FELDMAN, LIONEL D. "Approaches to Local Government Reform in Canada: The Case of Winnipeg," *Canadian Tax Journal*, XIX, 3 (May-June, 1971), 216–25.

FELDMAN, LIONEL D. and GOLDRICK, MICHAEL D., eds. *Politics and Government of Urban Canada: Selected Readings*. 2nd ed. Toronto: Methuen, 1972.

HANSON, ERIC. "The Changing Structure of Local Government in Alberta," *Canadian Public Administration*, I, 3 (September, 1958), 26–31.

KAPLAN, HAROLD. "The Integration of Metropolitan Federations: The Interaction of Political Theory and Urban Phenomena," in N. H. Lithwick and Gilles Paquet, eds., *Urban Studies: A Canadian Perspective*. Toronto: Methuen, 1968.

————. "Metropolitan Government," in Ralph R. Krueger and R. Charles Bryfogle, eds., *Urban Problems: A Canadian Reader*. Toronto: Holt, Rinehart and Winston, 1971.

————. *Urban Political Systems: A Functional Analysis of Metro Toronto*. New York: Columbia University Press, 1967.

KRUEGER, RALPH R. "The Provincial-Municipal Revolution in New Brunswick," *Canadian Public Administration*, XIII, 1 (Spring, 1970), 51–99.

PLUNKETT, THOMAS J. "The Report of the Royal Commission on Finance and Municipal Taxation in New Brunswick: A Review and Commentary," *Canadian Public Administration*, VIII, 1 (March, 1965), 12–23.

————. "Structural Reform of Local Government in Canada," *Public Administration Review*, 33, 1 (January-February, 1973), 40–51.

————. *Urban Canada and Its Government: A Study of Municipal Organization*. Toronto: Macmillan, 1968.

PRICE, TREVOR, ed. *Regional Government in Ontario*. Windsor: University of Windsor Press, 1971.

RICH, S. GEORGE. "Metropolitan Winnipeg: The First Ten Years," in Ralph R. Krueger and R. Charles Bryfogle, eds., *Urban Problems: A Canadian Reader*. Toronto: Holt, Rinehart and Winston, 1971.

ROSE, ALBERT. *Governing Metropolitan Toronto: A Social and Political Analysis 1953–1971*. Berkeley: University of California Press, 1972.

ROWAT, D. C. "The Concept of Regional Government and a Proposal for Ontario," in N. H. Lithwick and Gilles Paquet, eds., *Urban Studies: A Canadian Perspective*. Toronto: Methuen, 1968.

————. *The Canadian Municipal System: Essays on the Improvement of Local Government*. Toronto: McClelland and Stewart, 1969.

SMALLWOOD, FRANK. "Reshaping Local Government Abroad: Anglo-Canadian Experiments," *Public Administration Review*, 30, 3 (September-October, 1970), 521–30.

————. *Metro Toronto: A Decade Later*. Toronto: Bureau of Municipal Research, 1963.

5: Socio-Political Consequences of Urbanization: The Setting for Urban Political Life

BACHRACH, PETER and BARATZ, MORTON S. "Two Faces of Power," *American Political Science Review*, 56, 4 (December, 1962), 947–52.

Bureau of Municipal Research. *Citizen Participation in Metro Toronto: Climate for Co-operation?* Toronto, 1975.

————. *Neighbourhood Participation in Local Government*. Toronto, 1970.

DAHL, ROBERT A. "The City in the Future of Democracy," *American Political Science Review*, LXI, 4 (December, 1967), 953–70.

————. *After the Revolution? Authority in the Good Society*. New Haven: Yale University Press, 1970.

————. *Who Governs? Democracy and Power in an American City*. New Haven: Yale University Press, 1961.

————— and TUFTE, EDWARD R. *Size and Democracy*. Stanford: Stanford University Press, 1973.

FELDMAN, LIONEL D. and GOLDRICK, MICHAEL D., eds. *Politics and Government of Urban Canada: Selected Readings*. 2nd ed. Toronto: Methuen, 1972.

FINIFTER, ADA W. and ABRAMSON, PAUL R. "City Size and Feelings of Political Competence," *Public Opinion Quarterly*, XXXIX, 2 (Summer, 1975), 189–98.

HAMPTON, WILLIAM. "Local Government and Community," *The Political Quarterly*, 40, 2 (April-June, 1969), 151–62.

—————. *Democracy and Community: A Study of Politics in Sheffield*. London: Oxford University Press, 1970.

HAWLEY, AMOS. *Human Ecology: A Theory of Community Structure*. New York: Ronald Press, 1950.

HILLERY, GEORGE A. "Definitions of Community: Areas of Agreement," *Rural Sociology*, 20 (March, 1955), 111–23.

HUNTER, FLOYD. *Community Power Structure: A Study of Decision Makers*. Chapel Hill: University of North Carolina Press, 1953.

KAPLAN, HAROLD. *Urban Political Systems: A Functional Analysis of Metro Toronto*. New York: Columbia University Press, 1967.

KOTLER, MILTON. *Neighborhood Government: The Local Foundations of Political Life*. Indianapolis: Bobbs-Merrill, 1969.

LANGROD, GEORGES. "Local Government and Democracy," *Public Administration*, XXXI (Spring, 1953), 25–34.

MARTIN, ROSCOE C. *Grass Roots*. 2nd ed. New York: Harper and Row, 1965.

MCKENZIE, R. D. *On Human Ecology*. Chicago: University of Chicago Press, 1968.

PARK, ROBERT E. *Human Communities*. Glencoe: Free Press, 1952.

POLSBY, NELSON W. "Community: The Study of Community Power," in *International Encyclopaedia of the Social Sciences*, Volume 3. New York: Macmillan and the Free Press, 1968.

—————. *Community Power and Political Theory*. New Haven: Yale University Press, 1963.

TOCQUEVILLE, ALEXIS DE. *Democracy in America*, Volume I. New York: Vintage Books, 1954.

TÖNNIES, FERDINAND. *Community and Society*, translated by Charles P.

Loomis. Toronto: Ryerson, 1957.

TOSCANO, JAMES V. "Transaction Flow Analysis in Metropolitan Areas: Some Preliminary Explorations," in Philip E. Jacob and James V. Toscano, eds., *The Integration of Political Communities*. Philadelphia: Lippincott, 1964.

VERBA, SIDNEY. "Democratic Participation," in Bertram M. Gross, ed., *Social Intelligence for America's Future*. Boston: Allyn and Bacon, 1969.

WARREN, ROLAND L. *The Community in America*. Chicago: Rand McNally, 1972.

WHEATON, WILLIAM L. C. "Integration at the Urban Level: Political Influence and the Decision Process," in Philip E. Jacob and James V. Toscano, eds., *The Integration of Political Communities*. Philadelphia: Lippincott, 1964.

ZIMMERMAN, JOSEPH. "Community Building in Larger Cities," in L. Axworthy and James M. Gillies, eds., *The City: Canada's Prospects, Canada's Problems*. Toronto: Butterworths, 1973.

6: Participation in Urban Politics: Group Actors

AXWORTHY, LLOYD. "Winnipeg: An Experiment in Innovation," in L. Axworthy and James M. Gillies, eds., *The City: Canada's Prospects, Canada's Problems*. Toronto: Butterworths, 1973.

——— and CASSIDY, JIM. *Unicity: The Transition*. Future City Series, No. 4. Winnipeg: Institute of Urban Studies of the University of Winnipeg, 1974.

BARKER, GRAHAM; PENNY, JENNIFER; and SECCOMBE, WALLY. *High Rise and Superprofits: An Analysis of the Development Industry in Canada*. Kitchener: Dumont Press, 1973.

Bureau of Municipal Research. *Citizen Participation in Metro Toronto: Climate for Co-operation?* Toronto, 1975.

———. *Neighbourhood Participation in Local Government: A Study of the City of Toronto*. Toronto, 1970.

CAULFIELD, JON. *The Tiny Perfect Mayor*. Toronto: James Lorimer, 1974.

DRAPER, JAMES A., ed. *Citizen Participation: Canada, A Book of Readings*. Toronto: New Press, 1971.

FELDMAN, LIONEL D. and GOLDRICK, MICHAEL D., eds. *Politics and Government of Urban Canada: Selected Readings*. 2nd ed. Toronto: Methuen, 1972.

FRASER, GRAHAM. *Fighting Back: Urban Renewal in Trefann Court*. Toronto: Hakkert, 1972.

GRANATSTEIN, J. L. *Marlborough Marathon: One Street Against a Developer*. Toronto: Hakkert, 1971.

GROULX, L. H. J. "L'action communautaire: diversité et ambiguité," *Canadian Journal of Political Science*, VIII, 4 (December, 1975), 510–19.

GUTSTEIN, DONALD. *Vancouver Ltd*. Toronto: James Lorimer, 1975.

KAPLAN, HAROLD. *Urban Political Systems: A Functional Analysis of Metro Toronto*. New York: Columbia University Press, 1967.

LEY, DAVID, ed. *Community Participation and the Spatial Order of the City*. Vancouver: Tantalus, 1973.

LORIMER, JAMES. *A Citizen's Guide to City Politics*. Toronto: James Lewis and Samuel, 1972.

————. *The Real World of City Politics*. Toronto: James Lewis and Samuel, 1970.

NOWLAN, DAVID and NOWLAN, NADINE. *The Bad Trip: The Untold Story of the Spadina Expressway*. Toronto: New Press/Anansi, 1970.

PASTERNAK, JACK. *The Kitchener Market Fight*. Toronto: Samuel Stevens, Hakkert, 1975.

RICHARDSON, BOYCE. *The Future of Canadian Cities*. Toronto: New Press, 1972.

SEWELL, JOHN. *Up Against City Hall*. Toronto: James Lewis and Samuel, 1972.

————; CROMBIE, DAVID; KILBOURN, WILLIAM; and JAFFARY, KARL. *Inside City Hall: The Year of the Opposition*. Toronto: Hakkert, 1971.

STEIN, DAVID LEWIS. *Toronto for Sale: The Destruction of a City*. Toronto: New Press, 1972.

7: Participation in Urban Politics: Parties and Elections

Bureau of Municipal Research. *Parties to Change: The Introduction of Political Parties in the 1969 Toronto Municipal Election*. Toronto, 1971.

CAULFIELD, JON. *The Tiny Perfect Mayor*. Toronto: James Lorimer, 1974.

CLARKSON, STEPHEN. *City Lib: Parties and Reform*. Toronto: Hakkert, 1972.

CRAWFORD, K. GRANT. *Canadian Municipal Government*. Toronto: University of Toronto Press, 1954.

DONNELLY, M. S. "Ethnic Participation in Municipal Government: Winnipeg, St. Boniface and the Metropolitan Corporation of Greater Winnipeg," in Lionel D. Feldman and Michael D. Goldrick, eds., *Politics and Government of Urban Canada: Selected Readings*. 2nd ed. Toronto: Methuen, 1972.

Editors, "Reform Politics in Winnipeg: Opening Things Up," *City Magazine*, 1, 3 (February-March, 1975), 29–36.

GILSDORF, ROBERT R. "Cognitive and Motivational Sources of Voter Susceptibility to Influence," *Canadian Journal of Political Science*, VI, 4 (December, 1973), 624–38.

GUTSTEIN, DONALD. *Vancouver Ltd*. Toronto: James Lorimer, 1975.

———. "The Developers' TEAM: Vancouver's 'Reform' Party in Power," *City Magazine*, 1, 2 (December, 1974-January, 1975), 13–28.

HARRIS, IRENE. "How to Run and Win," *City Magazine*, 1, 3 (February-March, 1975), 14–23 and 26–7.

HOUGH, JERRY F. "Voters' Turnout and the Responsiveness of Local Government: the Case of Toronto, 1969," in Paul W. Fox, ed., *Politics: Canada*. 3rd ed. Toronto: McGraw-Hill, 1970.

JOYCE, J. G. and HOSSÉ, H. A. *Civic Parties in Canada*. Ottawa: Canadian Federation of Mayors and Municipalities, 1970.

KAPLAN, HAROLD. *Urban Political Systems: A Functional Analysis of Metro Toronto*. New York: Columbia University Press, 1967.

LORIMER, JAMES. *A Citizen's Guide to City Politics*. Toronto: James Lewis and Samuel, 1972.

———. *The Real World of City Politics*. Toronto: James Lewis and Samuel, 1970.

MASSON, JACK K. and ANDERSON, JAMES D., eds. *Emerging Party Politics in Urban Canada*. Toronto: McClelland and Stewart, 1972.

MICHAELSON, PETER. "Montreal's Civic Party: the King, the Duke and the Vassals," *Civic Administration* (April, 1968), 38–9 and 56.

MILNER, HENRY. "City Politics: Some Possibilities," *Our Generation*, 10,

4 (Winter, 1975), 47–60.

ROWAT, DONALD C. *Your Local Government*. 2nd ed. Toronto: Macmillan, 1975.

SEWELL, JOHN. *Up Against City Hall*. Toronto: James Lewis and Samuel, 1972.

VAISON, ROBERT and AUCOIN, PETER. "Class and Voting in Recent Halifax Mayoralty Elections," in Lionel D. Feldman and Michael D. Goldrick, eds., *Politics and Government of Urban Canada: Selected Readings*. 2nd ed. Toronto: Methuen, 1972.

WINN, CONRAD and MC MENEMY, JOHN. "Political Alignment in a Polarized City: Electoral Cleavages in Kitchener, Ontario," *Canadian Journal of Political Science*, VI, 2 (June, 1973), 230–42.

8: Urban Politicians

ANDREW, CAROLINE; BLAIS, ANDRÉ; and DES ROSIERS, RACHEL. "Le logement public à Hull," *Canadian Journal of Political Science*, VIII, 3 (September, 1975), 403–30.

AXWORTHY, LLOYD and CASSIDY, JIM. *Unicity: The Transition*. Future City Series No. 4. Winnipeg: Institute of Urban Studies of the University of Winnipeg, 1974.

Bureau of Municipal Research. *The Metro Politician: A Profile*. Toronto, 1963.

————. *Neighbourhood Participation in Local Government: A Study of the City of Toronto*. Toronto, 1970.

CAULFIELD, JON. *The Tiny Perfect Mayor*. Toronto: James Lorimer, 1974.

GIBBONS, KENNETH M. and ROWAT, DONALD C., eds. *Political Corruption in Canada: Cases, Causes and Cures*. Toronto: McClelland and Stewart, 1976.

GUTSTEIN, DONALD. *Vancouver Ltd*. Toronto: James Lorimer, 1975.

KAPLAN, HAROLD. *Urban Political Systems: A Functional Analysis of Metro Toronto*. New York: Columbia University Press, 1967.

KAY, BARRY J. "Voting Patterns in a Non-partisan Legislature: A Study of Toronto City Council," *Canadian Journal of Political Science*, IV, 2 (June, 1971), 224–42.

LONG, J. ANTHONY and SLEMKO, BRIAN. "The Recruitment of Local Decision-Makers in Five Canadian Cities: Some Preliminary

Findings," *Canadian Journal of Political Science*, VII, 3 (September, 1974), 550–9.

LORIMER, JAMES. *A Citizen's Guide to City Politics*. Toronto: James Lewis and Samuel, 1972.

————. *The Real World of City Politics*. Toronto: James Lewis and Samuel, 1970.

MASSON, JACK K. "Decision-Making Patterns and Floating Coalitions in an Urban City Council," *Canadian Journal of Political Science*, VIII, 1 (March, 1975), 128–37.

———— and ANDERSON, JAMES D., eds. *Emerging Party Politics in Urban Canada*. Toronto: McClelland and Stewart, 1972.

MORTON, DESMOND. "Mississauga: The Story of a Municipal Investigation," *City Magazine*, 2, 2 (June, 1976), 36–43.

SEWELL, JOHN. *Up Against City Hall*. Toronto: James Lewis and Samuel, 1972.

Index

Access, concept of, 166, 167, 168, 170
Accountability, 292–93; of elected representatives, 182, 243, 252, 264, 265; of special-purpose bodies, 107, 156, 291
Alberta, County Act, 152; Local Authorities Board, 72; local improvement districts, 33, 34; municipal functions, 58, 59; municipal history, 33–35; municipal reorganization, 34, 152, 153; North-West Municipal Ordinance, 33; statute labour and fire districts, 33
Alderman (see Councillors)
Alexander, Alan, 242
Allen, William R., 213
Amalgamation, 156, 157, 158, 164; British Columbia, 153; Halifax, 129; Hull–Outaouais Regional Community, 136; Laval, 135; Ontario, 146; Quebec, Province, 136–38; Quebec Urban Community, 136; Saint John, 131, 132; Thunder Bay, 146; Toronto, 138, 139, 141, 142; Winnipeg, 147
American influence, city manager structure, 94, 119, 207; council size, 97; "home rule", 48; in British Columbia, 35; reform movement, 207, 228, 236, 241; United Empire Loyalists, 15, 16, 19, 21, 26–28, 40, 41
Andras, Robert, 82, 83
Annexation, ·156, 157, 164; Calgary, 152, 153; Edmonton, 152, 153; Halifax, 129; Quebec, 136
Archer, William L., 146, 288
Associations, municipal, 75, 76, 87, 146
Autonomy, municipal, 48, 164; and municipal reorganization, 138, 155, 156; and special-purpose boards, 107; financial, 66–71, 88, 128, 132, 290; functional, 56, 57, 60, 290; in U.S.A., 49
Axworthy, Lloyd, 151

Baldwin, Robert, 28
Baldwin Act, 28, 29, 31, 36, 54

Basford, Ronald, 86
Beckett, Hollis E., 144
Betts, George M., 199
Blier, Camille, 133, 134
Board of commissioners, 112–15
Board of control, 115–19, 147, 244, 249
Boundaries, municipal, area, 132, 138, 144, 145, 148, 149, 150, 164, 293; blurring of, 125–27, 134, 147, 291; British Columbia, 154; determinants, 129, 130, 132, 139, 142, 144, 145, 148, 154, 167, 293; Montreal, 134; Nova Scotia, 129, 130; Ontario, 144, 145; Saint John, 132; Toronto, 138, 139, 142; Winnipeg, 147, 148, 149, 150, 293
Bourassa, Robert, 137
Brandon, 238
British Columbia, Consolidated Municipal Act, 35, 36; Municipal Act, 36; Municipal Clauses Act, 36; municipal functions, 58, 59, 153, 154, 155; municipal history, 35, 36; municipal reorganization, 153–55, 292; Natural Gas Revenue Sharing Act, 70; regional districts, 36, 128, 153–55
British influence, 52, 236; colonial administration, 16, 25, 26, 27, 41; councils, 34, 93, 108; Courts of Quarter Sessions, 19, 21, 25, 26, 40; immigrants, 15, 16, 40
British North America Act, 15, 52, 53
Brodie, J. L., 147
Bureau of Municipal Research, 185, 199, 211, 259, 260, 261
Bureaucracies, and citizen participation, 204, 205, 212; city manager, 119–22; organization, 103, 108–10, 112-14, 115–18, 119–22; roles, 102–04; size, 102, 103
Burke, Edmund, 270, 271
Burlington, 145
Byrne, Edward, 131, 132

Calgary, annexation, 152, 153, 157; area, 165; attitudes, 196, 197;